Dychweler y llyfr hwn erb[illegible] y dyddiad isod, neu
pan elwir amdano g[illegible]ellydd.
[illegible]wy'r [illegible]rhyw d[illegible] [illegible]tho ddychwel[illegible]

AF741186

INTERPRETING COMPANY REPORTS AND ACCOUNTS

Geoffrey Holmes and Alan Sugden

WOODHEAD-FAULKNER · CAMBRIDGE

Published by Woodhead-Faulkner Limited
8 Market Passage, Cambridge CB2 3PF

First published 1979

© Geoffrey Holmes and Alan Sugden 1979

339121

HF5681. B2 H63
FOLIO

ISBN 0 85941 059 5 (Cased)
ISBN 0 85941 062 5 (Paper)

Conditions of sale
All rights reserved. No part of this publication may be reproduced, stored in a retrieval system or transmitted, in any form or by any means, electronic, mechanical, photocopying, recording or otherwise, without the prior permission of the copyright owners.

Photoset by Millford Reprographics International Limited, Luton
Printed in Great Britain by Lowe & Brydone Printers Limited, Thetford, Norfolk

PREFACE

"Published accounts are utterly and absolutely useless."
Clive Jenkins

Many non-trade unionists might agree with Clive Jenkins on this point, but we believe they are wrong. Given a sound knowledge of the basic components of a balance sheet and profit and loss account, *anybody with a reasonably enquiring mind* can learn a great deal about a company by studying its report and accounts and by comparing it with other companies, and we have written this book to provide the basic knowledge required and to give the reader (be he student, investor, company director, or trade unionist) a line-by-line guide on how to take a set of reports and accounts to pieces.

A careful, systematic examination of accounts can also provide warning of when a company is taking undue risks, when it is "window dressing" to cover up a poor performance, or when it is "netting off" figures to hide embarrassing items.

In addition, an examination of accounts over several years can give a very good picture of the long-term trends of a company's fortunes, distinguishing between a company that is growing at an incredible speed (in which case don't believe it), is growing at a prudent speed (in which case consider investing), or is static or on the decline (in which case avoid or sell).

Analysing accounts, sorting out the good, well-run companies from the less reliable ones, all the time asking further questions and keeping an eye out for warning signals is, in our view, fun. We hope that once you have mastered the nuts-and-bolts of the process you will find it fun, too.

Acknowledgements

We would like to thank our friends in the City for providing and checking information for us, and in particular David Cole, Keith Niven and Charles Tallents for their detailed comments on our early drafts.

G.H.
A.S.

CONTENTS

Chapter 1

INTRODUCTION TO ACCOUNTING PRACTICE

This book is intended as a practical guide to the interpretation of reports and accounts. In it frequent reference is made to the legal, accounting and Stock Exchange requirements that accounts have to meet, but this is done in the context of what interesting information to look out for, rather than to show how a set of accounts should be prepared.

Useful guides to *compiling* accounts include:

Accounting Requirements of the Companies Acts, a summary of the statutory requirements published for the Institute of Chartered Accountants in England and Wales by Gee & Co.

Survey of Published Accounts, published annually by the Institute.

Blank Company Limited, a pro forma report and accounts with comprehensive referencing, published by Burrup, Mathieson, the Extel Group printers.

Information which reports and accounts must contain

The annual report and accounts is usually the principal way in which shareholders and others can keep themselves informed on the activities, progress and future plans of a company.

Although the style and content vary with the directors' views on the use of the report and accounts as a public relations vehicle – an increasing number of companies distribute a summary of their report and accounts to all employees or include one in their house newspaper, and some even produce a separate "company profile", while others argue the risks of disclosing anything in case it may be of use to competitors – there is a minimum amount of information that *must* be disclosed to comply with the Companies Acts. Amongst these requirements, the annual report and accounts has to contain four basic components: a directors' report, a profit and loss account, a balance sheet and an auditors' report.

In addition, when the company's shares are listed on the Stock Exchange, London, the Report and Accounts should also meet the requirements of the Stock Exchange Listing Agreement, which is contained in Chapter 2 of the Stock Exchange's *Admission of Securities to Listing,* known as the "Yellow Book". One of these requirements is the production of a half-yearly or interim report, in addition to the Companies Acts requirement for an annual Report and Accounts.

Accounting standards

The Institute of Chartered Accountants in England and Wales, in conjunction with the Scottish and Irish Institutes, the Association of Certified Accountants and the Institute of Cost and Management Accountants, has produced a series of papers giving guidance on the treatment and presentation of various aspects of a company's accounts. These papers are published in two series:

1. *Exposure Drafts* (EDs), which propose methods to be used, and form the basis for discussion and comment in the development of official standards. Once these standards are agreed they are published as:
2. *Statements of Standard Accounting Practice (SSAPs).* These place, on members who are directors or officers of companies, the onus of ensuring that the standards are

fully understood by other directors and within the company, and that significant departures are disclosed and explained in the accounts, while members acting as auditors are also required to justify any significant departures if they concur with them.

The production of these papers is a continuing process: a list of currently extant EDs and SSAPs is contained in Appendix 1. One of them, SSAP 10, requires the annual report and accounts to contain a fifth basic component, a Source and Application of Funds Statement.

Fundamental accounting concepts

Four fundamental concepts are laid down in SSAP 2 (*Disclosure of Accounting Policies*):

1. The *going concern* concept: the accounts are compiled on the assumption that there is no intention or need to go into liquidation or to curtail the current level of operation significantly.
2. The *accruals* (or matching) concept: revenue and costs are accrued (accounted for) as they are earned or incurred, not as the money is received or paid, and revenue and profits are matched with associated costs and expenses by including them in the same accounting period.
3. The *consistency* concept: accounting treatment of like items is consistent from one period to the next.
4. The concept of *prudence*, which is the overriding concept, demands that:
   (*a*) Revenue and profits are not anticipated;
   (*b*) Provision is made for all known liabilities (expenses and losses), whether the amount is known with certainty or has to be estimated.

Accounting policies

SSAP 2 requires the accounting policies (the various bases on which the accounts have been prepared) to be disclosed as a note to the accounts. The note is usually No. 1 and, typically, includes the basis for accounting for:

(*a*) sales (treatment of VAT and duties);
(*b*) deferred taxation;
(*c*) depreciation of fixed assets;
(*d*) investment grants;
(*e*) research and development;
(*f*) stocks and work in progress;
(*g*) extraordinary items;
(*h*) conversion of currencies;

plus any items specially related to the company's business, such as the treatment of long-term contracts, hire purchase transactions or growing timber.

The balance sheet and profit and loss account

(The remainder of this chapter provides an introduction to the balance sheet and profit and loss account for those who are not already familiar with them. Experienced readers may like to turn straight to Chapter 2.)

Example 1.1 The new company's balance sheet

Liabilities		Assets	
Ordinary share capital	£100,000	Cash	£100,000

Example 1.2 The balance sheet after acquisition of fixed and current assets

Liabilities		Assets	
	£		£
Ordinary share capital	100,000	*Fixed assets*	
		Freehold land and buildings	60,000[1]
		Fixtures and fittings	15,000[2]
		Motor vehicles	2,500[4]
Current liabilities		*Current assets*	
Creditors	20,000[5]	Stock (of goods)	40,000[3]
		Cash	2,500[6]
	120,000		120,000

The *balance sheet* is a statement of the assets and liabilities of a company on a given day, *i.e.*, on the balance sheet date. The *profit and loss account* is a record of the activities of a company for a given period of time; this period, which is called the accounting period, is normally a year, and the balance sheet always has to be drawn up on the last day of the company's accounting year.

When a company is formed the *members* (shareholders) subscribe for shares. For example, let us suppose that a company is formed with a share capital of 100,000 ordinary shares with a nominal value of £1 each, and that all the shares are issued at *par* (are issued to members at their nominal value of £1 each). The balance sheet will then look like Example 1.1.

Supposing the company then:

1. buys a freehold shop for £60,000,
2. fits it out for £15,000 and
3. stocks it with £40,000 worth of goods.

It also:

4. buys a van for £2,500.

The shop, the fittings and the van are all paid for with cash, and so are half the goods, but:

5. the other half of the goods are supplied on credit; *i.e.*, the suppliers do not require immediate payment, so they become creditors of the company (*Creditors* are people to whom the company owes money);
6. by this time most of the original £100,000 has been spent: £100,000 – 60,000 – 15,000 – 20,000 – 2,500 = £2,500 cash remaining.

The balance sheet would then look like Example 1.2 (superior figures refer to items in the above list).

Fixed assets are assets not held for resale but for use by the business. *Current assets* are cash and assets that the company expects to turn into cash (*e.g.*, stock), and *current liabilities* are liabilities that the company expects to have to meet within twelve months. In modern accounting practice the current liabilities are normally shown below the current assets on the assets side of the balance sheet, and the total of the current liabilities is deducted from the total of the current assets to give what is called *net current assets*.

Let us suppose that the company then trades for a year, during which time it:

7. sells goods for £300,000, their cost plus a profit margin, and
8. buys goods for £220,000 in addition to the initial purchase of £40,000, which is called the *opening stock* (except for the first year this is the stock on hand at the end of the previous year).
9. At the end of the year, on the last day of the company's accounting year, there is £85,000 of stock, valued at cost price, on hand. This is called the *closing stock*.
10. Wages and expenses for the year amount to £72,000. In addition,
11. a provision is made for the wear and tear on fixed assets during the year. This is calculated so that the cost of each fixed asset is written off over its expected life. The provision is called *depreciation* and, using the most common method of depreciation, the "straight line" method:

$$\text{Depreciation for the year} = \frac{\text{Cost of asset}}{\text{Expected useful life}}$$

For our company the depreciation charge for the year would be worked out as follows:

Fixed asset	*Cost*	*Life*	*Annual depreciation* £
Building	£50,000	50 years	1,000
Fittings	£15,000	10 years	1,500
Motor Van	£2,500	5 years	500
Depreciation charge for the year[11]			3,000

Notice that depreciation is only charged on the cost of the building (here assumed to be £50,000), not on the value of the land, because depreciation is provided only on assets with a finite useful life.

Example 1.3 overleaf shows how the profit and loss account for the first year's trading would be calculated.

During the year the company has also borrowed money to finance increased stock and to cover credit sales, where a company's customers are allowed to run accounts, normally payable monthly. The borrowings were of two types:

12. a twenty-year loan of £25,000 secured on the freehold land and buildings – this is called a mortgage debenture because the lender of the money (the debenture holder) has first claim on the property if the company goes into liquidation;
13. an overdraft facility with the company's bank, with a limit of £10,000 (*i.e.*, the bank allows the company to borrow on its

Example 1.3 The first year's profit and loss account

	£	£	£
Sales (or Turnover)			300,000[7]
less Cost of goods sold:			
Opening Stock	40,000[8]		
Purchases	+220,000[8]		
	260,000		
Closing Stock	-85,000[9]		
Cost of Goods Sold		175,000	
Wages and other expenses		72,000[10]	
Depreciation		3,000[11]	
			250,000
Profit before tax			50,000
Corporation Tax (assuming the company pays tax at a rate of 52%)			26,000
Profit after tax			24,000
Dividends (the directors recommend a further 10% on the nominal value of the issued share capital, having paid an interim dividend of 5%, making 15% in all)			15,000
Retained profits (to be ploughed back into the company)			9,000

current account any amount it likes up to a maximum of £10,000).

At the end of the year:

14. debtors (customers owing money to the company) owed a total of £24,000;
15. creditors were £38,000 – so a little less than half the stock was being financed by suppliers.

Our final illustration (Example 1.4) shows the balance sheet at the end of the year drawn up in the modern way, with the assets above the liabilities, rather than side by side. Notice that:

16. fixed assets are shown at cost *less* depreciation to date;
17. companies normally have a small amount of cash in hand, even if they have an overdraft;
18. the final dividend, 10% out of a total of 15% for the year, has not yet been paid;
19. net current assets current assets – current liabilities, *i.e.*, £109,500 – 50,000 = £59,500;
20. *ordinary shareholders' funds* ordinary share capital issued plus reserves.

Example 1.4 The balance sheet after the first year's trading

		£
Assets		
Fixed assets[16]		
Freehold land and buildings		59,000[11]
Fixtures and fittings		13,500[11]
Motor vehicles		2,000[11]
		74,500
Current assets		
Stock	85,000[9]	
Debtors	24,000[14]	
Cash[17]	500	
	109,500	
Current liabilities		
Creditors	38,000[15]	
Dividends payable[18]	10,000	
Overdraft[17]	2,000[13]	
	50,000	
Net current assets[19]		59,500
		134,000
Financed by		
Ordinary share capital		100,000
Reserves (retained profits)		9,000
Ordinary shareholders' funds[20]		109,000
Mortgage debenture		25,000[12]
		£134,000

Chapter 2

FORMING A COMPANY

Incorporation of a company

When a company is formed by incorporation under the Companies Acts a Certificate of Incorporation is issued and the company assumes a legal identity separate from its shareholders.

Before incorporation can take place, a Memorandum of Association and Articles of Association have to be drawn up and filed with the Registrar of Companies in England and Wales or with the Registrar of Companies in Scotland.

Memorandum of Association

The Memorandum lays down the rules which govern the company in its relations with the outside world. It states the name of the company; the country in which the Registered Office will be situated; the objects of the company (*i.e.*, activities the company may pursue); the authorised share capital, the nominal value of the shares; a list of initial subscribers and whether the liability of members (shareholders) is limited. An example is given in Table B of the First Schedule to the Companies Act 1948.

Articles of Association

The Articles lay down the internal rules within which the directors run the company. The main items covered are:

(*a*) the issue of shares, the rights attaching to each class of share, the consent required for the alteration of the rights of any class of shareholders, and any restrictions on the transfer of shares;

(*b*) the procedure for general meetings and for altering the authorised share capital;

(*c*) the election and retirement of directors, their duties and their powers, including borrowing powers;

(*d*) the declaration of dividends;

(*e*) the procedure for winding up the company.

A model set of Articles is given in Table A of the First Schedule to the Companies Act 1948.

Members' (shareholders') liability

The liability of members (shareholders) of a company can either be limited by shares or by guarantee, or the liability can be unlimited.

Limited by shares

This is the method normally used for a company engaged in business activities. If the shares are *fully paid*, the members' liability is limited to the money they have put up: the maximum risk a shareholder runs is to lose all the money he has paid for his shares, and no further claim can be made on him for liabilities incurred by the company. If the shares are only *partly paid*, shareholders (and to a limited extent former shareholders) can be called upon to subscribe some or all of the unpaid part, but no more than that.

Limited by guarantee

This method is used for charitable and similar organisations, where funds are raised by donations and no shares are issued. The liability is limited to the amount each member personally guarantees, which is the maximum each member may be called upon to pay in the event of liquidation. This form of incorporation is not normally used for a business.

Unlimited
This method is used by professional firms who want the tax advantages of being a company; the members have joint and several liability in the same way as a partnership (each member can individually be held entirely responsible).

Chartered company

Companies may also be established by Royal Charter, the method used before any Companies Acts existed; for example, the PENINSULAR & ORIENTAL STEAM NAVIGATION COMPANY was incorporated by Royal Charter in 1840. The legal position of a chartered company is similar to an incorporated company, except that any change to the Articles involves a petition to the Privy Council.

Private company

(Reference: Companies Act 1948, Section 28.)

A private company is one whose Articles:

(*a*) restrict the right to transfer shares, usually requiring existing shareholders to be given first refusal;
(*b*) limit the number of members (shareholders) to 50, not including employees and former employees;
(*c*) prohibit any invitation to the general public to subscribe for any shares or debentures.

Public company

Any company which is not a private company is a public company. A public company does not automatically have its shares listed on the Stock Exchange, but the process of obtaining a listing (*see* Chapter 3) is often referred to as "going public", as a private company cannot obtain a listing on the Stock Exchange, and the processes of obtaining a listing and of becoming a public company are often carried out together.

Close company

(Reference: Income and Corporation Taxes Act 1970, Section 282.)

Broadly speaking, a close company is one which is under the control of five or fewer persons or their associates *or* is under the control of its directors.

A close company is required to distribute at least 50% of trading income less Corporation Tax and all its investment income less tax, unless larger retentions can be shown to be needed for the continuing requirements of the business. If insufficient is distributed, the company is assessed as having distributed the required total: the difference is apportioned to the shareholders, treated as paid to them, and they are taxed accordingly. This process, called "apportionment", is sometimes still referred to as "shortfall", its correct name prior to 1973.

A listed company is not a close company if shares carrying not less than 35% of the voting power are unconditionally and beneficially held by the public.

The Listing Agreement requires a company to include, with its annual report, a statement showing whether or not, as far as the directors are aware, the company is a close company.

Chapter 3

ADMISSION TO LISTING

Stock Exchange listing – "quoted companies"

(Reference: The Stock Exchange, London's book *Admission of Securities to Listing* – known as "The Yellow Book".)

Provided that it meets certain criteria, a public company may have its shares and/or debentures, unsecured loan stocks and warrants "listed", *i.e.*, included in the Stock Exchange Official List, so that a market is "made" in the securities. Although it is usual for all the securities of a company to be listed, it is possible for this not to be the case. For example SAINSBURY's preference shares were listed for many years before their ordinary shares were offered to the public.

Companies which have securities that are listed are often referred to as "quoted companies", "having a quotation" or "being listed", although it is the company's securities that are listed, not the company itself. "Having a quotation" is simply the old term for being "listed", and the Stock Exchange department which deals with applications for listing is still called the Quotations Department.

Requirements for listing

Before admitting any of a company's securities to listing, the Stock .Exchange's Quotations Department has to ensure that the company makes available sufficient information on its history, current position and future prospects to enable the general public to assess the securities' value as an investment. The Companies Act 1948 requires any company wishing to invite public subscriptions for shares or debentures to issue a *prospectus* with the form of application. The prospectus must contain all the information and reports specified in Schedule 4 of the Act and, where a listing is sought, it must also comply with Schedule II in the Yellow Book.

The Stock Exchange also has to satisfy itself that sufficient dealings are likely to take place in the class of security for which application is being made to make a realistic market, and thus justify a listing. The Yellow Book lays down two minimum criteria for listing – the expected market capitalisation (the expected market price multiplied by the number of shares issued and to be issued: the current minimum is £500,000 for the company and £200,000 for each class of security) and the proportion of shares to be held by the public (currently 25% of any class of issued equity capital).

Finally, the Stock Exchange has to ensure that the general public will be kept satisfactorily informed of the company's activities and progress in the future, and that the shareholders' interests will be adequately protected; this is done by requiring the board of directors to pass a resolution by which the company enters into a "Listing Agreement" with the Stock Exchange.

The Listing Agreement

The Listing Agreement, which is contained in Chapter 2 of the Yellow Book together with notes on its application and use, is designed to protect shareholders and to keep them properly informed. It requires the company to submit to the Stock Exchange through the company's brokers proofs *for approval* of all circulars to holders of securities, notices of meetings, forms of proxy and notices by advertisement to holders of bearer securities. It also requires the company to notify the Stock Exchange of profit announcements, dividend declarations, material acquisitions, changes of directors, proposed changes in the nature of the business and "any other information necessary to enable the shareholders and the public to appraise the position of the company and to avoid the establishment of a false market in its securities".

In addition, amongst various requirements on interim reports, proxy voting, registration of securities and several other topics, *the Listing Agreement requires companies to circulate with the annual report:*

(*a*) the directors' reasons for any non-compliance with standard accounting practices;
(*b*) a geographical analysis of turnover and trading results of operations outside the United Kingdom;
(*c*) the name of the principal country in which each subsidiary operates;
(*d*) certain particulars of each company in which the group holds 20% or more of the equity capital;
(*e*) details of directors' beneficial and non-beneficial interests in the company;
(*f*) information on holdings, other than by directors, of 5% or more of any class of voting capital;
(*g*) a statement of whether the company is or is not a close company;
(*h*) particulars of significant contracts during the year in which any director is or was materially interested;
(*i*) particulars of the waiving of emoluments by any director;
(*j*) particulars of the waiving of dividends by any shareholder.

Companies are also expected to issue their report and accounts within six months of their year end, and to explain any delay in doing so to the Stock Exchange.

Methods of obtaining a listing

Chapter 1 of the Yellow Book describes the five ways in which a company can obtain a listing. Briefly, they are as follows:

1. *Offer for sale*, the most common method; both new and/or existing shares can be offered to the public. The issuing house or the sponsoring broker purchases the shares from the existing shareholders and/or from the company, and offers them on to the general public at a slightly higher price.
2. *Offer for sale by tender*, a variation on method 1 which allows applicants to bid for securities at or above a minimum issue price. The shares are then all sold at one price, the "striking price", which may be the highest price at which all the shares can be sold, or a little lower if this is necessary to ensure a good spread of shareholders.
3. *Public issue by prospectus*, a rare method; shares are offered direct to the public by the company. Only new shares can be offered.
4. *Placing*, used for small issues (under £1 million); the shares are sold to institutional investors, and the general public are not invited to subscribe. A proportion of the shares have to be offered to the jobbers to ensure that a reasonable market can be started in the shares, *i.e.*, so that other investors have an opportunity to buy the shares through any stockbroker.
5. *Introduction*, used where the company's shares are already widely held and/or are already listed outside the UK; there is no formal offer of shares.

Methods 1 to 4 are referred to broadly as "new issues", because the company's shares are new to the stock market, although methods 1, 2 and 4 do not necessarily involve the issue of any new shares.

Chapter 4

SHARE CAPITAL AND RESERVES

SHARE CAPITAL

Authorised and issued share capital

When a company is formed the authorised share capital and the nominal value of the shares are established and written into the company's Memorandum of Association. At the same time the procedure for increasing the authorised share capital is included in the company's Articles of Association; this procedure usually requires the passing by simple majority of an ordinary resolution at a general meeting of shareholders. Thereafter the directors of the company cannot issue new shares in excess of the authorised limits, nor can they issue any form of securities which have rights to subscribe for shares (*e.g.*, convertibles and warrants: see below) if the full exercising of these rights would involve the issue of shares in excess of the authorised share capital.

Both the authorised share capital and the issued share capital are shown in the company's balance sheet.

Types of share capital

Although all shares are referred to generally as "risk capital", as the shareholders are the first investors to lose if the company fails, the degree of risk can vary within the same company from hardly any more than that of an unsecured lender to highly speculative, with prospects of reward usually varying accordingly. The main types of shares, in increasing order of risk, the order in which they would rank for distribution in the event of liquidation, are

(*a*) Preference shares;
(*b*) Ordinary shares;
(*c*) Deferred shares;
(*d*) Warrants to subscribe for shares.

Unlike interest paid on loan capital, distributions of profits to shareholders are not an "allowable expense" for company taxation purposes; *i.e.*, dividends have to be paid out of profits *after* Corporation Tax has been deducted, although the present imputation tax system does concede to shareholders an associated tax credit on dividends, as explained in Chapter 13.

Preference shares

Preference shares carry a fixed rate of dividend, normally payable half-yearly, but unlike the holders of loan capital, who can take action against a company in default of interest payments, preference shareholders have no legal redress if the board of directors decides to recommend that no preference dividends should be paid. However, if no preference dividend is declared for an accounting period, no dividend can be declared on any other type of share for the period concerned, and the preference shareholders usually become entitled to vote at shareholders' general meetings. (Provided their dividends are paid, preference shares do not normally carry a vote.)

Varieties of preference shares can include one or a combination of the following features:

1. *Cumulative.* If the dividend on a cumulative preference share is not paid on time, payment is postponed rather than omitted. When this happens, the

preference dividend is said to be "in arrears", and these arrears have to be paid by the company before any other dividend can be declared. Arrears of cumulative preference dividends must be shown in a note to the accounts.

2. *Redeemable.* The shares are repayable, normally at their par value, in a given year, *e.g.*, 1990, or when the company chooses within a given period, *e.g.*, 1988/92.
3. *Participating.* In addition to receiving a fixed dividend, shareholders participate in an additional dividend, usually a proportion of any ordinary dividend declared.
4. *Convertible.* Shareholders have the option of converting their preference shares into ordinary shares, usually on an unchanged nominal value basis within a given period of time, the conversion period.

Example 4.1 Varieties of preference share

A company has four types of share, listed below. In 1975 it pays no dividends; in 1976 it pays preference dividends only, including arrears of cumulative preference dividends, and in 1977 and 1978 it also pays ordinary dividends of 4p and 12p respectively. The participating preference shareholders are entitled to half the ordinary dividend in addition to their fixed 3.5% per annum.

The net dividend payable on each type of share, all of £1 nominal value, would be

	1975	1976	1977	1978
5.6% Cumulative Preference	Nil	11.2p	5.6p	5.6p
7% Redeemable Preference 1976	Nil	7p	Nil (redeemed)	Nil
3.5% Participating Preference	Nil	3½p	5½p	9½p
Ordinary £1 share	Nil	Nil	4p	12p

(The rate of dividend on a preference share is quoted gross, or net of associated tax credit (*see* p. 86).)

Ordinary shares

Ordinary shares usually form the bulk of the share capital of a company. Ordinary shareholders are normally entitled to all the profits remaining after tax and preference dividends have been deducted although, as explained later, not all these attributable profits are likely to be distributed. Ordinary shareholders are entitled to vote at general meetings, giving them control over the election of directors.

Ordinary stock

Ordinary stock is a historic legacy from the days when every share in issue had to be numbered; some companies used to convert their shares into stock when they became fully paid (as this avoided the bother of numbers), and a few companies have carried on doing so.

Ordinary stock is equity capital. It can, in theory, be transferred in any monetary amount, while shares can only be bought and sold individually; in practice ordinary stock is normally traded in multiples of £1, so the terms "ordinary share" and "ordinary stock" are effectively synonymous.

Non-voting shares

A number of companies have more than one class of share (other than preference shares), with differing rights on voting and/or dividends and/or on liquidation. The most common variation is on voting rights, where a second class of share, identical in all other respects to the ordinary class, carry either no voting rights, (usually called N/V or "A" shares), or carry restricted voting rights (R/V shares).

The trend over the last few years has, however, been towards the abolition of non-voting shares, and it is becoming increasingly difficult (if not actually impossible) to raise new money by the issue of non-voting shares. Several companies, led by MARKS & SPENCER in 1966, and including SEARS and RANK, have enfranchised their non-voting shares, giving modest scrip (free) issues to voting shareholders by way of compensation.

Deferred shares

Another, but less common, class is the deferred share, where no dividend is payable either:

(*a*) until ordinary shareholders' dividends have reached a certain level,
or
(*b*) until several years after issue: *e.g.*, BRITISH-AMERICAN TOBACCO issued some deferred ordinary stock in 1972 in connection with the acquisition of INTERNATIONAL STORES. This deferred ordinary stock never ranked for dividends but became convertible into ordinary stock in 1976.

Partly paid shares

When a company does not need all the proceeds of an equity issue immediately (*e.g.*, an oil exploration company with a lengthy drilling programme) or wishes to have guaranteed recourse to further equity finance in certain circumstances (e.g., a merchant bank wanting ample cover for liabilities), it may issue partly paid shares, *i.e.*, shares for which subscribers pay for only part of the nominal price at the time of issue. Partly paid shares, once issued, place an obligation on the holder to subscribe the un-paid-up portion at the company's call, and there are legal safeguards to prevent the device of holders transferring their shares to a non-creditworthy person in order to avoid paying the call.

Details of partly paid shares issued by a company are shown in the balance sheet (*e.g.*, HAMBROS, as shown below).

Where a company holds partly paid shares, details must be shown under "contingent liabilities" (CA 1948, Sch. 8, para. 11 (5)), *e.g.*, BURMAH OIL, illustrated below.

Shares can be issued with part of the issue price payable on application and the remainder payable shortly afterwards, before registration (*i.e.*, before the company registers the shares in the holder's name). However, if shares are to remain partly paid after registration, the Stock Exchange will not normally allow them to be admitted to listing.

Warrants

Warrants are transferable options granted by the company to purchase new shares from the company at a given price, called the "exercise price". The warrant is normally exercisable only during a given time period, the exercise period, although one or two perpetual warrants have been issued.

Warrants can be issued on their own, but are usually issued attached to new issues of unsecured loan stock to give the stockholder an opportunity of subsequently participating in the equity of the company; the warrant element makes the issue more attractive and is sometimes referred to as the "sweetener" (*see* Chapter 5).

Once the loan stock plus warrants "package" is issued the warrants can be detached ("stripped") and sold separately, providing a high risk/high reward form of equity investment. For example, if the ordinary shares of a company stood at 100p, warrants with an exercise price of 75p would then be worth a minimum of 25p. If the ordinary shares doubled to 200p then the warrants would be worth a minimum of 125p, a fivefold increase. In practice warrants command a premium over the

HAMBROS LIMITED *Balance sheet*

	Authorised £	1978 £	1977 £
Share capital and reserves			
400,000 shares of £10 each fully issued £2.50 paid	4,000,000	1,000,000	1,000,000
20,000,000 shares of 25p each	5,000,000		
17,029,447 issued fully paid		4,257,000	4,257,000
510,500 issued 2½p paid		13,000	13,000
1,000,000 "A" shares of £1 each fully issued and paid	1,000,000	1,000,000	1,000,000
	10,000,000	6,270,000	6,270,000

BURMAH OIL *Balance sheet*

Note 37 Other commitments and contingent liabilities

	1974 £ thous Group	1974 £ thous Company	1973 £ thous Group	1973 £ thous Company
(a) Amounts uncalled on partly paid shares:				
Subsidiaries	–	1,092	–	1,122
Associates	2,261	2,261	2,261	2,261
Trade investments	216	180	276	180
	2,477	3,533	2,537	3,563

ordinary price minus exercise price, although this premium tends to fall over the life of the warrant, reaching zero at the end of the exercise period. Warrants are comparatively rare in the United Kingdom, where the majority have been issued in bid situations.

A very clear explanation of the behaviour of warrant prices in practice is given in R. A. Brealey's book *Security Prices in a Competitive Market.*

Share schemes for directors and employees

There are several types of scheme, listed below.

Share options
These are like warrants, except that they are not normally transferable, and may lapse on termination of the holder's directorship of or employment by the company. Details of the number granted, the period during which the options may be exercised and the subscription price payable must be shown in the accounts.

Partly paid shares
These are usually 1 or 2 pence paid, and holders are either entitled to dividends *pro rata* to the portion paid up or to no dividends until fully paid up. As the call on the unpaid portion is usually payable at the holder's request, partly paid shares issued under executive incentive schemes are very similar to options from the company's point of view, the unpaid-up portion being equivalent to the subscription price of the option, but the holder's tax position is different.

Details of all types of partly paid shares are shown in the balance sheet under "Share capital" (*e.g.*, CALOR GAS, shown here).

CALOR GAS *Balance sheet*

Note 12 Share capital	1974
	£000
Ordinary shares of 25p each:	
Authorised	9,000
Issued and fully paid	8,725
Issued under the terms of the share incentive scheme 1.25p paid	4
	8,729

The total of shares issued under the share incentive scheme at 31st March, 1974 was 346,000

Shares purchased with loans
Section 54 of the Companies Act 1948 allows loans to employees, but not to directors, for the purpose of purchasing fully paid shares in the company. A company may also make loans to a trust for the purchase of shares for the benefit of both employees and directors holding a salaried employment or office in the company. In either case the aggregate amount of any outstanding loans must be shown in the company's balance sheet.

Strictly speaking, options granted and partly paid shares issued to directors and employees under executive schemes produce potential dilution of equity earnings in the same way as warrants, but in practice they are usually sufficiently small in relation to a company's issued equity to be ignored.

Unfortunately the whole subject of these schemes is a political football, because they are designed to allow management the incentive of a lightly taxed capital gain rather than a heavily taxed salary increase; any measure introduced under the Conservatives is emasculated by the next Labour government.

Other types of scheme are aimed at wide share ownership amongst employees rather than to reduce taxation on higher management rewards, for example, SAYE and profit-sharing schemes:

SAYE (save as you earn) schemes
The employee enters a SAYE scheme for a period of at least five years and on entry is given the option to buy at the end of the period a given number of shares at a given price, using a lump sum he or she will receive through the scheme at that time. The total number of options outstanding under the scheme will be shown in the accounts (*e.g.*, GREENALL WHITLEY, illustrated here).

GREENALL WHITLEY *1975 report*

Employees' Share Scheme
Options over 424,305 Ordinary Shares were granted in April 1975 to employees and directors of the Group under the terms of the Savings Related Share Option Scheme approved at the Extraordinary General Meeting held on 27th February 1975. These options entitle the participants to purchase the shares at 36p per share between 1980 and 1982 but special arrangements apply to circumstances such as retirement after 3 years following the grant.

Profit-sharing schemes
Although several companies such as OWEN OWEN have been using a proportion of their profits to buy shares for employees for a number

of years, it was not until the April 1978 budget that Labour, under pressure from the Liberals, announced a major tax concession to encourage this type of scheme. With effect from the Financial Year 1979, companies will be allowed to allocate up to £500 per employee to be used to purchase shares at full market value through specially created trusts. The shares have to be held in trust for five years; Income Tax only has to be paid when the shares are sold, and then only on a reduced scale according to the length of tenure, but normal Capital Gains Tax is also payable on disposal.

Limitations on the issue of further equity

There are three limitations to the issue of further equity.

Firstly, as already mentioned, there must be sufficient share capital authorised.

Secondly, the Stock Exchange's Listing Agreement forbids the issue of equity, convertibles, warrants or options for cash, other than to the equity shareholders of the company, except with the prior approval of ordinary shareholders in general meeting, and the approval of the Stock Exchange. The Stock Exchange normally restricts issues of equity capital by way of placings to £1 million of equity or £3 million of convertible stocks, with an overall limit of 5% of the existing listed equity capital, but these restrictions can be relaxed when market conditions or the individual circumstances of a company justify doing so.

Thirdly, Section 57 of the Companies Act 1948 requires the approval of both shareholders and the court for the issue of shares for less than their nominal value, *i.e.*, at a discount.

A method of getting over this problem when the ordinary price is so low that a suitable discount would mean an issuing price below par is to issue shares that are partly paid by capitalising reserves. For example, in 1975 GORDON JOHNSON-RICHARD (HOLDINGS) made a 1-for-2 rights issue of 25p shares 10p paid at 17p, having passed a resolution at an EGM to capitalise £189,956.20 from the General Reserve Account and apply it in paying up 10p on each of the new shares. This can, of course, be done only when the company has sufficient reserves; companies whose shares are standing close to or below par may have little or no reserves left.

Rights issues

When a rights issue is made, new shares are offered to shareholders in proportion to their existing holdings at a discount to the current market price. The discount varies according to the "weight of the rights issue; 1 new share offered for every 8 or 10 shares already held would be regarded as a "light" issue, probably requiring a discount of around 15%, while more than 1-for-4 would be "heavy" and likely to need about 20% discount, or more if the company is in poor health. At these discounts underwriting would be arranged to ensure buyers for any shares not taken up by shareholders, but companies occasionally choose to make a rights issue at very much below the market price, the lowest price normally permitted being the par value of the shares.

The effect on the balance sheet of an issue at par is to add the total nominal value of the shares being issued to the issued share capital, and to show the cash received on the assets side. The expenses of the issue would normally be written off either to profit and loss account or against share premium account.

If the new shares are issued above par, the nominal value of the shares issued is added to the issued share capital and the difference between the issue price and the nominal price of each new share, *i.e.*, the premium at which the shares were issued, is added to the share premium account. For example, in June 1973 DE LA RUE made a 1-for-10 rights issue of 50p ordinary shares at 215p per share. The effect of the issue was shown in their subsequent report and accounts, illustrated here.

DE LA RUE *Balance sheet 1974*

Year end 31 March	1974	1973
	£000	£000
Ordinary shares	6,791	6,173
Share premium account	3,512	1,544

Note 12 The premium arising of £2,037,000 less expenses of £69,000 has been credited to the share premium account.

There are two methods of dealing with convertible stock in a rights issue. The holders are either offered new shares on the basis of the number of ordinary shares they would hold on full conversion, or the stock has its conversion terms adjusted to allow for the rights issue, whichever method is laid down in the convertible's trust deed (*see* Chapter 5). Similarly, warrant holders are either offered new shares or the warrant's exercise price is adjusted.

Scrip issues

A scrip issue, also known as a bonus or capitalisation issue, is a free issue of additional new shares to existing shareholders, made by capitalising reserves. For example, WATTS BLAKE BEARNE made a 1-for-2 scrip issue in 1978, with the following effect on the balance sheet:

	At 31 Dec 1977	*Post scrip*
	£000	£000
Share capital:		
preference	146	146
ordinary	2,154	3,231
Reserves	9,769	8,692
Shareholders' funds	12,069	12,069

As a scrip issue is purely a book-keeping transaction, the share price would normally be expected to adjust accordingly (*e.g.*, would fall from 150p to 100p with a 1-for-2), and it is open to debate as to whether scrip issues serve any useful purpose. The main arguments in favour are that:

(*a*) Scrip issues are popular with the investing public, and therefore enhance share prices. Research shows that shares tend to outperform the market after the announcement of a scrip issue, but that companies only make scrip issues when they are doing well, *i.e.*, when their share price would be expected to outperform just as much without the scrip issue.

(*b*) A "heavy" share price in the market, say over £2, tends to make the shares harder to trade and artificially depresses the price. Scrip issues can be used to scale the price down.

(*c*) A scrip issue, being "paid for" out of reserves, enables retained profits and/or the increased value of assets to be reflected by an increased share capital.

(*d*) The rate of dividends, expressed as a percentage of an unrealistically small share capital, can look excessive.

(*e*) An issued share capital of at least £1 million is needed for Trustee status.

The last argument appears to be the only factual one in favour of scrip issues; the remainder are psychological, although only a sound and flourishing company is likely to be able to make substantial scrip issues every few years. Watts Blake Bearne's record illustrates this well: the company also made a 1-for-2 scrip issue in 1970, a 1-for-3 in 1972 and a 1-for-4 in 1976.

The arguments against scrip issues are firstly the administrative costs incurred and secondly the increased risk of the share price subsequently falling very close to or below par, thus precluding a rights issue. The cost is relatively small, but reducing the market price can cause serious embarrassment if the company wants, at a later date, to make a rights issue only to find that its share price is too low to do so.

Share splits

Where a company feels its share price is "heavy" but does not want to capitalise reserves – *i.e.*, it does not want to make a scrip issue – it can split its shares into shares with a smaller par value. For example, in 1976 PATERSON ZOCHONIS split their 25p shares, which were standing at around 400p at the time, into 10p shares on the basis of 5 new 10p shares for every 2 old 25p shares held, and the share price moved to around 160p.

Stock (scrip) dividends

There are two types of stock or scrip dividends:

(*a*) where the company issues shares instead of paying cash dividends – shareholders have no choice (*e.g.*, ULTRAMAR);

(*b*) where each shareholder can choose whether he or she wishes to receive a cash dividend or a stock dividend.

Between 1973 and 1975 tax legislation enabled shares issued by companies in lieu of cash dividends at the choice of individual shareholders, *i.e.*, type (*b*) above, to be assessed for Capital Gains Tax on subsequent disposal rather than being treated as income received in the year of distribution. The number of shares was calculated to give the same value as the *net* dividend payable, and each shareholder could elect to receive a stock dividend in lieu of a cash dividend if he preferred the former.

An alternative method, adopted by one or two companies (for example, RIO TINTO-ZINC), was to create a separate class of *accumulating shares*, which ordinary shareholders could switch into so as to receive stock dividends automatically.

The tax concession was of considerable advantage to shareholders paying more than the standard rate of Income Tax, and was abolished when a Labour government returned to power. Thus stock dividends became fairly rare; they may still be paid in lieu of cash, but they can only avoid Income Tax assessment providing the stock dividend is not an alternative to cash, *i.e.*, type (*a*) above.

Vendor consideration

This is the use of new shares to pay for an acquisition. In the balance sheet the value of the shares issued is shown as an increase in liabilities under share capital and share premium account, balanced on the other side by the assets acquired.

ENGLISH CHINA CLAYS *Source and application of funds statement 1977*

ANALYSIS OF ACQUISITIONS

	£000		£000
Net assets acquired		**Discharged by**	
Fixed assets	5,064	Shares issued	4,364
Stocks	537	Cash paid	1,317
Debtors	2,568		
Creditors	(3,138)		
	5,031		
Goodwill	650		
	5,681		5,681

If the value of the tangible assets falls short of the market value of the shares issued, the difference (*i.e.*, the premium the acquirer has paid) is taken into the balance sheet as "goodwill" - an intangible asset. For example, in 1977 ENGLISH CHINA CLAYS made several acquisitions and, in amplification of the figure of £5.681 million shown for acquisitions in the source and application of funds statement, gave the details shown above.

Reduction of share capital

Under Section 66 of the Companies Act 1948 a company may, with court approval, reduce its share capital in any way and, in particular, may:

(*a*) reduce or extinguish liability on share capital not fully paid up;
(*b*) cancel any paid-up share capital which is lost or unrepresented by available assets; and
(*c*) repay any paid-up share capital in excess of its requirements.

Where the net assets no longer exceed the nominal value of the issued share capital, the reserves will appear negative in the balance sheet. Take, for example, the balance sheet of a company which has 1 million £1 ordinary shares in issue and reduces this to 1½ million 25p shares to remove a substantial accumulation of losses (Example 4.2):

Example 4.2 Share capital reduction on the balance sheet

	Before reduction	*After reduction*
	£000	£000
Issued share capital	1,000	375
Share premium account	206	-
Other reserves	(831)	-
Shareholders' funds	375	375

£625,000 nominal of capital and the share premium account of £206,000 have been cancelled.

Arrangements and reconstructions

If a company wishes to make an arrangement with its creditors or shareholders, including a reorganisation of the company's share capital by consolidation of different classes and/or division into different classes, it can do so under Section 206 of the Companies Act 1948. A meeting has to be called for each class of creditor or shareholder concerned, at which a resolution to make the arrangement requires at least three-fourths by value of those present to vote in favour; after subsequent sanction by the court, the arrangement is then registered with the Registrar of Companies and becomes binding on all creditors and shareholders concerned.

RESERVES

Reserves can arise in several ways:

(*a*) by the accumulation of profits, either by retained profits from the profit and loss account or from the sale of assets.
(*b*) by the issue of shares or loan capital at a premium, *i.e.*, at more than their nominal value: the issue can be either for cash or as consideration (payment) in an acquisition;
(*c*) by the purchase or repayment of loan capital below its nominal value;
(*d*) by upward revaluation of assets (*see* p. 33).

They can be reduced by losses, issue and

redemption expenses, revaluation deficits and the writing-off of goodwill. In addition, some companies charge foreign currency adjustments direct to reserves.

Under the Companies Act 1967 (Sch. 2, para. 27) reserves shall not include either provisions (as described in Chapter 11) or any sum set aside to prevent undue fluctuations in charges for taxation (*i.e.*, deferred taxation, dealt with in Chapter 13); reserves, provisions and deferred taxation must each be shown separately (Sch. 2, paras 6 and 7A).

Capital and revenue reserves

By law certain reserves are non-distributable (cannot be paid out as dividends) and the Articles of a company may further restrict distribution.

Prior to the Companies Act 1967 a company was required to distinguish between reserves available for dividend (revenue reserves) and those not available (capital reserves), and although in law this distinction is no longer compulsory some companies still make the division between capital reserves and revenue reserves in their accounts.

Share premium account

(Reference: Companies Act 1948, Section 56.)

When shares are issued at a premium over their nominal value, the premium element must, by law, be credited to the share premium account.

The share premium account has to be shown separately on the balance sheet and no part may be paid out to shareholders except on liquidation or under a capital reduction scheme authorised by the court. It is permissible, however:

(*a*) to capitalise the share premium account to pay up unissued shares for distribution to shareholders as a *bonus* issue (otherwise known as a scrip or capitalisation issue), for instance:

Ordinary share capital	£100,000
Share premium account	£85,000

Company makes 1-for-2 scrip issue:

Ordinary share capital	£150,000
Share premium account	£35,000

(*b*) to charge to the share premium account:
- (i) the preliminary expenses of forming a company;
- (ii) the expenses and commissions incurred in any issue of shares and loan capital;
- (iii) any discount on the issue of shares or loan capital (the issue of shares for less than their nominal value is very rare);
- (iv) any premium paid on the redemption of redeemable preference share or loan capital.

Foreign currency equalisation

Some companies with overseas borrowings and overseas assets keep a running total of the effect of currency exchange rates in a separate reserve.

Reserve funds

Where a reserve is represented by earmarked assets (*e.g.*, quoted securities, an endowment policy and/or cash specifically set aside), it is called a reserve *fund*.

For example, if a company issues a £250,000 debenture repayable in 20 years and decides to set aside £8,000 each year towards the cost of eventual redemption (the old-fashioned type of sinking fund as described in Chapter 5), it will treat it as a separate fund, investing the money in earmarked assets, usually risk-free gilt-edged securities, to earn interest between now and the redemption date.

Debenture redemption reserve funds are comparatively rare these days as almost all debenture issues now either have no sinking fund at all or provide for a small proportion of the debenture to be redeemed by drawings or repurchase each year, rather than setting the money aside in a fund.

Capital redemption reserve fund

Where redeemable preference shares are redeemed out of profits the Companies Act 1948 (S. 58) requires an amount equal to the nominal value of the shares to be redeemed to be transferred from distributable profits to a separately shown reserve which is called the "capital redemption reserve fund" although it is not really a reserve *fund* at all.

The idea behind the law is to prevent a company's overall share capital plus non-distributable reserves from being reduced when preference capital is repaid: the fund can never be distributed except upon liquidation or in a capital reduction scheme, but it can be capitalised by a bonus issue, as in Example 4.3 opposite.

Movements to and from reserves

The Companies Act 1967 requires the source of any increase and the application of any decrease in reserves to be disclosed (Sch. 2, para. 7), and SSAP 6 requires that a statement of retained profits/reserves should immediately follow the profit and loss account (*see* p. 97).

Example 4.3 Capital redemption reserve fund

1. Initial position	£		£
Issued share capital			
30,000 £1 Redeemable Preference Shares	30,000		
100,000 £1 Ordinary shares	100,000		
	130,000	Cash	**50,000**
Reserves			
Revenue reserve (retained profits)	75,000		

2. Company then redeems all the preference shares:

Issued share capital			
100,000 £1 Ordinary shares	100,000		
	100,000	Cash	20,000
Reserves			
Capital redemption reserve fund	30,000		
Revenue reserve (retained profits)	45,000		

3. Company then decides to make a 3-for-10 scrip issue:

Issued share capital			
130,000 £1 Ordinary shares	130,000		
	130,000	Cash	20,000
Reserves			
Revenue reserve (retained profits)	45,000		

4. The overall share capital is thus brought back to £130,000.

Chapter 5

LOAN CAPITAL

The advantages of borrowing

If a company confidently expects that its return on capital (*i.e.*, the trading profit expressed as a percentage of the capital the company employs), will exceed the cost of borrowing, then borrowing will increase the profit attributable to the ordinary shareholders.

There are, however, various limitations on the amount a company can borrow, which we will discuss later in this chapter, and borrowing also increases risk.

The risk of borrowing

The risk of borrowing is twofold: firstly the interest on most borrowings has to be paid promptly when due (unlike dividends on shares, which can be deferred or omitted altogether) and secondly most borrowings have to be repaid by a certain date (unlike most share capital, which is only repayable on liquidation).

In a poor year, interest charges can drastically reduce the pre-tax profits of a heavily borrowed company. Take, for example, two companies that are identical except that one, Company A, is financed entirely by shareholders while the other, Company B, is financed half by shareholders and half by borrowing, which bears a fixed rate of interest of 10% per annum.

The table in Example 5.1 shows the profitability of the two companies with varying rates of return on capital employed: in an average year Company B earns 15% on money borrowed at 10%, and so gains 5% on £500,000, adding £25,000 to pre-tax profits. This extra profit, after tax, adds 2.5p to the earnings attributable to each of the 500,000 shares that Company B has issued, making the earnings per share 10p compared with 7½p for Company A.

In a good year the advantage of borrowing will enhance Company B's earnings per share even more (20p compared with 12½p for Company A) but in a poor year, as our table shows, all the trading profit is used servicing the borrowings of Company B, while Company A still manages to earn £25,000 after tax for its shareholders.

The point at which the two companies do equally well as far as their shareholders are concerned is shown on the graph in Example 5.1. Their earnings per share are both 5p when the return on capital employed is 10% per annum: as one would expect, borrowing at 10% to earn 10% neither adds to nor detracts from Company B's profits. As the graph also shows, borrowing makes a company's profits more volatile, and the risk of borrowing is further increased when money is borrowed at a variable rate of interest (*e.g.*, on overdraft). If interest rates had risen above 10% in our example's "poor year", Company B would have actually made a loss.

We will come back to the effects of borrowing in Chapter 23, but let us now look in detail at various types of borrowing.

Types of borrowing

There are many ways in which a company can borrow money, the main characteristics of different types of debt being:

(*a*) the length of time for which the money is borrowed;
(*b*) the rate of interest paid;
(*c*) the security offered to the lender by way of

Example 5.1. Financing by share capital and by borrowing

	Company A			Company B		
Issued equity (£1 shares)	£1,000,000			£500,000		
Borrowings (10% interest)	Nil			£500,000		
	Good year	*Average year*	*Poor year*	*Good year*	*Average year*	*Poor year*
Rate of return	25%	15%	5%	25%	15%	5%
	£000	£000	£000	£000	£000	£000
Trading profit	250	150	50	250	150	50
Interest	–	–	–	50	50	50
Pre-tax profit	250	150	50	200	100	0
Taxation (50%)	125	75	25	100	50	0
Profit after tax	125	75	25	100	50	0
Earnings per share	12.5p	7.5p	2.5p	20p	10p	0p

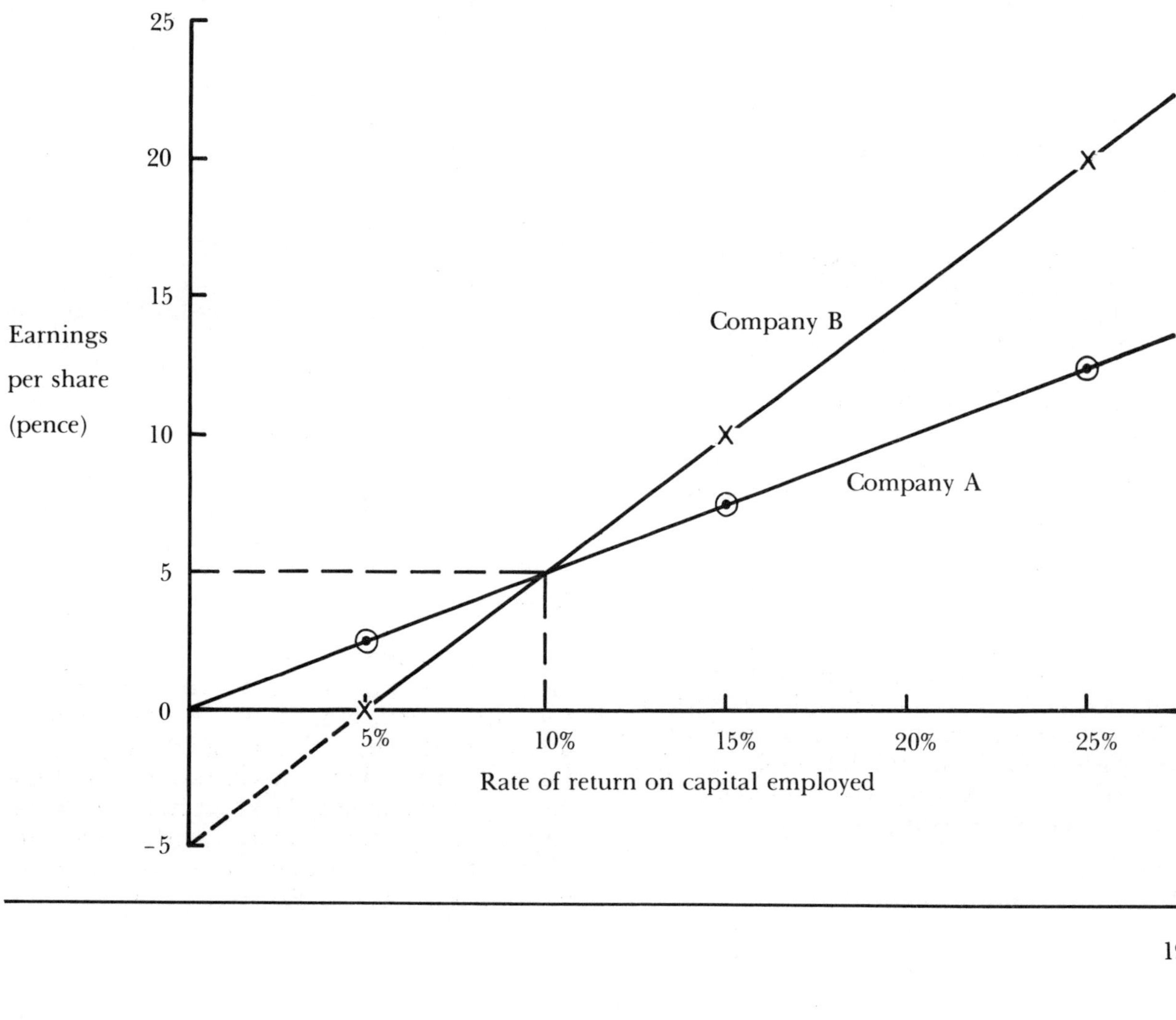

charges on the assets of the company;

(*d*) the negotiability of the debt instrument (*i.e.*, does the lender receive a piece of paper which he can sell if he wishes to disinvest before the date of repayment?);

(*e*) the flexibility to the company and to the lender in the timing of borrowing and repayment;

(*f*) any deferred equity option given to the lender.

A company's borrowings fall broadly into three categories:

1. Issues of debentures and unsecured loan stock, which can be held by the general public, and can be bought and sold in the same way as shares.
2. Loans from banks and other financial institutions.
3. Bank overdrafts (described in Chapter 10).

Categories 1 and 2 are shown in the balance sheet under a separate heading, usually called "loans" or "loan capital" (with a note describing the terms on which each loan is repayable and the rate of interest), dividing them into secured and unsecured loans, and giving the aggregate amount of:

(*a*) bank loans;

(*b*) other loans wholly repayable within 5 years;

(*c*) other loans, wholly or partly repayable more than 5 years after the balance sheet date.

Loans that are wholly repayable within one year should appear under "current liabilities", together with bank overdrafts, but may sometimes still be found under "loan capital". This is an important point to watch, because a loan coming up for repayment may significantly weaken the company's liquidity position, and can be a very serious threat to a company that is already short of funds if it is likely to have any difficulty refinancing the loan.

Security given to the lender debentures and unsecured loan stock

When a company wishes to issue loan capital it can offer the lender some specific security on the loan. If it does so, the loan is called a debenture (£100 units) or debenture stock (usually units of £1); if not it is an unsecured loan stock (ULS), and these are the two main types of loan capital raised from the general public.

Debentures

Debentures can be secured by fixed and/or floating charges described below, the most common type of debenture being one that is secured on specific land or buildings, sometimes called a mortgage debenture. Other examples are:

1. *Tonnage debenture*, secured on the revenues of specific long-term contracts between the company and their customers, *e.g.*, BRITISH OXYGEN COMPANY's series of Tonnage Debenture Stocks, 8½% 1988 and 1990 and 11% 1992.
2. *Wagon debenture*, secured on railway rolling stock. Although common in the United States there has only been one recent issue in the United Kingdom, the PROCOR (UK) 11¼% Wagon Debenture Stock 1993/98.

Fixed charge

A fixed charge is similar to a mortgage on a house. The company enters into a debenture deed which places a charge on specific identifiable assets. This gives the debenture holder a legal interest in the assets concerned as security for the loan, and the company cannot then dispose of them unless the debenture holder releases the charge (which he is unlikely to do unless he is offered some equally good alternative security). If the company defaults or falls into arrears on interest payments or capital repayments, the debenture holder can either:

(*a*) Appoint a Receiver to receive any income from the assets (*e.g.*, rents) *or*

(*b*) Foreclose, *i.e.*, take possession and sell the assets, using the proceeds of the sale to repay the debenture holders in full; any surplus remaining is then paid to the company, but if the proceeds of selling the assets charged are insufficient to repay the debenture holders in full, the debenture holders then rank equally with unsecured creditors for the repayment of the shortfall.

Floating charge

This is a general charge on the assets of a company. But the debenture holder has no legal interest in the assets unless and until an event specified in the debenture deed occurs; for example, if the company goes into liquidation or ceases trading, or falls behind with interest payments or capital repayments, or exceeds specified borrowing limits. In the event of default the debenture holder can then appoint a Receiver, who takes physical possession of the assets of the company. The Receiver can also be appointed as the Manager or a separate Manager can be appointed to continue running the company, or the Receiver can sell off the assets; the former course is adopted if possible, because a company can normally be sold as a going concern for more than the break-up value.

The ranking of ULS
In a liquidation the holders of unsecured loan stock rank equally with other unsecured creditors, that is after debenture holders and preferential creditors (tax, rates and certain obligations to employees). In practice trade creditors often restrict a company to "cash with order" terms if they see it running into difficulties, and to that extent a ULS tends to rank behind suppliers.

Typical characteristics of debentures and ULS

Interest
Most debentures and ULS carry a fixed annual rate of interest (known loosely as the "coupon") which is payable (normally half-yearly) regardless of the company's profitability. Interest is deductible before the company is assessed for tax, *i.e.*, it is an allowable expense for tax purposes, and therefore costs the company less than the same amount paid out in dividends on shares.

Redemption
Each issue is normally for a given term, and is repayable at the end of the term (at the redemption date) or, where there is a redemption period (*e.g.*, 1993/97) it is repayable when the company chooses within that period. A few irredeemable stocks do exist, *e.g.*, BRITISH ELECTRIC TRACTION 5% Perpetual Debenture, redeemable (at 130%) only in the event of voluntary liquidation, but they are rare.

Liquidation
In the event of liquidation, debenture holders are entitled to repayment in full from the proceeds of disposal of the charged assets. Then the ULS holders and other unsecured creditors, and the fixed charge debenture holders if not already fully satisfied, rank equally after preferential creditors, and have to be repaid before the shareholders are entitled to anything.

Specific characteristics – the trust deed

Where a debenture or loan stock is to be issued to more than a very small number of holders, and particularly when it is going to be listed on the Stock Exchange, a trustee or trustees are appointed to represent the holders collectively, and the company enters into a trust deed rather than a debenture deed.

For listing, the Stock Exchange also requires that at least one trustee must be a trust corporation which has no interest in or relation to the company which might conflict with the position of the trustee. A large insurance company or the specialist LAW DEBENTURE CORPORATION is often appointed as trustee.

The deed contains all the details of the issue, except the issue price, including:

(*a*) details of fixed and floating charges, together with provision for *substitution* (securing further assets to replace secured assets which the company may subsequently wish to dispose of during the term of the loan). Provision may also be made for '*topping up*' (securing further assets if the value of secured assets falls below a given limit);
(*b*) redemption price and redemption date or period, together with any sinking fund arrangements;
(*c*) conditions under which the company may repurchase in the market, by tender and from individual holders;
(*d*) redemption price in the event of liquidation;
(*e*) conditions for further *pari passu* (equal ranking) issues, restrictions on prior borrowings and, for ULS, overall borrowing limits;
(*f*) minimum transferable unit (nominal value);
(*g*) powers to approve modifications to the terms and conditions.

The trust deed may also include restrictive clauses, for example:

(*h*) to prevent the nature of the company's business being changed; this is known as a "Tickler" clause, after the celebrated case of the jam manufacturer who was taken to court by the holders of an unsecured loan stock;
(*i*) to prevent major disposals of the company's assets – a "disposals" clause;
(*j*) to restrict the transfer of assets between charging subsidiaries (those within the charging group, *i.e.*, included in the charge on assets) and other subsidiaries – sometimes known as a "ring fence".

Treatment of expenses on issue and of profit or loss on redemption

The expenses of issuing debentures and ULS, and any profit or loss on issues not made at par, are normally shown as an extraordinary item. For example, ARTHUR BELL, the whisky manufacturer, made a debenture issue of £3.5 million nominal in 1975 at £98½% and the accounts showed the discount on debenture placing (£52,500) and the expenses of the issue as extraordinary items.

Similarly, the loss on redemption above par or the profit on redemption below par is normally shown as an extraordinary item; for example, CLAYTON DEWANDRE in 1975 showed in the balance sheet under loan capital:

	1975	1974
7¼% debenture stock 1986/91	£1,799,010	£1,831,510

a reduction of £32,500 nominal, and showed under "extraordinary items" in the profit and loss account:

Profit on purchase of debenture stock	£15,155

(The analyst can thus calculate that the stock was purchased by the company at around £53 per £100 nominal).

On the other hand, in the same year, the same company issued £1.25 million nominal of a new debenture at £99%, and wrote off the discount and issue expenses directly against reserves, so there is no hard and fast rule in practice on the treatment of profit/loss and expenses arising from the issue and redemption of debt.

In fact, some companies treat profit on redemption as a *normal* item in their profit and loss account; for example, BICC GROUP's 1975 accounts showed operating profit as including:

Profit on redemption of debentures and bonds	£0.824m

In our view, profits of this nature should not be included in the calculation of a company's normal earnings.

Sinking funds

Some debenture and loan stock issues make provision for part or all of the stock to be redeemed gradually over a period of time by means of a sinking fund.

The normal method for a sinking fund to redeem stock is by annual or six-monthly drawings (lotteries of stock certificate numbers), with the company in some cases having the option of purchasing stock in the market if it can do so at or below the drawing price. The company may also be allowed to invite holders to tender stock for redemption.

There are three types of sinking fund, described below.

Original concept – no early redemptions
The sinking fund or redemption reserve fund, as originally conceived, was a fund into which a company put a given sum each year, the money being invested in government or other safe fixed-interest securities rather than being used to make early redemptions. The sums, together with interest earned, went on accumulating in the balance sheet year by year until the redemption date. This method is now rarely used.

Non-cumulative
Each year in which the sinking fund is in operation the company normally sets aside enough cash to redeem a fixed amount of stock, expressed as a given percentage of the total issue, and uses it to redeem stock on or by the date of the second interest payment (Example 5.2).

Example 5.2 Non-cumulative sinking fund

A 25-year stock with a 2% sinking fund starting at the end of the 5th year would be redeemed at the rate of 2% per annum at the end of years 5 to 24, leaving 60% of the stock to be redeemed at redemption date.

Providing redemptions each year are by drawings at par, the *average life* of a stock can be calculated by working out the average life of the stock redeemed by the sinking fund, in this case 14½ years, and then weighting it by the percentage redeemed by the sinking fund, in this case 40%:

$$\text{Average life} = \frac{(14\tfrac{1}{2} \times 40\%) + (25 \times 60\%)}{100\%}$$
$$= 20.8 \text{ years}$$

Cumulative
In a cumulative sinking fund the cash used for redemption each year is variable and normally consists of a fixed amount of cash plus the amount of interest saved by prior redemption (*see* Example 5.3 opposite).

Yields

The yield on an irredeemable security is the gross amount of income received per annum divided by the market price of the security. Redeemable securities have two yields, their running yield and their gross redemption yield.

Running yield
The running yield is the same as the yield on an irredeemable security: it measures *income* and is concerned purely with the annual gross interest and the price of the stock; for instance, an 8% unsecured loan stock issued at £98 per cent will yield 8% ÷ 0.98 = 8.16% at the issue price, or a 4½% debenture purchased at £50 per cent will

Example 5.3 Cumulative sinking fund

If our previous example had been a £10m issue of a 25-year stock with a 10% coupon and a cumulative sinking fund starting at the end of year 5, and if all redemptions were made by drawings at par, then the annual redemptions would be:

End of year	*Fixed amount of cash*	*Variable amount (interest saved)*	*Stock redeemed in year*	*Total stock redeemed*	*Stock remaining*
4	Nil	Nil	Nil	Nil	£10,000,000
5	200,000	Nil	200,000	200,000	£9,800,000
6	200,000	20,000	220,000	420,000	£9,580,000
7	200,000	42,000	242,000	662,000	£9,338,000
8	200,000	66,200	266,200	928,200	£9,071,800

and so on. The average life can be calculated by time-weighting each year's redemption, *e.g.*, 200,000 × 5 years plus 220,000 × 6 years, etc. ÷ 10,000,000. However, if redemptions are made by purchases in the market or by tender at below the redemption price, the amount redeemed will be greater, the amount of interest subsequently saved will be larger and the whole process of redemption will accelerate.

give the purchaser a yield of 9%, ignoring purchase expenses.

Redemption yield

The *gross* redemption yield is rather more complicated, as it measures "total return"; *i.e.*, it takes into account both the stream of income and any capital gain (or loss) on redemption. It is *not* just the sum of the running yield and the capital gain per annum, but is obtained by discounting the future interest payments and the redemption value at a rate that makes their combined *present value* equal to the current price of the stock. (The concept of discounting to obtain *present value* is explained in Appendix 2.) The rate required to do this is the gross redemption yield (Example 5.4).

Typical gross redemption yields for a well secured debenture are ¾% to 1½% above the yield on the equivalent gilt-edged security (*i.e.*, a UK Government stock of similar life and coupon), and 1% up to 5% or more for ULS, depending very much on the quality of the company and the amount of prior borrowings (borrowings that would rank ahead in a liquidation). *Net* redemption yields (*i.e.*, the yields after tax) vary with the individual holder's rate of income tax payable on the stream of interest payments and the rate of tax payable on any capital gain on redemption.

Example 5.4 Gross redemption yield

A 6% debenture due for redemption at £105 per cent in four years' time is standing in the market at £90. Interest is payable in the normal manner, half-yearly in arrears (at the end of each six months). The present value of the stock is the sum of the present values of the eight future six-monthly interest payments discounted at $\sqrt{1+i}$ per half-year (where i% = gross redemption yield).

$$\frac{3}{(\sqrt{1+i})} + \frac{3}{(\sqrt{1+i})^2} + \ldots + \frac{3}{(\sqrt{1+i})^8}$$

plus the present value of the sum received on redemption in 8 half-years' time =

$$\frac{105}{(\sqrt{1+i})^8}$$

Solving for i by trial and error:

Value of i		*Present value of income*		*Present value of redemption*		*Total*
10%	=	19.48	+	71.72	=	£91.20
11%	=	19.09	+	69.15	=	£88.24

Inspection suggests that the gross redemption yield on a market price of £90 is about 10½%, and a more accurate figure can be obtained by further manual calculation or by computer. Alternatively, the yield can be obtained from Bond Tables.

Redemption date

When a stock has a final redemption period, *e.g.*, 1999/04, it is assumed in computing redemption yields that the company will choose the earliest date for redemption, 1999, if the stock is currently standing above par, otherwise the latest date, 2004.

When there is a sinking fund which allows redemptions only by drawings, the average life can be calculated accurately and should therefore be used as the number of years to redemption in calculating redemption yields. However, if the company is allowed to redeem by purchase in the market or by inviting tenders, the stockholder can no longer be sure that early drawings at par will take place, and the average life is therefore ignored.

The amount a company can borrow

The amount a company can borrow may be limited by:

(*a*) Its borrowing powers. The directors' borrowing powers are normally limited by a company's Articles of Association, and cannot be altered except with the approval of shareholders at a general meeting. Borrowing powers are usually expressed as a multiple of shareholders' funds (issued share capital plus reserves, less goodwill).

(*b*) Restrictions imposed by existing borrowings. The terms of the trust deeds of existing loan capital may restrict or preclude the company from further borrowing. In particular the terms of an unsecured loan stock may include a clause preventing the company from issuing any loans that rank ahead of the stock concerned, and unduly restrictive clauses are often the reason for companies redeeming loan capital in advance of the normal redemption date.

(*c*) The lender's requirement for capital and income cover.

(*d*) The lender's general opinion of the company and its overall borrowing position.

Capital and income covers

These are two standard measures the intending purchaser of a debenture or loan stock may use to assess the security of his investment.

The *capital* or asset cover can be calculated in two ways, on a simple basis or on a "rolled-up" basis.

Using the simple basis, the cover is the total capital less all prior-ranking stocks, divided by the issued amount of the stock in question.

Using the "rolled-up" basis, the cover is the total capital divided by the stock in question plus all prior-ranking stocks.

As Example 5.5 shows, the two equal-ranking ULS issues are three times covered on a simple basis (£60 million total capital less £15 million prior-ranking debenture, divided by the total of £15 million ULS), but only twice covered on a rolled-up basis. The more conservative "rolled-up" basis is normally used for assessing capital covers.

For a floating charge debenture a rolled-up capital cover of at least 3 or 4 is expected by the lender, and 2½ times is the normal minimum for an unsecured loan stock, but both depend on the quality of the assets, *i.e.*, the likely realisable value of the assets on the open market in the event of a liquidation.

The *income* cover is normally worked out on a rolled-up rather than a simple basis: *i.e.*, it is the number of times the interest on a stock plus the interest on any prior-ranking stocks could

Example 5.5 Capital cover

Capital	*Amount*	*Cumulative total*	*Simple cover*	*Rolled-up cover*
	£000	£000		
6% Debenture	15,000	15,000	4.0	4.0
8% ULS	10,000	} 30,000	3.0	2.0
10% ULS	5,000			
Ordinary shares	12,000	} 60,000		
Reserves (less goodwill)	18,000			
Total capital	60,000			

Example 5.6 Income cover

A company has £5.76 million of earnings before interest and tax, and the following loan capital, with the ULS and the CULS ranking equally:

Nominal value of issue	*Annual interest*	*Cumulative interest*	*Times covered*	*Priority percentage*
£12m of 6% Debenture	£0.72m	£0.72m	8.0	0–12½%
£10m of 8% ULS	£0.80m	} £1.92m	3.0	12½–33⅓%
£8m of 5% CULS	£0.40m			

be paid out of profits before interest and tax. This cover can also be expressed as a *priority percentage*, showing the percentile ranking of a stock's interest, with earnings before interest and tax representing 100% (Example 5.6).

Interest should normally be several times covered, although a lower income cover may be acceptable in some highly geared situations *e.g.*, in some property companies, where assured rental income provides safe cover.

A company's overall borrowing position

There are a variety of methods of measuring a company's overall borrowing position: the two main ones are *gearing* and *debt/equity ratio* (which is known as "leverage" in the United States).

Gearing is most commonly defined as loan capital plus bank and other borrowings expressed as a percentage of capital employed.

Example 5.7 Gearing and debt/equity ratio

Loan capital	£24,000	£34,000
Bank overdrafts	£10,000	
Ordinary shares	£14,500	£36,000
Reserves (*less* goodwill)	£21,500	
Capital employed		£70,000

$$\text{Gearing} = \frac{34{,}000}{70{,}000} = 49.1\%$$

Debt/equity ratio = 34,000:36,000 = 0.94 or 94%

Gearing of 33.3% (debt/equity ratio of 50%) would be a reasonable level for an average company, although companies with steady profits can borrow more highly, while those in cyclical industries would be wise to have little or no gearing.

Convertible loan capital

Convertible loan capital, which is usually convertible unsecured loan stock (CULS) rather than convertible debentures, entitles the holder to convert into ordinary shares of the company if he so wishes (*see also* convertible preference shares, Chapter 4).

The coupon on a convertible is usually much lower than the coupon needed for the issue of a straight unsecured loan stock with no conversion rights. This is because a convertible is normally regarded by the market as deferred equity, valued on the basis of the market value of the shares received on conversion plus the additional income enjoyed before conversion (the coupon on issue being higher than the yield on the ordinary shares).

Because convertibles are a form of deferred equity, listed companies can issue them without shareholders' prior approval only as a rights issue or as part or all of the consideration in an acquisition. In a takeover situation the bidder can use a suitably pitched convertible to provide the shareholders of the company being acquired with a higher initial income than they would receive from an equivalent offer of the bidder's ordinary shares. This is particularly useful when a bidder with low yielding shares wants to avoid the shareholders of the company he wishes to acquire suffering a fall in income if they accept his offer.

In recent years CULS have become increasingly popular with investors, particularly with gross funds (*e.g.*, pension funds), which are attracted by their higher income and by the greater security a convertible provides for both income and capital compared with the equity. From a company's point of view, CULS is cheaper to service than convertible preference shares, as the interest on the former is deducted before Corporation Tax is assessed.

Terms of a convertible loan

The holder has the option of converting into ordinary shares during a given period in the life of the debenture or ULS (the conversion period), at a given conversion price per share, expressed as so many shares per £100 of stock, or as so much nominal stock per ordinary share:

Example 5.8 Convertible loan: MIDLAND BANK

MIDLAND BANK issued a 7½% convertible subordinated unsecured Loan Stock 1983/93 in 1973 and 1974 as part consideration for the acquisition of Montagu Trust and the Drayton Group respectively. The stock can be converted into 21 £1 Midland Bank ordinary shares per £100 on 31 May in any of the years 1977 to 1983, and these conversion terms will be adjusted for any *scrip issues* to the ordinary shareholders in the meantime. Any *rights issues* to ordinary shareholders will also be made to the holders of the convertible as if they had already exercised their outstanding conversion rights (rather than making an adjustment to the conversion terms, as is done in some convertible issues).

If more than 75% of the stock is converted, the Midland Bank have the right to force remaining stockholders to convert or redeem straight away; this is a fairly standard condition in a convertible stock, enabling the company to clear a convertible off its balance sheet once most of it has been converted.

Stock that remains unconverted at the end of the conversion period can be redeemed by the Midland Bank at any time after 31 December 1983 and all outstanding stock will be redeemed on 31 December 1993, the final redemption date.

The period between issue and the first date for conversion is sometimes called the "rest period" and the period from the last date for conversion and the final redemption date the "stub". Diagrammatically the Midland Bank convertible can be shown as:

Rest Period	Conversion Period	Stub	
1973	1977	1983	1993

A rest period of two or three years is normal, and most conversion periods run for at least four or five years. Some of the earlier convertible issues had little or no stub, but several years is now fairly standard because if convertible holders decide not to exercise their conversion rights the company concerned is probably not doing very well and would not want to be faced with having to redeem the stock immediately the conversion rights lapsed.

Another piece of convertible jargon is the *conversion premium.* This is the premium one pays by buying the ordinary shares via the convertible rather than buying them direct. For example, if the Midland Bank convertible in Example 5.8 was standing at £105 per cent (per £100 nominal) and the ordinary shares were standing at £4, the cost of getting into the ordinary shares through the convertible would be £105 ÷ 21 each = £5, a conversion premium of 25%.

A good indication of the likely market price of a convertible can be obtained by discounting the future income advantage to present value and adding it to the market value of the underlying equity. Where conversion terms are varied during the conversion period, sometimes called *stepped conversion* (*e.g.*, C.T. BOWRING's 10% CULS 1987), the calculation has to be done for each set of terms and the highest result taken. One caveat to this method is that if the price of the ordinary shares is very depressed the price of the CULS in the market can become mainly dependent on its value as a fixed-interest security, particularly if the conversion period has not long to run.

Finally, in our example, the Midland Bank convertible is called *subordinated,* because it ranks after unsecured creditors in the event of liquidation and ranks equally with the Midland Bank's other subordinated issue, the 10¾% SULS 1993/98, and the trustee is the PRUDENTIAL ASSURANCE COMPANY LIMITED.

Warrants

Where a company is reluctant to raise loan capital when very high long-term interest rates prevail, or investors are reluctant to commit themselves to purely fixed-interest securities, loan capital can be raised with a lower coupon by attaching warrants to issues of stock.

Warrants, already described in Chapter 4, are long-term options granted by the company, entitling holders to subscribe for ordinary shares during some specified period in the future at some specified price, called the exercise price. They are normally detachable and exercisable as soon as the stock to which they are attached is fully paid, and in some issues stock can be surrendered at its nominal value as an alternative to cash payment when the warrants are exercised.

In a takeover situation, warrants can provide a more flexible way for the bidder to give loan stock an equity interest than convertibles, because the number of warrants, sometimes called the "equity kicker", can be varied as the company wishes, while the quantity of ordinary shares to which convertible holders are entitled is defined within a narrow range by the limit the market will accept on the conversion premium.

On the other hand, a drawback to warrants is that they will seldom be exercised until close to the final exercise date, because they are bought by investors who want the gearing they provide, so the future flow of money into the company's equity is more chancy than a convertible. In addition the tendency for speculators to "strip" (detach) the warrants and dump the stripped stock on the market has led to more responsible investors regarding warrants with some distrust.

Chapter 6

FIXED ASSETS

(Reference: SSAP 12 *Accounting for Depreciation*, standard, except for investment properties, for accounting periods starting on or after 1 January 1978.)

Definitions

Fixed assets
Those long-lived assets not held for resale in the ordinary course of business but for the purpose, directly or indirectly, of earning revenue. Thus they include not only things like plant and machinery which are actually used to provide the product, but assets used to house or support its operations, such as land, buildings, furniture, vehicles, ships and aircraft.

Depreciation
A measure of the loss of value of an asset due to use, the passage of time and obsolescence, including the amortisation of fixed assets whose useful life is predetermined (*e.g.*, leases) and the depletion of wasting assets (*e.g.*, mines).

Book value
Traditionally fixed assets are shown in the balance sheet at cost less aggregate depreciation to date (*i.e.*, at net book value). This book value is not, and does not purport to be in any sense, a valuation, though fixed assets, particularly land and buildings, are quite frequently revalued. Sometimes, but by no means always, the valuation is taken into the books.

Companies Act requirements on fixed assets

The requirements of the Companies Act 1967 with regard to fixed assets are somewhat complex. In summary they are that:

(*a*) Fixed assets shall be classified under headings appropriate to the business.

(*b*) Land must be analysed into freehold, long leaseholds (over 50 years unexpired) and short leaseholds.

(*c*) Under each heading the aggregate figure for the following amounts must be shown:
   (i) cost or valuation;
   (ii) provision for depreciation since acquisition or valuation;
   (iii) the book value (i minus ii).

(*d*) Where fixed assets are included at a valuation, the amount so included must be shown, together with the years and amounts of the valuations and, for assets valued during the year, the names of the valuers and the basis of valuation (*see* p. 34, Example 6.9).

(*e*) Particulars of additions and disposals during the period.

Disclosure requirements on depreciation

Schedule 2 of the Companies Act 1967 requires companies to disclose:

(*a*) the amount of depreciation charged to revenue;

(*b*) if depreciation has been calculated on other than book value;

(*c*) any amounts, additional to depreciation, charged by way of provision for renewal of fixed assets;

(*d*) if no provision has been made for depreciation or replacement; or the method used if other than by depreciation charge or provision for renewals.

SSAP 12 requires companies to disclose the method of depreciation used for each category of asset, together with the effective useful lives assumed.

Rates of depreciation

The following are typical rates (using the straight line method of depreciation, described below):

Freehold land	Nil
Freehold buildings	2% = 50 year life
Leasehold property:	
Long leases (over 50 years)	2% = 50 years
Short leases	Over life of the lease
Plant and machinery	10% = 10 years
Vehicles	20% = 5 years
Ships, according to type	4–10% = 10–25 years
Furniture and equipment	10% = 10 years

Sub-normal depreciation charges
Where a company is charging a sub-normal rate of depreciation, or is omitting to charge depreciation on assets (other than freehold land), it will report higher than normal pre-tax profits, and the figures should be adjusted accordingly in any analysis.

Where depreciation is shown in the accounts

Depreciation can appear in several places; EDBRO (HOLDINGS) LTD provides an example of what a good set of accounts shows:

1. In the profit and loss account, as a note to the item "Trading profit" (*see* below);
2. In the balance sheet, as a note to the item "Fixed assets" (*see* below);
3. In the statement of accounting policies:

EDBRO (HOLDINGS) LTD *Statement of accounting policies*

Depreciation
The charge for depreciation is calculated to write off the cost of fixed assets, less government grants, over their expected effective lives.
Annual rates of depreciation used are on the straight line basis unless otherwise indicated. The rates used are generally as follows:

Freehold land	Nil
Freehold buildings	4% (reducing balance)
Leasehold land & buildings	4% (reducing balance)
Plant and machinery	10%
Office equipment	20%
Motor vehicles	20%

In addition the auditors' report may mention depreciation. For example, J.B. EASTWOOD'S 1976 accounts showed that the company had not provided for depreciation on freehold or long leasehold properties nor on poultry house equipment, but instead had charged the cost of all replacements (an unspecified amount) direct to revenue. If depreciation had been charged at say a modest 2% on the book value of the assets

EDBRO (HOLDINGS) LTD *Profit and loss account, note on trading profit*

	1976
	£
Trading profit is stated after charging	
Depreciation	299,604
Auditors' remuneration (etc. . . .)	

EDBRO (HOLDINGS) LTD *Balance sheet, note on fixed assets*

	Land and buildings: Freehold	Land and buildings: Long leasehold	Plant and equipment	Total
Aggregate depreciation at 1st April, 1975	85,289	331,872	1,209,286	1,626,447
Differences on exchange	5,320	22	8,712	14,054
Amount provided in the year	32,822	52,113	214,669	299,604
	123,431	384,007	1,432,667	1,940,105
less eliminations on disposals	1,495	–	23,133	24,628
Aggregate depreciation at 31st March, 1976	121,936	384,007	1,409,534	1,915,477

concerned, the profits would have been reduced by more than £0.4 million, material in relation to the reported pre-tax profits of £7 million, and even more material in the previous year, when the company reported a loss of £0.5 million. Their auditors, the leading firm of Peat, Marwick, Mitchell & Co., qualified their auditor's report accordingly.

J.B. EASTWOOD *Auditors' report*

. . . in our opinion the fixed assets concerned (other than land) depreciate by reason of use coupled with the effluxion of time and provision should therefore be made for such depreciation in arriving at the profit of the group.

In any analysis of Eastwood's accounts, the estimated depreciation omitted (£0.4 million) should be deducted from the reported figure for pre tax profits.

Methods of depreciation

The most common method or basis of depreciation, used by over 80% of major companies, is the straight line (or fixed instalment) method. Other methods include:

(*a*) the declining balance (or reducing balance) method;
(*b*) the sum of the years' digits method;
(*c*) the production unit method;
(*d*) the annuity method;
(*e*) the sinking fund method.

The straight line or fixed instalment method

Depreciation under the fixed instalment method is computed as follows (*see also* Example 6.1 below):

$$\text{Annual depreciation} = \frac{\text{Cost} - \text{Residual value}}{\text{Expected useful life}}$$

The straight line method is ideal where the service provided by the asset continues unabated throughout its useful life, as might be the case with a 21-year lease of a building; and it is *generally used wherever the equal allocation of cost provides a reasonably fair measure of the asset's service*, for example, for buildings, plant, machinery, equipment, vehicles and patents. It is easy to calculate, and conceptually simple to understand.

The declining balance or reducing balance method

The declining balance method used to be the most popular method of depreciation; but is has largely been supplanted in recent years by the straight line method.

Under the declining balance method, the annual depreciation charge represents a fixed percentage of the net book value brought forward (*i.e.*, cost less aggregate depreciation). The calculation of the annual charge is simple enough once the appropriate percentage has been determined, but this requires the use of tables, a slide rule or a calculator.

$$\begin{array}{l}\text{Depreciation rate}\\ \text{(as a decimal)}\end{array} = 1 - \sqrt[n]{\frac{\text{Residual value}}{\text{Cost}}}$$

where n = useful life in years.

Example 6.2 (overleaf) illustrates the calculation.

Example 6.1 Straight line depreciation

If a machine having an estimated useful life of five years is purchased for £10,000, and is expected to have a residual value of £1,000 at the end of that life, depreciation will be:

$$\frac{£10{,}000 - £1{,}000}{5} = \frac{£9{,}000}{5} = £1{,}800 \text{ per annum}$$

and the accounts will show:

End of year	*Depreciation for the year* (shown in the P & L account)	*Cost*	*Provision for depreciation to date*	*Net book value*
		←	shown in the balance sheet	→
	£	£	£	£
1	1,800	10,000	1,800	8,200
2	1,800	10,000	3,600	6,400
3	1,800	10,000	5,400	4,600
4	1,800	10,000	7,200	2,800
5	1,800	10,000	9,000	1,000

Example 6.2 Declining balance depreciation

The rate for the machine in Example 6.1 would be computed as follows:

$$\text{Depreciation rate} = 1 - \sqrt[5]{\frac{£1{,}000}{£10{,}000}} = 1 - 0.631 = 0.369 = 36.9\%$$

Thus the rate to apply is 36.9%.

End of year	*Depreciation for the year* (shown in the P & L account)	*Cost*	*Provision for depreciation to date*	*Net book value*
		← shown in the balance sheet		→
	£	£	£	£
1	3,690	10,000	3,690	6,310
2	2,328	10,000	6,018	3,982
3	1,470	10,000	7,488	2,512
4	927	10,000	8,415	1,585
5	585	10,000	9,000	1,000

Among the disadvantages of the declining balance method are these:

(*a*) Most users do not calculate the rate appropriate to each particular item of plant, but use standard percentages, which tend to be too low rather than too high.

(*b*) Unless notional adjustments are made to cost and residual value, it is impossible to calculate satisfactorily a declining balance rate if the residual value is nil – the net book value can never get to nil, as it can only be reduced by a proportion each year.

(*c*) Even if the asset is assigned a nominal scrap value (say £1 so that it is not overlooked in the books) or if there is some residual value but it is small in relation to cost, the method is unlikely to be satisfactory without notional adjustments, because it leads to such high charges in the early years, as Example 6.3 shows.

Example 6.3 Declining balance depreciation, small residual value

Taking our previous example of plant costing £10,000, but with a residual value of £200 instead of £1,000, we get:

Year	*Year's depreciation*	*Compared with*
	£	£
1	5,425	3,690
2	2,482	2,328
3	1,135	1,470
4	520	927
5	238	585
Accumulated depreciation at the end of year 5	9,800	9,000
Residual value	200	1,000

The sum of the years' digits method

The sum of the (years') digits method is not commonly found in Britain, though it is used a good deal as a method of allowing accelerated depreciation in the United States (where accounting depreciation, provided it is computed by an acceptable method, is used for tax purposes too). It is occasionally found in Britain in connection with activities like leasing which involve heavy outlays in early years, when it is often referred to as "the rule of 78" (since the digits of the twelve months in a year add up to 78).

In this method, the cost less any residual value is divided by the sum of the years' digits to give what, for the purpose of this explanation, may be termed a unit of depreciation. In the last year of expected life, one unit of depreciation is provided; in the next to last, two; in the one before that, three; and so on.

The sum of the years' digits is simply the sum of the series: $(1 + 2 + 3 + 4 + \ldots\ldots + n)$, where n represents the expected life of the asset.

The formula for computing the sum of the digits is $n(n + 1) \div 2$, where n is the number of years. Thus, to apply the sum of the digits to an asset having a life of 5 years, the divisor (*i.e.*, the sum of the years' digits) is $5(5 + 1) \div 2 = 15$, and the first year's depreciation is 5/15ths of (cost

Example 6.4 Sum of the years' digits method of depreciation

Taking our example of a machine costing £10,000, with an estimated life of 5 years and a residual value estimated at £1,000: the sum of the years' digits is 15, and a unit of depreciation is thus (£10,000 – £1,000) ÷ 15 = £600, so:

End of year	*Depreciation for the year* (shown in the P & L account)	*Cost*	*Provision for depreciation to date*	*Net book value*
		← shown in the balance sheet		→
	£	£	£	£
1	3,000	10,000	3,000	7,000
2	2,400	10,000	5,400	4,600
3	1,800	10,000	7,200	2,800
4	1,200	10,000	8,400	1,600
5	600	10,000	9,000	1,000

minus residual value), the second year's 4/15ths, and so on (*see* Example 6.4 above).

It is interesting to compare the balance sheet value of this asset year by year with the value under the straight line and the declining balance methods, as shown in Fig. 6.5.

Fig. 6.5 Comparison of depreciation methods (for an asset costing £10,000, residual value £1,000, useful life 5 years)

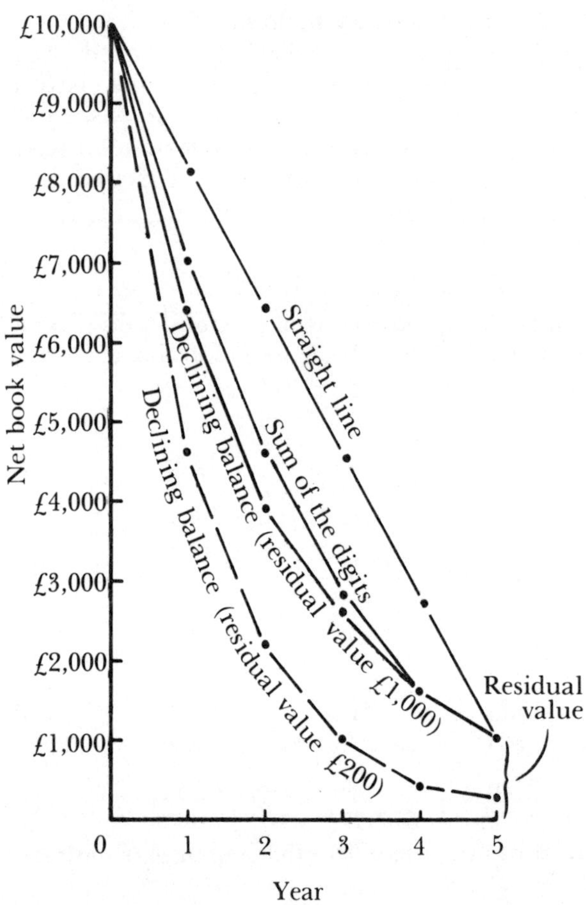

It can be seen that if the annual book value under the declining balance method is plotted, it follows a curve which in mathematical terms is asymptotic, that is, it gets nearer and nearer to the horizontal axis (*i.e.*, to 0) but if the residual value is zero it would never quite get there (*i.e.*, a charge for depreciation is made however long the asset lasts, be that charge ever so small), whereas the value under the sum of the digits method is reduced in decreasing steps, year by year, reaching residual value at the end of the asset's expected life, regardless of the size of the residual value, if any. Thus, although there is a similarity in the charges produced by the two methods, the sum of the digits method does not need the notional adjustments of the declining balance method to cope with small or nil residual values.

The production unit method

In this method, depreciation is charged according to the number of units produced in the period (*see also* Example 6.6):

$$\text{Charge per unit} = \frac{\text{Cost} - \text{Residual value}}{\text{Estimated number of units to be produced during the asset's effective lifetime}}$$

Example 6.6 Production unit depreciation

An asset costing £10,000 is estimated to have a residual value of £1,000 at the end of its useful life, which is 300,000 units.

$$\text{Depreciation per unit} = \frac{£10,000 - £1,000}{300,000} = 3\text{p}$$

Thus, the charge in a period in which 80,000 units were produced would be £2,400.

This method can only be used where all the units an asset produces are identical or involve the same "work value". It makes costing of machine costs simple; and has the result of charging high depreciation where a machine is being used round the clock (which is not unreasonable); but it can be very misleading in that there is no charge for depreciation if the machine lies idle – though clearly an unused asset still depreciates with the lapse of time, *e.g.*, through corrosion, and the idleness of a machine may indicate an earlier than estimated end to its useful life.

The annuity method

The annuity method is sometimes used for the amortisation of leasehold properties, *i.e.*, to write off the premium (the initial cost of the lease) over the term of the lease.

The annual depreciation charge under the annuity method is calculated by dividing the cost of the asset (less the present value of any expected residual value) by the present value of an annuity of 1 per annum for the estimated life of the asset.

An *annuity* is simply an annual payment, normally for a defined number of years (or for someone's lifetime), so the present value of an annuity of 1 for *n* years is the present value of 1 receivable in one year's time, plus that of a further 1 receivable in two years' time and so on, up to the last payment of 1 in *n* years' time.

Example 6.7 Calculating present value of an annuity

If $n = 3$ and the interest rate is 15%, then the present value of an annuity of 1 is

$$\frac{1}{(1.15)} + \frac{1}{(1.15)^2} + \frac{1}{(1.15)^3} = 2.283$$

(A more detailed explanation of the concept of present value is given in Appendix 2, together with examples of a present value table and an annuity table.)

Returning to the calculation of depreciation – as we said, the cost of the asset less the present value of any expected residual value is divided by the present value of an annuity of 1 per annum for the estimated life of the asset to produce the annual depreciation charge. At the same time notional interest on the net book value (cost less accumulated depreciation) is taken on the credit side of the profit and loss account (Example 6.8 below).

Alternative annuity method

An alternative way of using the method, at one time used by public utilities, and used by property companies in Canada, shows the net amount (*i.e.*, depreciation less notional interest) as "depreciation", and not a depreciation

Example 6.8 Annuity method of depreciation

Take the case of a five year lease costing £9,000, with no residual value: if interest is taken to be 15% the present value of an annuity of 1 for 5 years is 3.352 (see table in Appendix 2) and the depreciation charge is thus:

$$\frac{£9,000}{3.352} = £2,685$$

The computation then proceeds as follows:

Year	1	2	3	4	5
	£	£	£	£	£
Cost	9,000				
Balance b/f	–	7,665	6,130	4,364	2,334
Notional interest at 15% p.a.	1,350	1,150	919	655	351
	10,350	8,815	7,049	5,019	2,685
Depreciation charge	2,685	2,685	2,685	2,685	2,685
Balance c/f	7,665	6,130	4,364	2,334	–

This method puts the company in a position similar to investing the £9,000 rather than purchasing the lease, and renting the asset for £2,685 per annum.

charge and a separate credit for interest. This has the effect of producing a rising charge: a low charge in the early years and a high one in the later years.

The sinking fund method

The sinking fund method is similar to the "original concept" of a sinking fund to provide for the repayment of a loan, described in the previous chapter. A given sum of money is invested each year outside the business sufficient to provide, with interest, the amount of money required to replace the asset at the end of its useful life. The method is rarely used, for two main reasons:

(*a*) The cost of replacement is unlikely to be known with any accuracy when the asset is originally acquired.
(*b*) Most businesses have opportunities for investment within the business which will yield far more than is normally available from fixed interest stocks, in which sinking funds are normally invested.

When the method is used, the amount to be set aside annually is the sum required for replacement divided by the value of an annuity of 1 in arrears for the expected life of the asset (the value an investment of 1 per annum will reach, with compound interest, by the end of the period). The value of an annuity of 1 in arrears can be obtained from annuity tables, or can be calculated as follows:

$$\text{Value} = \frac{(1 + r)^n - 1}{r}$$

where r is the interest rate (expressed as a decimal), and n is the expected life of the asset.

Further points on depreciation

Change in expected useful life
Where, through experience or changed circumstances, it is considered that the original estimate of useful life of an asset needs to be revised, the unamortised cost of the asset (net book value less residual value) should be charged over the revised remaining useful life.

Irrecoverable cost
If, at any time, the unamortised cost of an asset is seen to be irrecoverable in full (for example where production on a purpose-built machine is about to cease) it should be written down immediately to the estimated recoverable amount.

Changing method
Under SSAP 12 a change from one method of providing for depreciation to another is permissible only on the grounds that the new method will give a fairer presentation of the results and of the financial position. Where such a change is made, the unamortised cost should be written off over the remaining useful life commencing with the period in which the change is made, and the effect of the change should be disclosed in the year of change, if material.

Freehold land and buildings
Traditionally freehold land and buildings used not to be depreciated, though the majority of companies have been depreciating freehold buildings in recent years, and SSAP 12 (effective for periods from 1978 onwards) makes this obligatory. In addition, freehold land should be written down if its value is adversely affected for any reason.

Excess depreciation

A few companies make an additional charge for depreciation to allow for the cost of replacing fixed assets, rather than just writing off the original cost of an asset over its useful life. Doing so is called "replacement cost accounting", which is discussed further in Chapter 22 on inflation accounting.

The amounts involved can be very large – for example, ASSOCIATED PORTLAND CEMENT (now BLUE CIRCLE) charged an additional £10 million in 1977 – and they should be added back for the purposes of inter-company comparison.

The revaluation of assets

Traditionally, under historical cost accounting, assets appear at cost less depreciation, and they are not revalued to show their current worth to the company. But because of the effects of inflation, the practice has grown up in the United Kingdom of revaluing assets, particularly freehold land and buildings, from time to time.

Indeed, Section 16(1)(a) of the Companies Act 1967 requires the difference between the market value of property assets and the balance sheet amount to be disclosed in the directors' report if, in the opinion of the directors, it is significant. UK companies thus face the choice: they must either:

(*a*) incorporate any revaluation in the accounts, *or*
(*b*) disclose it in the directors' report.

Where assets are revalued and the revaluation is incorporated in the accounts, both sides of the balance sheet are affected, and depreciation from then on is based on the revalued amounts, as Example 6.9 illustrates.

Example 6.9 Effects of revaluation

Freehold land at cost	£100,000
Revaluation at 1 January 1978	£380,000
Buildings at cost	£420,000
Revaluation at 1 January 1978	£810,000

Let us assume that the buildings were 10 years old on 31 December 1977. Depreciation to that date would thus have been 2% p.a. on £420,000 = £8,400 p.a. for 10 years = £84,000, so the balance sheet would show:

Freehold land and buildings at cost	£520,000
less depreciation to date	£84,000
Book value	£436,000

After the revaluation the accounts would show freehold land and buildings at the valuation figure of £1,190,000, an increase of £754,000. The corresponding adjustments on the other side of the balance sheet would at one time have been made on the basis that if the gain was realised it would be subject to Corporation Tax at an effective rate of 30%; 30% o. £754,000 (£226,200) would have been credited to the deferred tax account, with the remaining £527,800 being credited to reserves. Under SSAP 15 no provision need be made until a liability to pay the tax is foreseen. The 1978 accounts would be required to disclose:

(*a*) the basis of valuation used and the name or qualification of the valuer (CA 1967, Sch. 2, para. 11 (6A));

(*b*) the effect of the revaluation on the depreciation charge, if material (SSAP 10, para. 20).

The revaluation will affect the company in Example 6.9 in several ways:

1. The annual depreciation charge on the buildings, based on the new value and the current estimate of the remaining useful life (40 years), will increase from £8,400 to £20,250 (2½% p.a. on £810,000), thus directly reducing the pre-tax profits by £11,850 in future years.
2. The overall profitability of the company, as measured by the ratio Return on Capital Employed (ROCE, described in Chapter 23) will also appear to deteriorate because the capital employed will have increased by £754,000. For instance, if the company in our example went on to make £300,000 before interest and tax in 1978, and had £2 million capital employed before the revaluation, the 1978 return on capital employed would be:

No revaluation $\frac{311,850}{2,000,000} = 15.59\%$ *Revaluation* $\frac{300,000}{2,754,000} = 10.89\%$

3. The borrowing powers of most companies are expressed as a multiple of share capital and reserves, so the increase in reserves will raise the borrowing limits, and improve the capital cover of existing lenders.
4. The higher property value may give more scope for borrowing on mortgage.
5. The increase in reserves will also increase the n.a.v., the net asset value per share, described in Chapter 23.

Revaluation deficits

Although unrealised surpluses on the revaluation of fixed assets should be credited direct to reserves, revaluation deficits should be charged to the profit and loss account to the extent that they exceed any surplus held in reserves identified as relating to previous revaluations of the same assets (SSAP 6 and its supplement, ED 16).

Sales and other disposals of fixed assets

Where fixed assets are disposed of for an amount which is greater (or less) than their book value, the surplus (or deficiency) should be reflected in the results of the year, and should be disclosed separately if material (SSAP 12).

Some companies, for instance MARKS & SPENCER, habitually include an item "profit (loss) on sale of fixed assets" in a note to their profit and loss account. If the profit or loss on disposals is not disclosed it may be possible to calculate it, but companies often adjust the depreciation charge for the year to bring the net book value of the assets sold into line with the proceeds of the sale, thus hiding any profit or loss on disposal in the depreciation charge, for example in the 1977 accounts of AARONSON BROS, shown opposite.

It is fairly unlikely that the proceeds of sale of fixed assets happened to be exactly the same as their normally written-down book value, so it is pretty certain that the depreciation charge for 1977 was adjusted to make the figures balance.

There is nothing particularly significant in a company making small gains or losses on disposals, but it may give some indication of whether fixed assets tend to be worth more or less than their net book value.

When disposals arise because of the discontinuation of a significant part of the business, they should be dealt with as extraordinary items (see Chapter 14); in these cases the release of capital and the profit or loss previously being made by the discontinued part are probably more important than the amount by which the proceeds of the sale varied from the book value of the assets sold.

AARONSON BROS *Disposal of fixed assets in 1977 accounts*

(*a*) In the note on fixed assets

	£000
Cost – 1 October 1976	13,085
Additions at cost	1,397
	14,482
Cost of disposals	465
	14,107
Aggregate depreciation – 1 October 1976	3,070
Amount provided this year	1,021
	4,091
Eliminated in respect of disposals	283
	3,808

The net book value of disposals is thus 465,000 – 283,000 = £182,000.

(*b*) In the Source and Application of Funds Statement

Net additions to fixed assets	1,215

The proceeds of disposal can be calculated as additions at cost – net additions = 1,397,000 – 1,215,000 = £182,000.

Government grants

(Reference: SSAP 4 *The Accounting Treatment of Government Grants.*)

Accounts are still being affected by investment grants, though these ceased to apply in the case of expenditure after 26 October 1970. In addition, regional development grants, introduced by the Industry Act 1972, are still being made, and similar grants are found in other countries.

All these grants, which provide a refund of part of the purchase price of fixed assets, are called *capital-based* grants and SSAP 4 requires such capital-based grants to be credited to revenue (*i.e.*, to profit) over the expected useful life of the asset concerned. There are two ways of achieving this:

1. By deducting the grant from the cost of the fixed assets (and thus reducing the subsequent annual depreciation charges). The grants received each year are deducted from the cost of fixed assets, and some companies show this deduction, as the extract below from BUNZL PULP & PAPER'S accounts shows.

2. By treating the grant as a deferred credit, and transferring it to revenue by annual instalments over the life of the asset concerned. Under this method government grants normally appear in three places in the accounts; for example ROYAL WORCESTER'S 1975 balance sheet showed a figure of £402,069 for Investment and Regional Development Grants, explain-

BUNZL PULP & PAPER *Deduction of grants*

Fixed assets	*Total*	*Land and buildings*			*Plant*	*Patents*
		Freehold	*Leasehold*		*machinery*	*and trade*
		properties	*Short term*	*Long term*	*vehicles*	*marks*
Group	£000	£000	£000	£000	£000	£000
Cost						
31st December 1974	58,346	14,372	265	1,090	42,328	291
Subsidiary sold	*(33)*	–	–	–	*(33)*	–
Currency conversion gain	3,050	790	4	–	2,237	19
Additions	9,561	3,816	35	30	5,641	39
Grants	*(720)*	*(416)*	*(2)*	*(6)*	*(296)*	–
Disposals and adjustments	*(554)*	*(17)*	*(1)*	–	*(501)*	*(35)*
31st December 1975	69,650	18,545	301	1,114	49,376	314

ing this in notes (illustrated here) to the balance sheet and profit and loss accounts.

ROYAL WORCESTER *Notes to 1975 accounts on government grants*

Investment and Regional Development Grants

	Group
	£
As at 31 December 1974	318,898
Grants receivable	165,945
Credited to Profit and Loss Account	(82,774)
	402,069

The amount shown in the Group Balance Sheet consists of the balance of investment grants received and regional development grants receivable on capital expenditure up to 31 December 1975 after deducting the total so far credited to income.

Trading Profit before Interest	1975	1974
	£	£
is stated after crediting:		
Investment and Regional Development grants	82,774	66,297
Proceeds of consequential loss claim relating to 1974	43,713	-

However, some companies using this method, like DUNLOP, deduct the balance in their government grants account from the net book value of their fixed assets in a note, rather than showing it in the balance sheet, while others like ICI deduct the annual amount transferred to revenue from the taxation charge, rather than crediting it in the calculation of trading profit.

Companies are almost equally divided as to which of the two basic methods they employ. Indeed, since the introduction of regional development grants, some companies use more than one method of accounting.

The arguments in favour of method 1 are, first, that commercial decisions on capital investment are (or should be) made on a "net of grants" basis, *i.e.*, the return on capital employed to consider is the return on the capital the company would have to put up, not the "gross" cost, and, second, that method 1 makes accounting so much simpler. Method 2 has the advantage of showing more clearly the extent to which government grants are contributing to and may be influencing the company's investment programme.

Revenue based grants, *e.g.*, regional employment premiums, are simply credited straight to revenue in the same period as the related expenditure and are seldom shown in the accounts.

Chapter 7

INVESTMENTS

Types of investment

Investments fall into three categories:

(*a*) Investment in subsidiaries.
(*b*) Investment in associated companies.
(*c*) Other investments, which may appear in the balance sheet as fixed assets, or as current assets, but which are usually shown between the two under a separate "Investments" heading.

Investment in subsidiaries
In simple terms, a subsidiary company is a company which the company owning the investment (the holding company) is able either by virtue of its voting power or of its ability, in some other way, to control the board of directors of the subsidiary. The holding company is required by law to produce group accounts, in which the profits, assets and liabilities of the subsidiary are merged with those of the holding company, as described in detail in Chapter 15.

Investment in associated companies
For accounting purposes, an associated company is defined by SSAP 1 as a non-subsidiary company in which the investing group or company's position in it is:

(*a*) effectively that of a partner in a joint venture or consortium; *or*
(*b*) long-term and substantial (*i.e.*, not less than 20% of the equity voting rights).

In each case the investing group must participate (usually through representation on the board of directors) in commercial and financial policy decisions of the associated company, including the distribution of profits.

The investing group's share of the associated company's profits before tax, taxation, extraordinary items and net profit retained are shown separately in the group's consolidated accounts, as described more fully in Chapter 16.

Other investments
While at first sight it may seem that these will consist entirely of investments of less than 20% in other companies, this is not the case. Many public companies have holdings greater than 20% in other companies which are not treated as associated because the investing group is not represented on the board of directors and does not participate in commercial and financial policy decisions. These and other long-term investments are normally shown separately in the holding company's balance sheet after fixed assets, and are often described as "trade investments". They usually appear in the balance sheet at cost, less any provisions that have been made.

Companies sometimes use surplus cash to make short-term investments in the securities of listed companies, and show these under current assets, at cost less any provision necessary to reduce them to market value.

Disclosure requirements of the Companies Act

The Companies Act 1967 requires the following information to be given on *investments other than investment in subsidiaries:*

1. The aggregate amount of quoted and unquoted investments, shown under separate headings (Sch. 2, para. 8(1) (a)).

In respect of quoted investments:
2. The aggregate market value where it differs

from the book amount, and the Stock Exchange value of any investment of which the market value is shown and is taken to be higher than the Stock Exchange value (Sch. 2, para. 11(8)).

In respect of unquoted investments:

3. If the investments are shown as fixed assets, the accounts must *either*
   (*a*) show the values estimated by the directors, *or*
   (*b*) give the cost or valuation, as shown in the company's books, and the aggregate provision for depreciation (Sch. 2, paras 5(1) and (2)(c)).
4. If the investments are in equity share capital, the accounts must *either*
   (*a*) show the values estimated by the directors, *or*
   (*b*) give details of income, the investing company's share of the year's profits/losses before and after tax, its share of undistributed profit/losses accumulated and the treatment of any losses in the investing company's accounts (Sch. 2, para. 5A).

Because of the amount of detail required under (*b*) in each case, most companies give (*a*), the directors' valuation of unquoted investments.

In respect of substantial holdings:

5. Section 4 of the Companies Act 1967 requires that where at the end of its financial year a company:
   (*a*) holds in excess of one-tenth in nominal value of the issued shares of any class of equity share capital of another company; *or*
   (*b*) holds shares in another company, not its subsidiary, stated in its accounts at an amount in excess of one-tenth of the amount of the investing company's total assets;

   then the accounts must include:
   (i) the name of the other company;
   (ii) the country in which it is incorporated (if other than Great Britain); *or* (if incorporated in Great Britain) the country in which it is registered (England or Scotland) if not the same as the investing company;
   (iii) the description of each class held, and the proportion held.

Such holdings are occasionally referred to as "associated companies", though they may or may not be associated companies for the purpose of SSAP 1 (*see* Chapter 16).

This information need not be disclosed in respect of companies incorporated or carrying on business outside the United Kingdom if the directors of the investing company consider disclosure would be harmful and the Department of Trade agrees.

Disclosure requirements of the Stock Exchange Listing Agreement

The Listing Agreement has different, overlapping requirements. Where the investment company or group interest in the equity capital amounts to 20% or more, the following information should be given:

(*a*) principal country of operation;
(*b*) its issued share and loan capital and, except where the group's interest is dealt with in the consolidated balance sheet as an associated company, the total amount of its reserves;
(*c*) the percentage of each class of loan capital attributable to the company's interest (direct or indirect).

Balance sheet presentation

Companies differ widely in the way in which they present information about investments. Most companies which have both subsidiaries and other investments, show two separate headings in the balance sheet, "subsidiaries" and "investments". Many include "associated companies" under the heading "investments", though this is not universal, and some companies have three or more items in the balance sheet proper. BARROW, HEPBURN GROUP's 1975 balance sheets (shown opposite) illustrate this.

Investments held as current assets

Investments held as current assets may be described as "securities", or something similar. For example, ICI's group balance sheet shows "liquid resources" as a subheading under "current assets", explaining, in a note, the breakdown of liquid resources into:

Quoted investments	£ 29m
Short-term deposits	£266m
Cash	£ 51m

Most companies are not in business to deal in shares, nor are equities really suitable as a holding medium for liquidity (notice ICI's holdings of quoted investments represented only 8% of liquid resources), and the investor should be wary of any substantial amount of short-term investments (other than short-dated government stock): they may indicate a wheeler-dealer style of management.

BARROW, HEPBURN GROUP *Balance sheets*

	Company		*Group*	
	1975	1974	1975	1974
	£000	£000	£000	£000
Assets employed				
Fixed assets				
Land and buildings	27	28	7,648	6,700
Plant and equipment	23	37	5,641	4,638
	50	65	13,289	11,338
Subsidiary companies	15,712	12,601	–	–
Associated companies	1,434	1,052	1,434	1,083
Investments	753	1,153	1,429	1,750
Goodwill arising on consolidation	–	–	1,406	1,442
Current assets . . . etc.				

[and a note amplified this:]

	Company		*Group*	
	1975	1974	1975	1974
Investments	£000	£000	£000	£000
At cost less provision	753	1,153	1,429	1,750
Valuation:				
Quoted – on UK Stock Exchange	–	237	–	294
Overseas	29	–	172	19
Unquoted – directors' valuation	1,190	871	1,265	1,436
	1,219	1,108	1,437	1,749

Points to watch on substantial holdings

A holding of 5% or more may indicate:

(*a*) the possibility of an eventual bid, particularly if the holder is predatory by nature;

(*b*) a blocking position taken by the holder to protect his trade interests from the risk of the company concerned being taken over by some (larger) competitor.

There is no hard and fast rule about which is which, and a holding could indicate a blocking position pending a possible bid in the distant future. In this context it is worth checking whether directors have substantial holdings and, if so, whether any are nearing retirement age.

If the holding is of *20% or more* and the company is *not* treated as an Associate, the chances are probably more in favour of a bid than a blocking position – the unwelcome holder of a substantial stake being unlikely to be given a seat on the board. If the holding is of *25% or more* the holder is in the strong position of being able to block any arrangements and reconstructions that the company might wish to make with creditors and members under Section 206 of the Companies Act 1948, which require three-fourths to vote in favour.

A substantial holding may also be the tombstone of an unsuccessful bid. For example, for several years ALLIED BREWERIES had a holding of over 20% in TRUST HOUSE FORTE which was built up in the abortive takeover attempt they made at the end of 1971.

Interlocking holdings

Where a number of companies under the same management have substantial holdings in each other or in another company the holdings may be entirely innocent, but interlocking holdings can give scope for manipulation to the detriment of outside shareholders and should be viewed with caution.

A classic illustration of the dangers of interlocking holdings was provided by the affairs of several companies in the LOWSON GROUP, which came under investigation by the Department of Trade in 1973. The appointed inspectors found that a number of defaults in the management "were knowingly committed by Sir Denys [Lowson] and constituted grave mismanagement of the affairs of the companies concerned" and that in some transactions "his motive was to obtain a very substantial gain for himself and his family".

Chapter 8

STOCKS AND WORK IN PROGRESS

(Reference: SSAP 9 *Stocks and Work in Progress*. Standard for periods commencing on or after 1 January 1976.)

Three different classes of stock

Most companies have traditionally shown in their balance sheet a single figure described either as "stocks" or as "inventories" or as "stocks and work in progress", but these terms cover three very different classes of asset:

(*a*) items in the state in which they were purchased (colloquially termed "stock");
(*b*) items in an intermediate stage of completion ("work in progress", or in the United States "work in process");
(*c*) finished goods ("finished stock" or again simply "stock").

A distinction is sometimes drawn between "goods purchased for resale", "raw materials" to be used in manufacture, "components" which will be incorporated in the product at a later stage, and "consumable stores" (like paint or oil) which will be used in making it.

Subclassification required by SSAP 9

SSAP 9 calls for the accounts to show the subclassification of stocks and work in progress "in a manner which is appropriate to the business and so as to indicate the amounts held in each of the main categories".

Some, but not many, companies have given this information in the past; for example BASS CHARRINGTON's 1975 accounts gave a subclassification of stocks in a note:

BASS CHARRINGTON *Note to the 1975 accounts*

	£m
Raw materials	8.1
Work in progress	8.7
Finished stocks	52.3
Bottles, cases and pallets	10.2
Consumable stores	7.8
	87.1

The matching principle

Where a business incurs in one accounting period expenditure on stocks which remain unsold or unconsumed at the balance sheet date, or upon work in progress which is incomplete at that date, these costs are carried forward into the following period so that they may be set against the revenue when it arises. This is an application of what accountants term the matching principle: that of matching cost and revenue in the year in which the revenue arises rather than charging the cost in the year in which the cost is incurred.

If, however, there is no reasonable expectation of sufficient future revenue to cover costs already incurred (for instance because of deterioration, obsolescence or a change in demand pattern) any irrecoverable cost should be charged to revenue in the year under review, and not carried forward. For this reason the value of stock and work in progress in the balance sheet at the end of the year (*i.e.*, the book value), should be the lower of cost and net realisable value.

Consistency

The method of valuing stock should be consistent, and most sets of accounts include a brief statement in the notes on how stocks have been valued, *e.g.*

AARONSON BROS: "Stocks and work in progress have been valued, as in previous years, at the lower of cost and net realisable value. Cost comprises the actual cost of raw materials and attributable overheads in the case of work in progress and finished goods. Provision has been made for obsolete and non-moving stock and also for unrealised profits on intra group stocks."

MARKS & SPENCER: "Stock is valued at the lower of cost and net realisable value. Cost is computed by deducting the gross profit margin from the selling value of stock and also takes into account an allowance for future markdowns."

A particular point to look for is any statement of a change in the basis between year-ends and, when one is made, whether any indication is given of how much difference the change has made to the year-end stock figure and to profits.

The importance of stock valuation

The accurate valuation of stock on a consistent basis is important, because quite small percentage variations can very significantly affect the profits reported in any period (Example 8.1):

Example 8.1 Stock valuation

	£	£
Sales		2,000
less Cost of goods sold:		
Opening stock	600	
add Purchases in period	1,500	
	2,100	
less Closing stock	400	
		1,700
		300
less Wages, overheads, etc.		200
Trading profit		£100

If the closing stock had been valued 10% lower at £360 and the opening stock 10% higher at £660, the cost of goods sold would have increased by £100 and the trading profit would have been wiped out.

Problems in valuing stock

Three main problems arise in valuing stock:

(*a*) the price to be used if an item has been supplied at varying prices.
(*b*) the value added in manufacture both to incomplete items (work in progress) and to completed items (finished goods).
(*c*) the assessment of net realisable value.

Stocks in a large retail business

Having defined the main principles and problems, let us now look at stocks in practice, beginning with the control of stocks in a large retail business, where all stocks are goods purchased for resale and the complications of WIP (work in progress) and finished goods do not arise.

The central management of most supermarkets controls the efficiency and honesty of local stores by charging goods out to those stores at *selling* price, and by maintaining overall stock control accounts in terms of selling price by broad product groups. It might, for instance, divide sales into five classes: groceries, meat, greengroceries, chocolate and sweets, and cigarettes and tobacco. By suitably analysing takings it will then be possible, for each of these product groups, to work as follows:

Opening stock at selling price + Deliveries at selling price − Takings = Theoretical closing stock at selling price

Every 28 or 42 days the central management of many supermarket chains sends round a team of specialist stocktakers to check whether the actual stock is in broad agreement with the theoretical stock. There will inevitably be differences, not simply because of pilferage by customers, sometimes euphemistically called "shrinkage", but because of breakages by customers and staff and errors on the part of staff marking up goods and upon the part of check-out staff. There may also be pilferage on the part of staff, including the local management.

With this sort of operation, it is usual for the purpose of monthly, quarterly, half-yearly and annual accounts to deduct from the value of stock at selling price the normal gross profit margin upon that particular class of goods. But SSAP 9 (about which we shall have much to say later) requires that before such a figure is used for the purposes of the annual accounts, it be tested to ensure that it gives a "reasonable approximation of the actual cost".

Stocks in the manufacturing business

Most manufacturing businesses employ a system of cost accounting. They do so:

(*a*) as an aid to price fixing (so that they can charge the customer with the materials used and the time actually taken to complete his job – as is the case with a motor repair garage, or jobbing builder;) *or*

(*b*) in order to provide the estimating department with information on which to base future estimates or tenders; *and/or*

(*c*) as a means of controlling operating efficiency.

The type of record employed varies widely, from a few scribblings on the back of an envelope, to a cost system parallel to the normal financial system, reconciled with it but not part of it, right up to a completely integral cost and financial accounting system. In all but the first of these there would normally be some form of stock record.

A problem often arises in the case of the manufacturing business over the pricing of issues from stock. When there are relatively few items, and where they are easily identifiable and can each be kept separate, each stock issue can be priced at its *specific price,* and no problem arises. But in many cases it is not possible, or not convenient, to keep identical items from different purchase consignments separate.

Several different methods of pricing issues from stock are commonly employed, and the value of the stock remaining depends on the pricing method used, as we will illustrate with Example 8.2.

Example 8.2 "STOCKOUT LTD"

"STOCKOUT LTD" purchased the following quantities of a raw material called "Expel" during 1976:

1 February	4,800 lb	at 10p per lb	£480
14 March	10,000	11p	£1,100
16 June	7,200	12p	£864
10 December	8,000	14p	£1,120
	30,000		£3,564

There was no stock on 1 January 1976. Issues during 1976 totalled 24,600 lb, leaving a closing stock on 31 December 1976 of 5,400 lb. The value of the closing stock under different pricing methods is dealt with below.

First-in first-out (FIFO)

Good storekeeping demands that goods should, so far as is possible, be used in the order in which they are received; that is to say, that those which came in first should be the first to go out, otherwise the danger of being left with stock which has deteriorated through lapse of time is greatly increased. The first-in first-out method of stock pricing merely assumes for accounting purposes that the normal rules of good storekeeping have been followed.

On a FIFO basis, all the stock at 31 December 1976 in Example 8.2 would be deemed to be out of the delivery on 10 December 1976, which cost 14p per lb:

Stock at 31 December 1976 =
5,400 lb at 14p = £756.

Average or weighted average price

When an organisation receives a number of deliveries during an accounting period at a series of different prices, it is reasonable to take the average price or, for more accuracy, the weighted average price.

Taking the *average price* for the year, Stockout Ltd's issues will be priced at:

(10p + 11p + 12p + 14p) ÷ 4 = 11.75p per lb

Stock at 31 December 1976 =
5,400 lb at 11.75p = £634.50.

On a *weighted average price* basis, Stockout Ltd's issues would be priced at:

£3,564 ÷ 30,000 = 11.88p per lb

Stock at 31 December 1976 =
5,400 lb at 11.88p = £641.52.

Standard price

Many businesses employ a standard cost system; that is to say, they predetermine for each type of unit manufactured the price which ought to be paid for material, the material usage, the wage rate of the personnel employed to produce it, the time they should take, and so on. In such a system materials issued from store are priced at standard cost, as are work in progress at all stages and any finished goods in stock. Any variances from standard are written off as operating losses (or profits) at the time they occur.

If Stockout Ltd adopted a standard costing system and employed a standard price of 11.5p per lb for "Expel", a material price variance of £114 (adverse) would be written off, computed as follows:

Cost of material acquired (30,000 lb)	£3,564
Standard cost of 30,000 lb at 11.5p per lb	£3,450
Material price variance (adverse)	£114

Provided the standard price represents fairly the average cost of the material in stock, it may be employed for financial accounting purposes.

Where it does not, it may be adjusted by adding back the proportion of the material price variance appropriate to the stock on hand:

Stock at 31 December 1976 at standard cost:	
5,400 lb at 11.5p	£621
add $\frac{5,400}{30,000}$ × £114	£20.52
Stock adjusted to a weighted average cost basis	£641.52

These different methods of pricing issues each give rise to a slightly different closing stock value and thus to a slightly different profit for the year. But this is not important *provided* that a company adopts the same method consistently in each accounting period. It is not permissible to chop and change.

Replacement price and NIFO
In the past, items in stock were occasionally stated in the accounts at replacement price when this was lower than both cost and net realisable value. The effect of this was to take a loss greater than that which it was actually expected would be incurred. The statement of stocks at the lowest of cost, net realisable value and replacement price is no longer (under SSAP 9) an acceptable basis of stock valuation. However, for pricing purposes (but not for either stock valuation or costing purposes) some companies employ a next-in first-out basis (NIFO) when estimating and pricing, taking account of the price they expect to pay to replace items to be taken from stock, rather than the price they themselves paid for them.

LIFO
Another method of valuation, acceptable in the United States though not in Britain, is the last-in first-out (LIFO) basis in which issues are charged at the latest price at which they could conceivably have come. This has the advantage of charging the customer with the most recent price; but in the balance sheet stocks appear at the price of the earliest delivery from which they could have arisen, on the basis that the rule of good store-keeping is (in theory only) reversed, and goods received latest are used first, and those in stock remain in stock.

In Example 8.2, the closing stock of "Expel" would have been deemed on a LIFO basis to be from the earliest purchases:

Stock at 31 December 1976 = (4,800 lb at 10p) + (600 lb at 11p) = £546

compared with £756 on a FIFO basis, reducing profits by £210.

Thus, in a time of rising prices LIFO has the effect of:

(*a*) showing stocks in the balance sheet at a cost appropriate not to recent purchases but to those many months or even years earlier; and, consequently,
(*b*) reducing profits.

Stocks in an inflationary period

Supposing that, in Example 8.2, Stockout Ltd had, in fact, had a closing stock of 5,400 lb of "Expel" at the end of 1975, valued on a FIFO basis at 9p per lb = £486, then:

Stock at 31 December 1976: 5,400 lb at 14p	£756
Stock at 31 December 1975: 5,400 lb at 9p	£486
Stock profit	£270

Until recently, Stockout Ltd would have been taxed on the profit of £270 even if the company's normal stock level of "Expel" needed for the business was around 5,000–6,000 lb, *i.e.*, even if the company was in no position to realise any of the profit by running stocks down. The effect of the general rise in prices from 1971 onwards hit very hard companies that needed to carry large stocks: they were taxed on their stock profits and had to find more working capital each year just to maintain the same *volume* of stock. Their plight was eventually recognised by the government, who introduced a temporary measure of stock relief in the Finance Act 1975 (*see* Chapter 13).

The problems of stocks in an inflationary situation, including possible measures for more permanent relief on stock profits, will be discussed further in Chapter 22.

Requirements of SSAP 9 on stocks and WIP

SSAP 9 requires that the amount at which stock and work in progress, other than long-term contracts, are stated in periodic financial statements should be "the total of the *lower of cost and net realisable value* of the separate items of stock and work in progress or groups of similar items", *i.e.*, each item or each group of similar items should be assessed separately.

The inclusion of overheads in cost
It was at one time accepted that companies should be free to choose whether to value work in progress and finished goods:

(*a*) at prime cost (that is to say, to exclude all overheads), *or*
(*b*) at variable (or marginal) cost: that is to say to exclude all *fixed* overheads, but include prime cost plus variable overheads, *or*

(*c*) at the full cost of purchase plus the cost of conversion (including fixed overheads too).

SSAP 9 regards only (*c*) as a proper method. The classification of overheads between fixed and variable is regarded as an unsuitable one for determining whether or not they should be included in the cost of conversion: the dividing line is considered too imprecise. Costs of general management, as distinct from functional management, are excluded unless directly related to current production (as they may be to some extent in smaller companies).

Net realisable value

Net realisable value is "the actual or estimated selling price (net of trade but before settlement discounts) less:

(*a*) all further costs to completion; and

(*b*) all costs to be incurred in marketing, selling and distributing."

When stocks are held which are unlikely to be sold within the turnover period normal to the company (*i.e.*, where there are excess stocks) the impending delay in realisation will increase the risk of deterioration and/or obsolescence, and this needs to be taken into account in assessing net realisable value.

The danger of rising stocks

Although SSAP 9's requirement to include production overheads in costing finished goods gives a fair picture when stocks are being maintained at prudent levels in relation to demand, their inclusion can produce unduly optimistic profits when a manufacturer leaves production unchanged in periods of lower demand. This is illustrated by Example 8.3.

Example 8.3 Rising stocks

Let us look at a single-product factory facing a year in which demand is forecast to fall by 30% due to an economic recession:

Production overheads (rent of factory, etc.) = £1 million
Production capacity 100,000 units per annum.
Variable costs = £10 per unit. Selling price = £25 per unit.
Sales last year 100,000 units.

The management is faced with the decision of whether

(*a*) to continue at full production, hoping that demand will pick up sharply the following year if not sooner, and that it possibly won't fall quite so sharply as forecast; *or*

(*b*) to cut production by up to 30%.

Under SSAP 9, assuming demand does fall by 30%, the figures that will be reported at the end of the year under these two choices will be:

	(*a*) *Full production*	(*b*) *Production cut by 30%*
	Units	Units
Opening stock	20,000	20,000
Units manufactured	100,000	70,000
	120,000	90,000
Units sold	70,000	70,000
Closing stock	50,000	20,000
	£	£
Fixed costs	1,000,000	1,000,000
Variable costs (£10 per unit)	1,000,000	700,000
Total costs (cost per unit made)	2,000,000 (£20)	1,700,000(£24.28)
less Addition to stock	600,000	–
Cost of goods sold	1,400,000	1,700,000
Sales (£25 per unit)	1,750,000	1,750,000
Profit (Sales *less* Cost of goods sold)	350,000	50,000
Opening stock value	400,000	400,000
Closing stock value	1,000,000	400,000

In practice, the profit from full production would be likely to be reduced by interest charges to finance carrying increased stock, but even so management can bolster profits a great deal in the short term by continuing high production in the face of falling demand. Rising stocks unmatched by rising turnover may give some warning here, and this can be monitored by the ratio Stocks/Turnover (Example 8.4).

Example 8.4 Stocks/Turnover ratio:
A. ARENSON

A. ARENSON, the office furniture manufacturer, reported:

Year to 31 July	1972	1973	1974	1975
	£000	£000	£000	£000
Turnover	2,501	4,927	7,675	6,437
Stocks	656	782	1,605	3,305
$\frac{\text{Stocks}}{\text{Turnover}}$	26.2%	15.8%	20.9%	51.3%

The strain of rising stocks and falling turnover in 1975 was reflected by a sharp jump in borrowings (despite £750,000 raised by an issue of convertible preference shares), higher interest charges and a very sharp fall in profits:

Amount due to bankers	183	217	356	1,110
Interest payable	24	73	141	248
Pre-tax profits	385	661	868	317

Demand was slow to recover, and the company ran into loss in the first six months of the following accounting year.

With SSAP 9's requirement to sub-classify stocks and WIP, the cause and likely effect of rising stocks will be more easily analysed. For example, suppose we had had two otherwise identical furniture companies, both with exactly the same previous record as Arenson, reporting in 1975 as follows:

	Company A	*Company B*
	£000	£000
Turnover	6,437	6,437
Stocks		
Raw materials	318	2,232
Work in progress	605	605
Finished goods	2,232	318
	3,305	3,305

There is a great deal of difference between Company A, where stocks of finished goods are clearly excessive, and Company B, which has managed to trim back production in line with sales, and may well have been very shrewd in buying timber and chipboard forward at a time of rapidly rising raw material prices.

Long-term contracts

A *long-term contract* is defined by SSAP 9 as "a contract entered into for manufacture or building of a single substantial entity or the provision of a service where the time taken to manufacture, build or provide is such that a substantial proportion of all such contract work will extend for a period exceeding one year."

Shipbuilders, constructional engineers and the like frequently engage in long-term contracts. Because of the length of time such contracts take to complete, to defer taking profit into account until completion would result in the profit and loss account reflecting not a true and fair view of the activity of the company during the year, but rather the results of those contracts which, by the accident of time, were completed by the year end. Traditionally, there are two ways of computing the profit to be taken.

It is normal with long-term contracts to have an arrangement under which the contractor receives payment on account on the basis of the "work certified" by an architect or surveyor. The "work certified" is an essential piece of information whichever of the two ways of arriving at the profit to date is adopted.

Under the first method, profit to date is computed as follows:

$$\text{Work certified at balance sheet date} - \text{Costs incurred on contract to date} = \text{Profit to date}$$

The second method takes a proportion of the overall profit expected:

$$\left\{\text{Total contract price} - \text{Total costs incurred on contract to date} - \text{Total estimated further costs to completion}\right\} \times \frac{\text{Work certified to date}}{\text{Total contract price}} = \text{Profit to date}$$

If the first formula is used it is still necessary to have regard to the costs likely to be incurred in completing the job, for it is clearly wrong to take a profit on the first stage of a contract if the profit is likely to be lost at a later stage. In either case, in considering future costs, it is necessary to allow for likely increases in wages and salaries, likely increases in the price of raw materials and rises in general overheads in so far as these items are not recoverable from the customer under the terms of the contract: inflation can play havoc with the profitability of fixed-price or inadequately protected contracts, as many companies have learned to their cost.

In neither case is it usual to take up the entire profit to date. Some companies take only two-

---

Example 8.5 Long-term contracts "COMMERCIAL CONTRACTS LTD"

"COMMERCIAL CONTRACTS LTD" is engaged in a long-term bridge-building contract.

	£
Work certified to 31 December 1978	1,250,000
Total contract price	2,000,000
Costs incurred on contract to 31 December 1978	1,025,000
Estimated further costs to completion	575,000
Amount received from customer by 31 December 1978	1,125,000
Profit taken on the contract in 1977	45,000

The company takes up three-quarters of the profit earned to date, reduced by the fraction: amount received to date ÷ work certified to date. What profit will be taken up on the contract in 1978?

Using the first formula:

$$\text{Work certified at balance sheet date} - \text{Costs incurred on contract to date} = \text{Profit to date}$$

Profit to date = £1,250,000 - £1,025,000 = £225,000

$$\text{Of which: } \tfrac{3}{4} \times \frac{1{,}125{,}000}{1{,}250{,}000} = 67\tfrac{1}{2}\% \text{ will be taken up} = £151{,}875$$

but £45,000 of this was taken up in 1977, so only £106,875 remains to be taken up in 1978.

Using the second formula:

$$\left\{ \text{Total contract price} - \text{Total costs incurred on contract to date} - \text{Total estimated further costs to completion} \right\} \times \frac{\text{Work certified to date}}{\text{Total contract price}} = \text{Profit to date}$$

$$\text{Profit to date} = (£2{,}000{,}000 - £1{,}025{,}000 - £575{,}000) \times \frac{1{,}250{,}000}{2{,}000{,}000} = £250{,}000$$

Of this £250,000 profit, 67½% will be taken up (as before) *i.e.*, £168,750, less the £45,000 already taken up in 1977 = £123,750.

The difference between the two figures for profit to date is due to the difference between the profit margin on that part of the contract completed to date (£225,000 on £1,250,000 in the first formula = 18%) and that estimated on the contract as a whole (£400,000 on £2 million in the second formula = 20%).

The second formula requires an estimate to be made of future costs and is therefore open to subjective judgement. Results should be viewed with caution if the overall profitability margin is estimated to be higher than the margin to date; *i.e.*, if the second formula allows a higher profit to be taken now than the first formula would allow.

thirds, others only three-quarters. Many multiply by a further fraction:

$$\frac{\text{Amount received to date}}{\text{Work certified to date}}$$

Where the customer is entitled (as is usually the case) to retain, say 10% of the amount certified as "retention monies", so as to ensure satisfactory rectification of any defects, the use of this further fraction of, in this case, 9/10ths, has the effect of disregarding that part of the profit appropriate to the amount retained.

The amount reflected in the year's profit and loss account will be the appropriate proportion of the total profit by reference to the work done to date, less any profit already taken up in prior years on the contracts still on hand. The aim of using a multiplying factor of two-thirds or three-quarters is to ensure that unless the remaining work on a contract is disastrous, some profit remains to be taken when the contract is finally completed. Example 8.5 illustrates the treatment of long-term contracts in the accounts of an imaginary company, "COMMERCIAL CONTRACTS LTD".

Requirements of SSAP 9 on long-term contracts

In the past, accounting treatment of long-term contracts has varied enormously from company to company. BOVIS, for example, in its 1972 accounts noted that "no provision is made for anticipated future losses" and a year later had to be rescued by P. & O. At the other end of the scale companies like JOHN LAING pursued policies of extreme prudence: all losses were taken when they occurred, but no account was taken of profits on contracts unfinished at the end of the year.

SSAP 9 requires that "The amount at which long-term contract work in progress is stated in periodic financial statements should be cost plus any *attributable profit,* less any foreseeable losses and progress payments received and receivable." Attributable profits on contracts are, however, only required to be taken up when "it is considered that their outcome can be assessed with reasonable certainty before their conclusion"; if the outcome cannot be reasonably assessed, "it is prudent not to take up any profit", so management is still left with a certain amount of latitude, and the key point to watch for is undue anticipation of profits.

SSAP 9 also requires balance sheets to show how the amount included for long-term contracts is reached by stating:

(*a*) the amount of work in progress at cost plus attributable profit (*i.e.*, profit or loss taken to date), less foreseeable losses;
(*b*) cash received and receivable at the accounting date as progress payments on account of contracts in progress.

Thus, if the bridge contract we have discussed in Example 8.6 was the only contract of Commercial Contracts Ltd to appear in the balance sheet at 31 December 1978, and if the first formula is used, it would appear as follows:

Work in progress, at cost *plus* Profit taken to date	£ 1,176,875	£
less Cash received from customer	1,125,000	
		51,875

Chapter 9

DEBTORS

TRADE DEBTORS AND OTHER DEBTORS

Debtors (termed "receivables" in the United States and Canada), represent amounts owing to the business.

A distinction should be made between *trade debtors, i.e.*, those arising from the sale of goods on credit, which appear in the balance sheet among current assets, and *other debtors* – for example, debts due from the sale of fixed assets or investments; other debtors should be shown separately if material or if *not* a current asset:

Example 9.1 Distinction between types of debtors: WIMPEY

WIMPEY in 1972 sold a large block of shares in OLDHAM ESTATES; the consideration included two deferred instalments of £12.15 million each, payable in May 1973 and May 1974. The outstanding amount was shown separately from debtors in the company's balance sheet under current assets:

	1973	1972
Balance of consideration for sale of shares in the Oldham Estate Company Limited	£12,150,000	£24,300,000
Debtors	£19,555,504	£11,625,957

and the details of the Oldham transaction were explained in notes to the accounts.

Prepayments

Debtors are normally lumped together with any prepayments, for example, rent or rates prepaid by the company, and the item is sometimes described as "debtors and prepayments" or "debtors and payments in advance".

Bad debts and doubtful debtors

The granting of credit inevitably involves some risk that the debtor will fail to pay, that is, will become a bad debt. When a business recognises that a debt is bad, the debt is written off to profit and loss account. That is to say, the balance appearing as "debtors" falls by the amount of the debt, and "bad debts" appears as an expense. This expense is normally only shown separately in the published accounts if the amount is material.

In addition, it is normal to set up a "provision for doubtful debtors". To do so a charge is made to profit and loss account and, in the balance sheet, the provision for doubtful debtors is deducted from the total debtors. Once again, the provision for doubtful debtors is only disclosed separately in the published accounts if it is material.

A provision for doubtful debtors may be *specific*, that is to say based upon the businessman's estimate of the probable loss, studying each debt in turn; for instance, there is a 10% probability that Smith will fail to pay his debt of £12,100, therefore we must provide £1,210; or it may be *general, e.g.*, 2½% of total debtors; or a combination of the two.

The importance of debtors

Companies such as supermarket chains, whose turnover is almost entirely for cash, will have very few debtors; the figure appearing in the balance sheet is likely to be largely prepayments and non-trade debtors, and will have no particular significance. At the other extreme are companies whose entire turnover is on credit terms and very large amounts of working capital may be tied up in debtors. Here the efficiency with which credit accounts are handled, and the timing of the taking of profit where payments are by instalment, are of considerable interest to the analyst.

Debt collection period

The ratio Debtors/Turnover can be used to monitor a company's credit control, as we describe in Chapter 23, and this is possibly a more meaningful measure if expressed in terms of time, as the *debt collection period*:

$$\text{Debt collection period (in days)} = \frac{\text{Debtors (preferably only trade debtors)}}{\text{Sales (Turnover)}} \times 365$$

e.g. Sales during the year = £7,300,000
Trade debtors at the end of the year = £860,000
Debt collection period = £860,000 ÷ £7,300,000 × 365 = 43 days

Some companies and analysts take 360 days to the year, or compute in terms of, say, 260 *working* days.

In a seasonal business it is more accurate to compute the collection period on a month-by-month basis, but this is not possible without inside knowledge. Indeed, the analyst can tell comparatively little about debtors unless more information than usual is available. Among the things which one would like to find out are:

1. What is the customer concentration? Is an undue proportion due from one major customer, or from customers in one important industry? Would failure of one or two customers have a material effect upon the company's financial future?
2. What is the age pattern of debtors? Are some unduly old? Is there adequate provision for bad and doubtful debts?
3. Are any of the debts long-term in nature? Traditionally in Britain debtors appear at their face value even if they are not currently due. In the United States, if a debt is not due within one year, it may be necessary to discount it, *i.e.*, to take account of imputed interest. Thus, a debt of $1 million due three years hence might appear, taking interest into account at 10%, as $751,300.

Factors affecting the debt collection period

A short debt collection period is, other things being equal, preferable to a longer one; but as with many ratios one has to qualify this general principle. For by restricting credit, and selling entirely for cash, a business can have a zero debt collection period; but if this drives its customers into the arms of competitors it is scarcely an improvement so far as the business as a whole is concerned. Subject to that qualification, any improvement in collection period, since it represents a reduction in overall debtors, means that more capital is available for other purposes, or that there is less need to borrow money from the bank.

At first sight it may seem that an increase in collection period represents a fall in the efficiency of the debt collection section. This is likely to be the case, but it is not necessarily so. The debt collection period may increase (decrease) between one period and another for a number of reasons:

1. If there is a *policy change* with regard to:
   (*a*) credit terms to existing customers; if, for example, the board of directors, to obtain a valuable order from a major customer, offers two months' credit instead of one;
   (*b*) the granting of credit; for instance, if potential customers whose credit rating was formerly insufficient for them to be granted credit, are granted credit – for such customers are unlikely to be among the fastest payers.
2. If there is *poor credit management*:
   (*a*) If credit is given to unsatisfactory customers.
   (*b*) If the invoicing section falls behind. Customers will not pay until they receive an invoice and, in general, pay at a fixed time determined by the date on which they receive an invoice, *e.g.*, at the end of the month in which they receive an invoice.
   (*c*) If statements are late – some businesses wait until they receive a statement.
   (*d*) If there is no consistent follow-up of overdue debts, by letter and/or telephone, or even in person.

Why it is important to keep a watch upon collection period

Although it is necessary for most businesses to offer some credit, any unnecessary credit is bad management, because it ties up money which (normally) earns no return, but which is subject to increased risk. The customer who is short of money, and who finds he can order things from a company without having to pay for them at the end of the month, tends to place more and more of his orders with that company; if he subsequently goes into liquidation, he is likely to do so owing a hefty amount.

HIRE PURCHASE AND CREDIT SALE TRANSACTIONS

Definitions

A *hire purchase transaction* is a transaction in which the *hirer* agrees to hire goods from their *owner* in return for which he pays (usually) a deposit and a series of weekly, monthly, quarterly or yearly payments. The intention is that when the hiring period comes to an end, the ownership of the goods will pass to the hirer, sometimes on the payment of a nominal sum, sometimes with the final instalment; ownership, therefore, does not pass to the hirer until all payments have been made.

A *credit sale* is an outright sale (usually by a retailer) where payment by instalments is agreed in writing as a condition of the sale. Under a credit sale arrangement the property in the goods passes immediately to the purchaser, who becomes the owner of the goods, but payment is required to be made over a period. If the purchaser defaults, the seller can sue for payment but is not entitled to reclaim the goods. Because of government controls over consumer credit, credit sales with no deposit are currently limited to a maximum period of nine months; nine equal monthly, or 39 weekly, instalments are normally made, the first one being on purchase.

Interest is normally charged by the seller both in credit sale and hire purchase arrangements; the great difference between them is that in a credit sale the "purchaser" owns the goods from the outset, whereas in the case of a hire purchase sale, they do not become his until the final payment is made. Thus the seller cannot reclaim the goods in the case of a credit sale if the purchaser defaults whereas, subject to the terms of the agreement and the law on hire purchase, he can in the case of a hire purchase transaction.

Amounts due under credit sale transactions are debtors, and normally appear with other trade debtors, though they may be shown separately. In the case of a hire purchase transaction, since there has, strictly speaking, been no sale, the goods involved are still an asset of the seller, and some companies do describe it in the balance sheet in this way as "stock out on hire purchase", but most refer to the item as "hire purchase debtors" or "instalments due under hire purchase agreements"

Timing of profit taking

Whether the sale is by credit sale arrangement or on hire purchase, there are two elements of profit: the profit on the sale of the goods themselves and interest upon the amounts outstanding. There are a number of ways in which these two forms of profit can be spread over the accounting periods involved; but essentially these break down into two:

1. take all the profit on the sale immediately, and spread only the interest element;
2. spread both the profit on the sale and the interest over the life of the agreement.

Although method 1 is permissible for credit sales, method 2 is the more prudent. Method 1 is not recommended for hire purchase, as the goods have not actually been sold.

Where a credit sale is made on truly "interest-free" terms, there is no interest to spread; though logically there is an interest cost so far as the selling company is concerned. This is not normally taken into account, though it could be, by taking into account imputed interest. But it is always necessary to make provision for collection costs. Such a provision might, for instance, be 10% of the credit sale account debtors outstanding on balance sheet date.

The rule of 78

Finance companies frequently apply the "rule of 78" in spreading either the interest alone, or the whole profit and interest, over the life of the agreement. This is simply a form of the "sum of the years' digits method" already discussed in connection with depreciation in Chapter 6. What happens is this: the period of the agreement is set down in months (or it could be weeks in the case of a weekly agreement, or years where payments were on an annual basis), and the sum of the digits represents the sum of 1 + 2 + 3 + 4 . . . to n, where n is that number of months (or weeks or years). It is called the rule of 78 because for a year's agreement, the sum of 1 + 2 + 3 + . . . + 12 is 78. Any interest charge is then spread as follows (in this case a year's agreement):

First month 12/78ths of total interest
Second month 11/78ths
Third month 10/78ths
. . .
Twelfth month 1/78th

Example 9.2 Credit sale, method 1: "VOLUME UNLIMITED LTD"

Hi-fi equipment costing £425 is sold by "VOLUME UNLIMITED LTD" to S.O. Loudwater for £600, to be spread by means of a credit sale agreement over nine months. Taking into account interest and collection costs of £45, Loudwater is to pay a total of £645, *i.e.*, £71.67 per month, commencing with delivery of the goods on 1 November 1977. Volume Unlimited Ltd prepares accounts to 31 December annually. How much profit will be taken upon Loudwater's agreement in 1977 (assuming he pays two instalments, one on 1 November and one on 1 December) and how much in 1978, the final payment being made on 1 July 1978?

All the profit on selling goods, purchased for £425, for £600 - *i.e.*, £175 - will fall into 1977, the year in which the sale was made, as will the interest for two months, computed as follows:

November 9/45ths of £45 = £9
December 8/45ths of £45 = £8
(Since the sum of the digits 1, 2, 3 . . . 9 is 45.)

At 31 December 1977 there would appear among debtors seven instalments of £71.67 (£501.69) less a provision for unearned interest and collection costs (£45 - £9 - £8 = £28) = £473.69.

Some companies use this same method for hire purchase transactions, but it is generally considered more prudent to spread both profit and interest over the life of the transaction (method 2), rather than to take profit at the outset.

Example 9.3 Hire purchase, method 2: "DEFERRALS LTD"

The hire purchase trading account of "DEFERRALS LTD" for 1978 is as follows:

Hire purchase sales	£120,000
less Cost of goods sold	£ 80,000
Gross profit on HP Sales (33⅓ %)	£ 40,000

Receipts from 1978 HP Sales = £36,000
Profit to be taken in 1978
£36,000 × 33⅓ % profit margin = £12,000
Provision for unearned profit
carried forward on 1978 HP Sales
= £40,000 - £12,000 = £28,000

HP Sales in 1978	£120,000
less Cash received	£ 36,000
	£ 84,000
less Provision for unearned profit	£ 28,000
Hire purchase debtors (from 1978 sales)	£ 56,000

If, say, £63,000 is received in 1978 in respect of transactions from 1977; and £42,000 from 1976, when the profit margins were 30% and 35% respectively; the total profit from HP sales to be taken in 1978 would be:

From 1978	£12,000
From 1977 (30% of £63,000)	£18,900
From 1976 (35% of £42,000)	£14,700
Total profit	£45,600

Hire purchase information given in accounts

A good set of accounts will give quite a lot of information on hire purchase and credit sale business; *e.g.*, GREAT UNIVERSAL STORES state how the profit is taken and how the interest is brought in, and show the amount of provisions made and describe what they cover (*see* illustration here).

Some companies arrange for their credit sales and hire purchase transactions to be handled by a separate finance company, so that they receive payment for goods at once and thus reduce their requirements for working capital. In these cases, of course, the amounts outstanding are of no concern to the selling company and do not appear in their accounts.

GREAT UNIVERSAL STORES *Information on hire purchase*

	Notes	1976	1975
		£000	£000
Current Assets			
Stocks		111,445	93,869
Instalment and Hire Purchase Receivables (after providing for doubtful accounts)		307,683	282,118
less:			
Provisions for unearned profit, service charges and collection costs	*1 (e)*	73,305	67,873
		234,378	214,245
Trade, banking and finance receivables		78,749	50,798
Bank deposits, current accounts and cash		74,857	67,290
		499,429	426,202

Notes to the accounts

1. **Accounting Policies**

(e) **Instalment and Hire Purchase Receivables**

The gross profit and service charges on goods sold under hire purchase and certain instalment agreements are brought into profit as and when instalments are received. Interest on hire purchase finance and short term personal loan agreements is brought into profit on a straight line basis over the period of the agreements. Interest on other personal loan agreements is brought into profit in proportion to the reducing balance outstanding.

The provision for unearned profit, service charges and collection costs in the Balance Sheet represents the unearned proportion of gross profit, service charges and interest and is required in part to cover future costs of instalment collection and commission payable to catalogue agents.

FACTORING

Factoring represents the outright sale of a company's trade debtors to a factoring house.

In general, factoring houses offer three facilities:

1. *A sales accounting service,* taking over from the company responsibility for credit control, sales accounting and debt collection.
2. *A guarantee against bad debts,* the factor paying whether or not the customer does. Factoring tends to provide greater protection against credit risks than credit insurance, which is normally limited to a proportion of the debt, say, 70%. The factor charges a commission for these services of around 2%, but much depends upon the nature and volume of the business. Clearly, the service costs more where the business has a large number of smaller accounts, and is in a risky industry, and less where it has few, large, accounts, all of whom are companies with household names.
3. *An improvement in liquidity.* The factor assesses the client's business and arrives at an agreed debt collection period. Suppose the client offers 30–day terms, but, in fact, is taking 60 days to collect the average debt. A reasonable assessment might be 45 days. The factor therefore undertakes to make

payment 45 days after the invoice is raised thus improving the liquidity of the client's business by 15 days' debtors, and the factor will doubtless aim to get the average collection period down to below 45 days. If the client wishes the factor will, upon receiving invoices, forward 75–90% of their value immediately, charging interest at, say, 3–4% over bank overdraft rate from that date to the normal collection date (in our example the 45th day).

Factoring can be especially useful to the seasonal business, which does not need to raise the additional money mentioned in (3) above (upon receiving invoices) except at certain times of the year. It is also of advantage to companies with foreign customers. Most factors tend to be either subsidiaries of UK clearing banks or part of an international factoring organisation. In either case, the factor tends to have expert knowledge of the credit standing not only of customers in this country, but also of those abroad, whereas the ordinary company has some difficulty running a credit check upon a potential customer overseas.

As explained earlier, most factoring is upon a non-recourse basis, the factor taking the entire credit risk; but it is possible to make other arrangements, especially where debt collection might prove a problem, and the client wishes to handle this himself. In the case of non-recourse factoring, the existence and identity of the factor are both known to the customer. In what is termed confidential invoice discounting (or confidential factoring), the company maintains its own accounting records, and collects the money from customers in the ordinary way; but each time an invoice is raised, a copy is forwarded to the factor, who advances, say, 80% of the value of the invoice. As cheques are received from customers, they are passed to the factor, who banks them, deducts the amount already advanced, plus his charges, and remits the balance. The customer then does not even know of the existence of the factor.

In general, it is impossible from an inspection of published accounts to say with certainty whether or not a factor is involved; but a single sharp reduction in collection period and total debtors outstanding might make one suspect that factoring had been introduced.

Chapter 10

BANKING

Bank facilities

There are three main methods by which a company can borrow money from a bank: by overdrawing on its current account, by loans and by the use of acceptance credits. The bank normally agrees with a company the maximum amount that can be borrowed under each method, and this is called granting a facility. For example a company that has the bank's permission to run an overdraft of up to £1 million has overdraft facilities for that amount.

What is shown in the balance sheet is, however, not the limit of each facility but the amount the facility is being used at the year end; only the amounts actually borrowed from the bank on the balance sheet date appear in the balance sheet, although some idea of the average amount overdrawn during the year can be gained from the interest charges reported in the profit and loss account. The bank facilities available to a company are not normally published, although broad statements may be made about the company having "ample overdraft facilities" or being "well within its bank facilities".

By law only the aggregate amount of bank loans and overdrafts need be shown, but the normal practice is to show bank overdraft and bank loans repayable within a year under current liabilities and to show other bank loans separately. The use being made of acceptance credit facilities will appear under current liabilities, but may not be shown separately.

Overdrafts

The traditional method of clearing bank lending is to allow the customer to overdraw on his current account. It was originally designed to cover fluctuations in the company's cash during the year and gives the company complete flexibility of drawing within a given limit, which is normally reviewed annually.

Bank advances on overdraft are technically repayable on demand and, although this is seldom enforced, the bank when granting overdraft facilities does expect the customer to produce budgets and cash flow forecasts to show the purposes for which the facilities are intended and the plans for eventual repayment. Bank lending on overdraft is traditionally short-term in character, designed to cover fluctuations in working capital requirements rather than to provide permanent capital for the company.

In recent years, however, long-term interest rates have been driven so high by inflation that finance directors have been unwilling to commit their companies to long-term debt. Instead they have resorted more and more to borrowing from their banks, where interest on an overdraft is charged at an agreed percentage over the clearing bank's base rate (see below) which they hope will average less than current long-term rates, and where the company is free to reduce its borrowing whenever it wishes. Although it is now quite common for companies to finance a large part of their working capital in this way, clearing banks are usually reluctant to let companies increase their overdraft *ad lib*, even against a floating charge, preferring their clients to convert any "hard-core" borrowing that has built up on overdraft into loans.

The cost of borrowing on overdraft

The interest a company has to pay on its overdraft is usually set at a given percentage above its bank's base rate, depending on the standing of the customer; a financially stable medium sized company might pay a fixed 1½% above base.

The base rate, the datum on which the rates of interest are based, is adjusted up and down, to reflect fluctuations in short-term interest rates, and in particular the Minimum Lending Rate (MLR), which is the rate set by the Bank of England as the lender of last resort to the money market. Each bank sets its own base rate according to supply and demand and the fluctuations of MLR, though in practice the clearing banks' base rates keep very much in line with each other.

Fluctuations of the overdraft
As we have said, the overdraft figure given in the balance sheet is the amount the overdraft facility is being used at the year end; as companies normally choose their year end to fall when business is at its slackest, the balance sheet figure is unlikely to be the maximum amount the company has overdrawn during the year.

For example, a company in a seasonal business, with peak sales in the summer, could be expected to build up stocks from early spring and to carry high debtors across the summer. With an annual turnover of say £15 million, an overdraft of £100,000 at its year end (31 December) and £150,000 bank interest paid (reflecting an average overdraft of £1,500,000 during the year, bearing interest on average at 10%), the amount the company was actually overdrawn during the year would be likely to fluctuate with the sales cycle as shown in Fig. 10.1.

In practice, profit and depreciation would accumulate during the year, steadily improving the overdraft position, but sharp increases would be expected with the payment of dividends and Corporation Tax, and capital expenditure would also have an immediate effect on the overdraft position.

Vulnerability of borrowing on overdraft
Companies which rely heavily on borrowing on overdraft are vulnerable to rising interest rates, particularly if their profit margins are small, and those which let their overdrafts steadily increase year by year without raising further equity or fixed interest capital are steadily increasing their risk.

Another hazard of financing on overdraft is that the government can and does from time to time clamp down on bank lending; in addition, the banks are also liable to restrict credit on their own account when they find themselves up against their own overall lending limits or too heavily lent in the particular sector in which the company operates. As credit controls often come when conditions are unfavourable for capital raising, a company which is financed extensively on overdraft can all too easily find its operations severely constrained by its immediate cash position.

Fig. 10.1 Example of annual fluctuation in overdraft

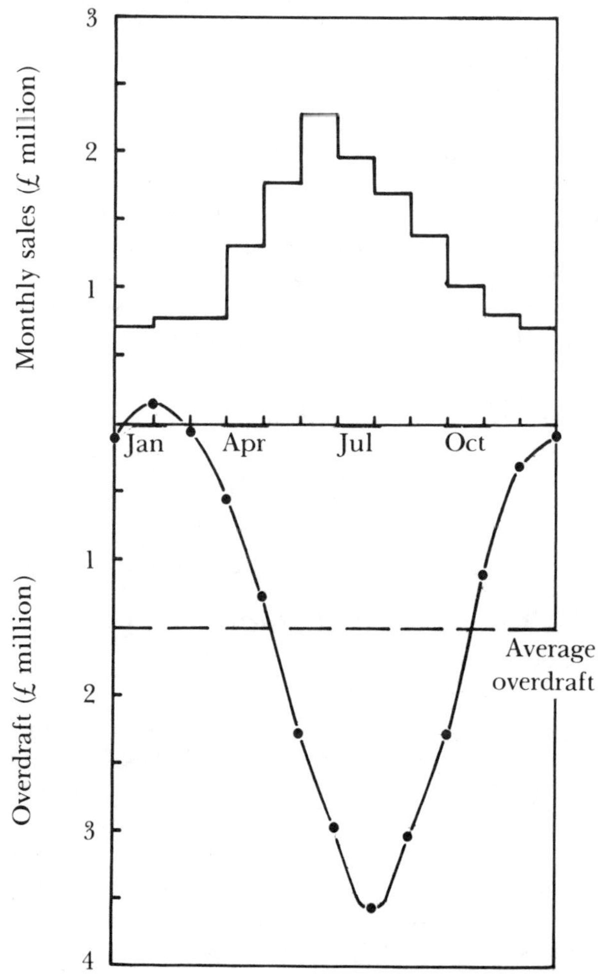

Bank loans

The simplest type of bank loan is one where the full amount is drawn by the borrower at the outset and is repaid in one lump sum at the end of the period. The duration (or "term") of the loan is seldom more than five years (seven years in Europe) but, unlike an overdraft, a bank loan cannot be called in before the end of the term unless the borrower defaults on any condition attached to the loan. Interest is charged either at a fixed rate or, more frequently, at a *floating* rate: an agreed percentage over base rate, or LIBOR (London Inter-Bank Offer Rate, usually the three-month rate).

Drawing and repayment by instalments
Where the borrower doesn't need all the money at once, the bank may allow the loan to be drawn down in *tranches* (specified instalments). Repayments may also be arranged in instalments, which may often be a stipulation of the lender; banks like to see money coming back gradually to make repayment easier for the borrower and to give early warning of a borrower getting into difficulties over repayment. Details of drawing down and repayment are agreed in advance, together with the rate of interest payable and the security to be given, although any of these features can be altered subsequently by mutual agreement.

Security
Bank loans are sometimes secured on assets acquired by the loan or on other assets of the company, but a floating charge is more usual or, if the loan is not secured at all, the company may be required to give a *negative pledge, i.e.*, to undertake not to give security to any new creditor or to increase security to any existing creditor without the bank's prior agreement in writing.

Loan facilities

There is an increasing trend, particularly in European banking, to provide companies with more flexible financing by means of loan facilities. Drawing down (usually with a minimum limit on any one drawing) can be allowed at any time given a little notice, repayment is flexible, and subsequent redrawing may possibly be allowed, but the borrower will be charged for this flexibility by a *commitment commission* payable on any unused portion of the facility for as long as the facility is left open.

FINANCING OVERSEAS INVESTMENT

If a UK company wishes to finance direct investment overseas it can:

(*a*) ask the Bank of England for permission to use official exchange, *i.e.*, foreign currency purchased at the current market rate without any premium – permission is only given if very stringent criteria are satisfied;
(*b*) purchase investment currency – purchase foreign currency at a premium through the investment currency market;
(*c*) borrow foreign currency by obtaining loans and/or overdraft facilities in the currency concerned;
(*d*) take out a back-to-back loan – borrow foreign currency and in the same transaction lend an equivalent amount of sterling;
(*e*) carry out a currency swap, swapping sterling for a foreign currency with an agreement to reverse the transaction at a given date in the future.

Repayment of foreign currency borrowings – matching benefits

As described in more detail in EC 18 (the Bank of England notice on direct investment overseas), the Exchange Control Act 1947 and subsequent Treasury Orders control the use of official exchange for repaying foreign currency borrowed by UK companies to finance direct investment overseas. On repayment the company has to demonstrate that the amount to be repaid has been matched by net benefits received in the United Kingdom from the investment concerned. This is known as the principle of *matching benefits*.

If the matching benefits (net of any interest paid on the loan) fall short of the amount of the loan, the balance has to be repaid with investment currency (purchased at a premium through the investment currency market), or refinanced out of further currency borrowings.

From the analyst's point of view, a company with unprofitable overseas activities financed by foreign currency borrowings may eventually have to make up the overall deficit with premium currency.

Back-to-back loans

A back-to-back or "parallel" loan (where a borrower of foreign currency lends an equivalent amount of sterling), does not avoid or reduce the matching benefit requirements, but usually enables a UK company to obtain finance for a longer period and on better terms than are normally available to a borrower.

As the loans are matched, they are usually omitted (netted out) from a company's balance sheet, details being given in a note (*e.g.* SLOUGH ESTATES, shown here).

SLOUGH ESTATES *Note on unsecured loans*

	£000
US $ Variable Interest Loan 1986	2,372
less Reciprocal Sterling Variable Interest Loan 1986	2,372
	–

Netting out avoids the double counting that would otherwise occur if a UK company borrowed sterling to lend on in a back-to-back arrangement.

Currency swaps

An alternative method of lending sterling in exchange for foreign currency is to swap currencies with an agreement to reverse the transaction after a given period. The method has some technical advantages, the main one being that the UK company's sterling loan is secured by the foreign currency, as the subsequent reversal of the swap is conditional upon both parties honouring the agreement.

In a back-to-back loan, if the borrower of the sterling defaults, the UK company's right to set off the foreign currency it had borrowed against the sterling debt would depend on the way in which the loan had been set up, and the law of the foreign country.

Currency swaps normally appear in a note to the accounts.

BILLS OF EXCHANGE

Definition

A bill of exchange is, briefly, an order in writing from one person (the *drawer*) to another (the *drawee*) requiring the drawee to pay a specified sum of money on a given date. When the drawee signs the bill he becomes the *acceptor* of the bill, and the person to whom the money is to be paid is the *payee*.

The main legislation on bills is contained in the Bills of Exchange Act 1882, and their use in practice is clearly and concisely described in a book, *The Bill on London*, produced by Gillett Brothers, one of the discount houses.

Purpose

The primary purpose of a bill of exchange is to finance the sale of goods when the seller or exporter wishes to obtain payment at the time the goods are despatched and the buyer or importer wants to defer payment until the goods reach him, or later.

In these circumstances A, the supplier of goods to B, would draw a bill of exchange for the goods, which B "accepts", acknowledging the debt and promising payment at some future date, normally three months ahead. Bills of this type are called *trade bills.*

A can then sell the bill to a third party, C, at a discount to the face value of the bill; and C in turn can endorse it and sell it on to D. In this case if B subsequently defaults, D can claim payment from A, and if A also defaults D can then claim on C.

Alternatively A can retain the bill, which gives a legal right to payment at a given date in the future (the date of maturity), or the bill can be deposited at a bank as a security against borrowings.

Presentation in the balance sheet

If Company A's year ends before the bill has reached maturity then:

(*a*) if A still holds the bill, it would usually be included in debtors, but may be shown separately as *bills receivable; or*

(*b*) if A has discounted the bill, it would not appear in the balance sheet, but should be shown as a contingent liability, in case B subsequently defaults on payment.

In Company B's balance sheet the outstanding bill would be shown under current liabilities, either as *bills payable* or included in the creditors total.

Discounting

When a bill of exchange is discounted, *i.e.*, sold to a third party, this is usually done through one of the discount houses, who will trade it in the money market. The discount on a trade bill depends on prevailing interest rates, on the creditworthiness of the drawer, the acceptor and any subsequent endorsers, and on the nature of the underlying transaction. In the case of a *bank bill,* that is one where a bank is the acceptor of the bill, or has endorsed it, the discount rate will be less than on a trade bill. The finest rates are obtained in discounting bills drawn against exports or imports and accepted by "eligible banks" (*i.e.*, those banks whose acceptances are eligible for re-discount at the Bank of England, which include the clearing banks and accepting houses).

Acceptance credits

Certain merchant banks (accepting houses) specialise in accepting bills for customers. They provide this type of short-term finance by granting the client an acceptance credit facility up to a given limit (usually reviewed annually), and the client can then draw bills of exchange on the bank as he wishes, providing the running total of bills outstanding does not exceed the prescribed limit (in other words, it is a revolving credit facility). The bank "accepts" the bills, which can then be discounted in the money market at the finest rate, and the customer receives the proceeds of the sale, less the acceptance commission he has to pay to the accepting house (normally 1% p.a. or more). When the bill falls due for payment (usually three months later) the bank will honour the bill on presentation by the eventual purchaser, and will claim payment of the full face value from the customer.

The acceptance of bills by banks is normally related to commercial transactions, either specifically matched or linked to the general volume of business, so that the bills are self-liquidating.

Unlike an overdraft, the interest on discounted bills is paid *in advance* by the deduction of discount charges from the face value of the bill and, in addition, if the bills have been accepted by a bank, the company will also have to pay the acceptance commission in advance. In spite of these extra costs, variations of interest rates may from time to time make the use of acceptance credit facilities cheaper than running an overdraft.

Acceptance credits in the balance sheet
The future obligation of a company to provide cash cover to meet bills that have yet to mature under an acceptance credit facility will normally appear in a company's balance sheet under current liabilities, and may be:

(*a*) shown separately as "acceptance credits" (as in BURMAH's accounts); *or*
(*b*) included with trade bills as "bills payable" (as RMC); *or*
(*c*) shown as "bank loans, overdrafts and acceptance credits" (as HAWKER SIDDELEY); *or*
(*d*) included in the overdraft figure, with no indication that acceptance credit facilities are being used.

Points for analysts to watch on bills

The discounting of bills is a traditional method of providing finance for many businesses, particularly importers and exporters, and acceptance credits are a standard form of short-term finance available to companies, so there is nothing inherently wrong with finding "bills payable" or "bills receivable" in a company's accounts, but a sharp change in the amounts involved can be a symptom of cash shortage:

Bills payable
If bills are not normally used by the company or in the particular trade, or if there is a marked increase in the total involved, the company may be resorting to the use of bills in lieu of cash to satisfy creditors or to the use of bills to borrow more money.

Bills receivable
A drop from normal levels in bills receivable is also of interest: the company may be discounting bills (selling them at a discount in advance of their maturity date) to obtain cash in order to ease liquidity problems.

Chapter 11

OTHER CURRENT LIABILITIES AND CONTINGENT LIABILITIES

The term current liability is not defined either in the Companies Acts or by accounting standards; but a current liability is normally taken to be any liability falling due for payment within one year of the date of the balance sheet.

Typical current liabilities

Under the balance sheet heading "Current liabilities" may be found:

(*a*) bank loans and overdrafts (as discussed in Chapter 10);
(*b*) dividends proposed;
(*c*) term borrowings falling due for redemption or repayment within twelve months;
(*d*) provisions;
(*e*) creditors;
(*f*) current taxation.

Items (*a*) to (*d*) are required by Schedule 2 of the Companies Act 1967 to be shown separately, though most companies go further than this, and show creditors and current taxation separately. Other items that may occasionally be found include:

(*g*) bills payable (bills of exchange, described in Chapter 10);
(*h*) accruals;
(*i*) deposits received;
(*j*) prepayments received.

For example, BASS CHARRINGTON's 1977 accounts show only a single figure for net current assets (current assets less current liabilities) in the balance sheet but give a breakdown of both current assets and current liabilities in a note (*see* extract below).

Dividends proposed
Under Section 157(1) of the Companies Act 1948, the directors' report must state any amounts which the directors recommend be paid by way of dividend. These proposed dividends appear in the balance sheet as a current liability.

The Advance Corporation Tax (ACT) on a

BASS CHARRINGTON *Extract from note on current assets and current liabilities, 1977 balance sheet*

	1977		1976	
	Group	Company	Group	Company
	£m	£m	£m	£m
Current liabilities				
Creditors and accruals	114.8	4.4	103.8	5.8
Deposits and short-term loans	8.8	1.2	7.2	–
Taxation	34.6	8.9	24.7	7.4
Bank overdrafts	10.1	10.5	18.5	16.1
Proposed ordinary dividend	8.9	8.9	7.9	7.9
	177.2	33.9	162.1	37.2

proposed dividend becomes payable a few days after the end of the quarter in which the dividend is paid and, under SSAP 8, should be shown as a current liability. It is normally included in the overall figure for current taxation.

This ACT is normally also an asset in that it can usually be offset against the company's Corporation Tax liability at a later date, as described in Chapter 13.

Borrowings due for redemption or repayment within twelve months
These are a current liability, though not all companies show them as such. Some companies retain them as medium-term liabilities and simply show the redemption date alongside. It is important to include them as current liabilities in any analysis of the company's liquidity position, especially in the calculation of liquidity ratios, as described in Chapter 23.

Provisions
A "provision" (as defined by CA 1967, Sch. 2, para. 27) is either:

(*a*) any amount written off or retained by way of providing for depreciation, renewals or diminution in the value of assets (the amount would normally be deducted from the value of the assets, rather than being shown separately); *or*
(*b*) any amount retained by way of providing for any known liability of which the amount cannot be determined with substantial accuracy, in which case the amount will be shown as a liability, and if due within twelve months as a current liability.

Under (*b*) some companies set up a provision for deferred repairs or deferred maintenance with a view to equalising the charge against profits from year to year. For example, the balance sheet of claymining company WATTS, BLAKE, BEARNE shows an amount described as "Provision for deferred repairs and overburden removal" as a current liability.

Creditors
A creditor is an existing liability of known amount. A distinction is sometimes drawn between *trade creditors* (people owed for *goods* supplied) and *expense creditors* (those in respect of everything else).

Current taxation
This is the total of all taxes due within twelve months of the balance sheet date. It will normally include one year's mainstream Corporation Tax (see Chapter 13), ACT on any dividends recently paid, ACT on any proposed dividends, and any foreign tax due.

Other terms
An *accrual* (or accrued liability) is an apportionment of a known or determinable future liability in respect of a service already partly received. Thus a business paying rent of £600 half-yearly in arrears on 30 June and 31 December would, if it had an accounting year ending 30 November, show each year in its balance sheet "Rent accrued", "Accrued charges" or "Accruals", £500 (the five months' rent from 1 July to 30 November unpaid at the end of its accounting year).

Deposits are a major item in financial companies, representing money deposited by customers to earn interest. In other businesses deposits may arise in two ways:

1. Where the customer is asked as a sign of good faith to deposit money in respect of a contemplated purchase. If the purchase goes through, the deposit becomes a part payment, and ceases to be a current liability. Should the sale not be consummated, the deposit would normally be returned, though it could conceivably be forfeited under certain circumstances.
2. Where goods are despatched in containers, drums, barrels or boxes, to ensure their return. The container, etc., remains part of the stock of the despatching company, until it becomes apparent that it will not be returned, *e.g.*, when the return period elapses, when it is treated as having been sold.

Contingent liabilities

A contingent liability is a potential liability which had not materialised by the date of the balance sheet. By their nature, contingent liabilities are insufficiently concrete to warrant specific provision being made for them in the accounts.

Under the Second Schedule the Companies Act 1967 a company must show by way of note or otherwise:

(*a*) any arrears of cumulative dividends (para. 11 (3));
(*b*) particulars of any charge on the assets of the company to secure the liabilities of any other person, including, where practicable, the amount secured (para. 11 (4));
(*c*) the general nature of any other contingent liabilities not provided for and, where practicable, the aggregate amount or the

OCEAN TRANSPORT & TRADING LTD *Note on contingent liabilities, 1977 accounts*

Contingent liabilities	Group	*Group*	Parent Company	*Parent Company*
	£000 1977	*£000 1976*	£000 1977	*£000 1976*
Guarantees in respect of shipbuilding and other loans and bank overdrafts of Overseas Containers Limited, its subsidiaries and associated companies of which £3,827,000 *(1976 £5,376,000)* is joint and several with other shareholders of Overseas Containers Limited	25,311	*22,251*	25,311	*22,251*
Group's share of amount payable if a subsidiary of Overseas Containers Limited is unsuccessful in resolving a dispute with the Inland Revenue	5,331	*6,162*	5,331	*6,162*
Guarantees on behalf of				
Subsidiary companies	–	–	33,898	*32,000*
Associated Companies	4,306	*3,787*	851	*645*
Other guarantees, mainly performance bonds	21,031	*10,995*	–	–
	55,979	*43,195*	65,391	*61,058*

estimated amount of those liabilities, if it is material (para. 11 (5)).

Examples of contingent liabilities include:

(*a*) bills of exchange discounted with bankers;
(*b*) guarantees given to banks and other parties;
(*c*) potential liabilities on claims (whether by court action or otherwise);
(*d*) goods sold under warranty or guarantee;
(*e*) any uncalled liability on shares held as investments, (*i.e.*, the unpaid portion of partly paid shares held).

The extract above from the 1977 accounts of OCEAN TRANSPORT & TRADING LTD will serve to illustrate this.

The expression "joint and several" in Ocean's first lot of contingent liabilities means that Ocean or any of the other shareholders of OCL acting as guarantors can be held individually liable for the whole amount.

Note that the guarantees on behalf of subsidiary companies are nil in the group accounts. Parent companies often guarantee the borrowings of their subsidiaries, but as these borrowings appear in the group accounts as part of the debt of the group, no further liability can arise as far as the group is concerned.

Court actions

There is some reluctance in the United Kingdom to disclose potential liability in actions before the court, though this is normal practice in the United States and is becoming more common in the United Kingdom. The note from TURNER & NEWALL's accounts illustrated here is an example of this.

TURNER & NEWALL *Note to the 1977 accounts*

Contingent liabilities

The Company and certain other Group companies are among many companies who have been named as defendants in pending court actions concerning alleged asbestosis in various States of the USA. Many of the actions do not specify the amount of damages claimed but the total amount of damages claimed in those actions where the claims are quantified is approximately $2,000m. The actions are being vigorously contested on the Group's behalf by US legal counsel who are of the opinion that the amounts claimed are grossly exaggerated. The Group companies should not ultimately be called upon to satisfy more than a small fraction of the total amount, if any, awarded by final judgments in these pending actions and no provision has been made in the accounts for the year ended 31st December 1977.

In many cases notes on contingent liabilities are of no real significance, for no liability is expected to arise, and none does. Occasionally, however, they are very important indeed, and points to watch for are a sharp rise in the total sums involved, and liabilities that may arise outside the normal course of business. In particular, experience suggests that any contingent liability (*e.g.*, in the form of guarantees) in respect of an investment (*e.g.*, a subsidiary) that has been disposed of, can be particularly dangerous. For there is an implication either that the new owners are not prepared to give their guarantee, or that it is unacceptable to the other party – a definite sign of weakness. And to guarantee the liabilities of someone, or some company, over which one has no control entails some risk.

Leasing commitments

There is as yet no UK requirement to show future commitments to rentals for leased assets, but many companies do so because large commitments are clearly material. For example, a note to the ROYAL DUTCH/SHELL GROUP's accounts includes the information on leased assets shown here.

ROYAL DUTCH/SHELL GROUP *Note on leased assets*

Group companies have a number of non-cancellable leases under which the minimum rental commitments (after deducting rentals to be received from non-cancellable sub-leases of £127 million) total £2,188 million. Of this total, £1,224 million relates to tanker charters and £631 million to land and buildings.

The rental commitments by time period are as follows:

	£ million		£ million
1977	378	1982–1986	469
1978	344	1987–1991	179
1979	25	1992–1996	98
1980	188	1997 and after	120
1981	154		

Capital commitments

Schedule 2, 11(6) of the Companies Act 1967 requires that, where practicable, the aggregate amounts or estimated amounts, if they are material, of

(*a*) contracts for capital expenditure (not already provided for) *and*

(*b*) capital expenditure authorised by the directors, which has not been contracted for,

be shown by way of note or otherwise, as the second extract from OCEAN TRANSPORT & TRADING shows (*see* facing page).

Such a note provides *some* indication of the extent to which the directors plan to expand (or replace) the facilities of the group, and thus of the potential call upon its cash resources. It should be read in conjunction with the directors' report and chairman's statement and any press announcements by the company, but it is not a particularly reliable guide to cash flows unless it gives some information on timing. It is impossible to tell from the note above how long the various ships to which Ocean is committed will take to build, or when payments will fall due.

OCEAN TRANSPORT & TRADING LTD *Note on capital commitments, 1977 accounts*

Capital commitments	Group 1977 £000	*Group 1976 £000*	Parent Company 1977 £000	*Parent Company 1976 £000*
Capital expenditure for which contracts have been placed but which is not otherwise provided for in these accounts	91,028	*24,017*	65,596	-
Capital expenditure authorised by the Directors but for which contracts had not been placed at balance sheet date	329	*137*	-	-
	91,357	*24,154*	65,596	-

Chapter 12

TURNOVER, TRADING PROFIT AND PRE-TAX PROFIT

INTRODUCTION

As described briefly in Chapter 1, the profit and loss account, sometimes called the revenue account, is a scorecard of how the company has done over the last year (or whatever period is being reported on). It can conveniently be divided into three parts:

(*a*) how the profit (or loss) was earned;
(*b*) how much was taken by taxation;
(*c*) what happened to the profit (or loss) that was left after taxation.

This chapter covers the first part, and the next two chapters will cover the second and third parts.

How the profit was earned

In calculating profits before tax, a company's *internal* accounts will start with the sales invoiced (the turnover) and deduct all expenses and provisions to arrive at profit before tax, but the company is only obliged to present some of the details in its report and accounts.

Example 12.1 shows the sequence of the calculation; items requiring disclosure are in italics, and those normally contained in the profit and loss account itself rather than in the notes to the accounts are asterisked. The remaining items do not normally appear so there tends, in British practice, to be an information gap in published accounts: little or nothing is disclosed about most of the expenses of the business. There is nothing, for instance, about the cost of the material used in a manufacturing business or the cost of the goods sold in a wholesale or retail one; nothing about the wages *charged* against profits (for this is not quite the same thing as the wages *paid*, especially so in the case of, say, a building contractor or shipbuilder engaged in long-term contracts).

It is however likely that, as Britain becomes subject to Common Market directives on accounts, more information will have to be disclosed, so that the gap will eventually disappear; meanwhile some companies do already help to fill the gap by publishing a separate

Example 12.1 Internal profit and loss account

		Amount disclosed £000
**Sales (Turnover)*		1,406
less	Cost of materials used	
	Wages and salaries charged against profits	
	Rent of premises	
	Hire of plant and machinery	46
	Depreciation	106
	Directors' emoluments	34
	Auditors' remuneration	14
	Other overheads	
	Bad debts written off	
	Discounts allowed for prompt settlement (etc., etc.)	
plus	Any credit from *Government grants*	
=	**Trading profit*	141
plus	**Investment income*	1
less	**Interest paid*	13
=	**Profits before tax*	129

value added statement along the lines of the RECORD RIDGWAY statement illustrated here, but for most companies turnover is shown as an entirely separate figure at the top of the profit and loss account or elsewhere.

RECORD RIDGWAY *Extract from value added statement*

	£
Turnover	11,992,956
less Bought-in materials and services	6,159,203
Value added	5,833,753
less	
Wages, salaries, pension contributions	4,094,482
Directors' salaries, pension contributions	86,552
Bank interest	148,756
Depreciation of assets	139,239
Profit before taxation	1,364,724

Effect of accounting policies on profitability

Before going on to discuss individual components, it is worth noting three important points of interaction between the profit and loss account and the balance sheet, where abnormal accounting policies can materially alter the reported profits:

1. *Valuation of stock* The higher the value at the end of the period the lower the cost of goods sold and the higher the profits.
2. *Depreciation* The lower the charge for depreciation in a particular year, the higher the book value of fixed assets carried forward and the higher the profits.
3. *Capitalising expenditure* All expenditure incurred by a company must either add to the value of the assets in the balance sheet or be charged in the profit and loss account. In the sense that it would otherwise be a charge against profits, any amount that can be capitalised will increase profits directly by the amount capitalised. Items which are sometimes capitalised include:

(*a*) research and development;
(*b*) interest on a capital project;
(*c*) starting-up costs.

Research and development
Under SSAP 13, the standard accounting practice on research and development, all expenditure on research and development should normally be written off in the year in which it is incurred. However, where development is for clearly defined projects on which expenditure is separately identifiable and for which commercial success is reasonably certain, companies may if they wish defer charging development expenditure "to the extent that its recovery can reasonably be regarded as assured". Deferred development expenditure should be separately disclosed.

Interest on a capital project
Capitalising interest on a project during construction is a normal and reasonable practice providing interest is not capitalised outside the planned timescale of the project. It would be reasonable, for example, to capitalise interest on a new refinery while it was being built, but not on the cost of the site before work had begun (it might lie undeveloped for years), nor on the overall cost once the refinery was completed but hadn't been put into production because demand for the product had slumped. For example, LADBROKE GROUP's accounting policies on interest charges are:

(*a*) Interest accruing on hotel and chalet expenditure to the date of availability for occupancy is capitalised.
(*b*) Interest accruing on investment and dealing properties prior to full letting is capitalised to the extent that it exceeds income receivable, and provided that the capital value of each individual property does not exceed its market value. Once fully let, all income and expenditure is taken to profit and loss account.

Policy (*a*) is prudent, but policy (*b*) could raise difficulties if properties remain unlet, or only partially let with income falling short of interest payments. Interest is then capitalised up to "market value", but market values are very much a matter of subjective judgement, and can fall disastrously, as many property companies discovered in the big shake-out in 1973/74.

Starting-up costs
The starting-up costs of a new factory, including the costs of removal from old premises, the initial losses of a new unit (*e.g.*, an hotel or supermarket), and the advertising, promotional and other expenses of launching a new product, should normally all be charged to revenue as they are incurred.

Consequences of abnormal accounting policies

If a company does overstate its profits in the year being reported on, the assets carried forward in the balance sheet will make future profits harder to earn: the opening stock for next year will be the figure for this year's overvalued closing stock, underdepreciated plant will wear out before it has been written off, and capitalised expenditure will inflate capital values, thus reducing the apparent return on capital employed and increasing the provision for depreciation. (Understating liabilities also has the same effect: profits for the year are inflated, but the liability will catch up with the company later on.)

The company's accounting policies, which appear either as "Note 1" to the accounts, or as a separate statement, should be read carefully to see if there are any unusual features that might affect the company's reported profits. The statement should also point out any changes to policies, and companies are required to report "any material respects in which any items shown in the profit and loss account are affected by any change in the basis of accounting" (CA 1967, Sch.2, para.14(6)(b)). For example, ROWNTREE MACKINTOSH in 1976 reported that, to conform with SSAP 9, the basis of valuation of stocks had been changed to include fixed production overheads. Comparative figures had been adjusted accordingly, resulting in an increase in profit before taxation of £1.012 million for 1975.

Any changes that are not explained, or that increase profits without reasonable accounting justification, should be viewed with caution, and with downright suspicion when "new and thrusting" management is involved.

We now turn to the individual items on the profit and loss account.

SALES (TURNOVER)

Statutory requirements

All companies with a turnover of more than £250,000, except banking and discounting companies, are required by the Companies Act 1967 (Sch.2, para.13A) to disclose turnover. The method used to arrive at the figure for turnover should be given, together with the following additional information:

1. If a company carried out *two or more classes of business* during the year which in the directors' opinion differ substantially from each other, it must describe the classes and show each one's turnover and pre-tax profit (S.17(1)). Similar information is required for a group of companies (S.17(2)).
2. Unless the directors can satisfy the Department of Trade that it would be harmful to the national interest, companies must state the *value of goods exported* from the United Kingdom during the year, or the fact that no goods were exported (S.20). Exports made as an agent of another person are excluded.
3. Net income from *rents of land* must be shown separately if it forms a substantial part of the company's revenue (Sch.2, para.13A(5)).

Definition of turnover

The Companies Acts do not, in fact, define turnover, but it is generally taken to be the total amount receivable by the company in the ordinary course of its business for goods sold or supplied by it as a principal and for services by it. Internal sales in a group should not be included, and turnover may thus sometimes be described as "external sales" or as "sales to customers".

VAT and Excise Duty

SSAP 5, *Accounting for Value Added Tax*, requires published accounts to show turnover net of VAT, or if for some reason it is desirable to show the gross amount, VAT should be shown and deducted explicitly to give the net sum. Excise Duty is normally included in turnover, even though doing so very much inflates the value of goods sold by brewers, distillers and tobacco companies and may make comparison of one year with another difficult if rates of duty have changed.

Stock Exchange requirements

Under the *Listing Agreement* a listed company is required to circulate with the annual report of the directors a geographical analysis of turnover and of contribution to trading results of those trading operations carried on by the company (or group) outside the United Kingdom. Although the requirement says a "geographical analysis" it does not specify in what detail, and some groups content themselves with no more than the sort of information shown in Example 12.2, which is better than nothing, but scarcely an indication of where exactly the trouble lies. Fortunately, a rather more typical presentation is that of COPE ALLMAN, illustrated opposite.

Example 12.2 Minimal geographical analysis

	Turnover	*Contribution to trading results*
	£	£
UK	10,600,768	45,234
Outside the UK	4,567,987	(51,456)
	15,168,755	(6,222)

Analysis of profitability

The analyst can do a good deal of work upon an analysis such as Cope Allman's, comparing the group operating profit as a percentage of sales for each product division and seeing how it varies from year to year, as well as calculating the profitability of trading in different parts of the world. Note should also be taken of the directors' report or chairman's statement as, in a good set of accounts, these will contain comment on the reasons for marked changes in profitability, and may indicate future trends.

It can, for example, be calculated from Cope Allman's table that:

(*a*) packaging in the year was a relatively unprofitable activity (profit only 3.5% of sales in 1975) compared with the business as a whole (5.8% in 1975), and that its profitability has fallen sharply (since it produced 7.8% in 1974);

(*b*) engineering, on the other hand, improved in profitability from 3.3% in 1974 to 8.0% in 1975;

(*c*) sales in Australia are marginally more profitable (6.6%) than those in the United Kingdom (6.4%), and much more so than sales in Europe (3.6%).

These facts can be linked with comments from the chairman's report where he deals with current prospects.

(*a*) "Trading in the packaging companies continues at low levels" [*i.e.*, scope for recovery, but unlikely in the current year].

(*b*) "One engineering company is being affected by a downturn in strip steel, contract engineering is operating at low levels, but specialist products are still buoyant" [*i.e.*, no increase in profits likely this year].

(*c*) "Overall, it will require a positive upturn in demand, particularly in Europe, to match last year's profits."

Note that, in Cope Allman's table, divisional profit is shown after the allocation of bank

COPE ALLMAN *Product division and geographical analysis*

Analysis of Turnover and Profit

An analysis of the Turnover and Profitability of the Group is as follows:

(*a*) *By Major Product Divisions*	1975		1974	
	Sales	*Group operating profit**	*Sales*	*Group operating profit**
	£000	£000	£000	£000
Packaging	54,572	1,968	49,138	3,823
Engineering	16,711	1,342	14,695	489
Fashion	16,046	1,226	12,929	1,186
Leisure	16,990	1,584	14,101	2,420
Miscellaneous	3,084	128	3,316	298
	107,403	6,248	94,179	8,216

**After allocation of Bank Interest and Central Group Expenses*

(*b*) *Geographically*	£000				
United Kingdom: Home	64,270				
Export	10,455				
		74,725	4,791	66,068	5,202
Europe		22,962	812	18,453	1,785
Australia		9,716	645	9,658	1,229
		107,403	6,248	94,179	8,216

interest and central group expenses: in comparing one company's profitability with another it is important to ensure that like is being compared with like: that the treatment of bank and other interest and central expenses is the same in each case.

There is no requirement to provide a geographical analysis of net assets or to show the proportion employed in each class of business, but a number of companies do so.

TRADING PROFIT

The next item in most published profit and loss accounts is trading profit, (sometimes termed "trading surplus" or "operating profit", though some companies call their profit before tax "operating profit"). Strange as it may seem, neither the Companies Acts nor the Stock Exchange calls for the disclosure of trading profit, nor does either define it.

Trading profit is generally taken to be the profit from trading activities, *i.e.*, excluding interest received and investment income generally, before charging interest paid, but after depreciation, directors' remuneration, auditors' remuneration, and the hire of plant etc; and after taking appropriate credit for any Government grants received (see p. 35). Computed in this way, trading profit is independent of the way the company is financed; that is to say, it is arrived at before all interest charges.

Unfortunately, the term is not used in the same way by all companies and it is essential to check in any individual case what is and what is not included. It is possible, for instance, to find companies which take trading profit to be the profit *before* depreciation, directors' remuneration, auditors' remuneration, and the hire of plant, etc., which is not particularly sensible, since such a figure can scarely be termed "profit". Again, some companies deduct all interest paid, or some of it (say, interest on bank overdrafts) in arriving at trading profit. Other companies do not show "trading profit" at all, but begin the profit and loss account with the "profit before tax", giving details of prior deductions in a note, so trading profit can only be found by working backwards, as shown in Chapter 24.

Disclosure of various expenses – statutory requirements

The Companies Acts require that the following be shown separately in the profit and loss account or the notes annexed – and they are normally shown in a note explaining the composition of the trading profit.

1. *Chairman's emoluments* for each person acting as chairman during the year, unless the duties were wholly or mainly discharged outside the United Kingdom. The aggregate emoluments of the highest-paid director should also be shown if they exceed those of the chairman, (CA 1967, S.6).
2. *Directors' emoluments,* including the aggregate amount of pensions and of compensation for loss of office paid to past and present directors, (CA 1948, S.196); the number of directors who fall into each bracket of £2,500, (*i.e.*, between £0 and £2,500, £2,501 and £5,000 and so on, (CA 1967, S.6)); the number of directors who have waived rights to receive emoluments, and the aggregate amount waived (CA 1967, S.7).
3. *Employees' emoluments*: the number of employees with emoluments of £10,000 or more, shown in brackets of £2,500 (CA 1967, S.8).

Emoluments of directors and employees working wholly or mainly outside the United Kingdom are excluded.

Most companies combine the information required by items 1 to 3 above into one note, and an increasing number are showing emoluments both before and *after* tax.

4. *Auditors' remuneration.* This includes expenses (CA 1967, Sch.2, para.13). A sharp increase in the auditors' remuneration (*i.e.*, more than merely keeping pace with inflation) may be an indication of accounting difficulties within the company, although the extra work involved in these circumstances can be billed separately as fees for professional advice and thus avoid disclosure or, where a marked increase is shown, the company's problems may have become more conspicuously apparent in other ways. For example in 1974, the year in which FIRST NATIONAL FINANCE CORPORATION plunged from pre-tax profits of about £18 million to a loss of £6 million, the auditors' remuneration jumped 48%, having gone up less than 20% in the previous year.
5. *Hire of plant and machinery:* to be shown if material (CA 1967, Sch.2, para.12(1) (gb)). There are basically two types of hiring or

leasing: the first is where equipment is hired on a temporary basis and can be returned when no longer required (sometimes known as *operational leasing*). The second type is where equipment is leased for its useful life (sometimes called *financial leasing*). Although some companies normally incur substantial hire charges of the latter type as a deliberate policy to reduce the amount of capital tied up in fixed assets, doing so will increase the effective gearing of the company, because borrowing fixed assets has the same effect as borrowing the money with which to purchase them: the company merely incurs standing rental charges instead of standing interest charges. Extensive leasing may also reflect a shortage of cash – the company resorts to off-balance sheet financing because it can't afford the capital outlay.

One or two companies, for example the engineering company ASH & LACY, show their outstanding liabilities under hire purchase agreements in the balance sheet as a deferred liability, but this is not yet commonplace.

6. *Depreciation*, renewals and diminution in value of fixed assets (*see* Chapter 6).

OTHER PRE-TAX ITEMS

Investment income

Statutory requirements

Companies must distinguish in their profit and loss account (or in the notes) between income from quoted investments and that from unquoted investments. Until 1967 it was necessary to distinguish between income from trade investments and other investments, and many companies continue to do this. A *trade investment* is an investment made for a trade reason, rather than purely as a means of earning income. It might for example, be an investment in a supplier (to help the supplier, to obtain information, or to act as a lever in dealing with him), in a competitor, or in a customer.

Franked and unfranked income

Investment income may be *franked* (dividends paid by another UK company out of profits which have already borne UK Corporation Tax) or *unfranked* (received from a source that has not borne UK Corporation Tax, which includes almost all types of interest received and any dividends from overseas companies). Under SSAP 8, incoming dividends from UK resident companies should be included before tax in the profit and loss account at the amount of cash received or receivable plus the tax credit (see Chapter 13).

Interest paid

The cost of servicing (paying the interest on) all debt is normally allowed to be deducted before profits are assessed for Corporation Tax.

The Companies Act 1967, (Sch.2, para. 12(1)(b)), requires the disclosure of the interest paid on bank loans and overdrafts, on loans repayable within five years both by instalments or otherwise, and on other loans. Most companies show a single figure in their profit and loss account, giving details in a note which may include some netting out of interest received or other adjustments, as, for example, in the note from RIO TINTO-ZINC's accounts shown here.

RIO TINTO-ZINC *Note on interest payable*

Interest payable	£million 1976	£million 1975
Interest paid on borrowings by the Group:		
Loans not wholly repayable within 5 years	26.4	22.0
Loans wholly repayable within 5 years	2.5	3.5
Bank loans	18.2	10.1
Bank overdrafts	6.0	3.8
Short term borrowings	0.4	0.6
	53.5	40.0
Less: Amount capitalised relating to projects during construction	3.6	2.1
	49.9	37.9

Profit before taxation

As we showed at the beginning of this chapter, trading profit *plus* investment income *minus* interest paid leaves the profit before taxation, or "pre-tax profits".

Chapter 13

TAXATION

(References: SSAP 8, *Taxation under the Imputation System;* SSAP 15, *Accounting for Deferred Taxation.*)

INTRODUCTION

Taxation is an item that appears both in the profit and loss account and in the balance sheet; it includes Corporation Tax on the company's income and capital gains, Advance Corporation Tax (ACT) which the company has to pay when it distributes dividends, and overseas tax.

VAT, Excise Duty, employee PAYE and other forms of taxation that the company may be involved in are not normally shown, though some companies give supplementary information on their role as unpaid tax collectors; for example, MARKS & SPENCER gives details, under a separate heading, of taxes it has been obliged to collect during the year, while other companies give details of government charges peculiar to their business (*e.g.*, LADBROKE show that their "profit before tax" is stated after charging so much betting and gaming duty and so much betting levy).

The profit and loss account usually shows a single figure for taxation, with a note giving details, which may include:

(*a*) UK taxation:
  (i) Corporation Tax charge for the year;
  (ii) tax credit on dividends received;
  (iii) deferred tax (sometimes called tax equalisation);
  (iv) irrecoverable ACT;
  (v) *less* relief for overseas taxation;

(*b*) Overseas taxation, specifying unrelieved overseas taxation arising from dividend distribution;

(*c*) taxation on share of profit of associated companies (*see* Chapter 16);

(*d*) over/under-provision for prior years' taxation.

Items under (*a*) and (*b*) are required by SSAP 8.

In the *balance sheet*, taxation can appear in several places:

(*a*) as a deferred liability, "deferred taxation", which may include:
  (i) deferred tax due to capital allowances exceeding depreciation,
  (ii) tax on the capital gains which would arise if revalued assets were sold at valuation, *and*
  (iii) deferred tax on stock appreciation;

(*b*) as a current liability - tax payable within the next twelve months, including ACT payable on proposed dividends;

(*c*) as a non-current liability - tax payable more than twelve months hence;

(*d*) as an asset - Advance Corporation Tax (i) recently paid and (ii) payable on proposed dividends, and which has not yet been offset against the company's Corporation Tax liability (this is normally offset temporarily against deferred tax, but may occasionally appear separately as a deferred asset).

Details of (*b*) and (*d*)(ii) are required by SSAP 8.

The original concept of Corporation Tax

Corporation Tax was introduced by the Finance Act 1965 to replace a somewhat complex system under which companies suffered two taxes: Income Tax and Profits Tax.

Introduced at the rate of 40% of the company's taxable income, the single tax left 60% which the company was free to distribute, or to plough back by way of retentions, without incurring any further tax; though it was required to deduct Income Tax at the standard rate of 38.75% from any dividends paid out to shareholders, and to hand that tax over to the Inland Revenue.

As the upper part of Table 13.1 shows, a company with pre-tax profits of £100,000 paid £40,000 in Corporation Tax regardless of

Table 13.1 Effects of changes in the tax system

The 1965 Corporation Tax system	*No dividend*	*Some dividend*	*Maximum dividend*
	£	£	£
Pre-tax profits	100,000	100,000	100,000
Corporation Tax (40%)	40,000	40,000	40,000
	60,000	60,000	60,000
Dividends (gross)	Nil	35,000	60,000
Retentions	60,000	25,000	Nil
Gross dividend per share (1m shares issued)	Nil	3.5p	6p
Income Tax at 38.75%	Nil	1.356p	2.325p
Net dividend	Nil	2.144p	3.675p
Government receive:	£	£	£
Corporation Tax	40,000	40,000	40,000
Income Tax on dividends	–	13,562.50	23,250
Total tax	40,000	53,562.50	63,250

The imputation system			
	£	£	£
Pre-tax profits	100,000	100,000	100,000
Total Corporation Tax (52%)	52,000	52,000	52,000
	48,000	48,000	48,000
Dividends (net)	Nil	22,750	48,000
Retentions	48,000	25,250	Nil
Net dividend per share	Nil	2.275p	4.8p
Associated tax credit (35/65ths)		1.225p	2.585p
Gross dividend equivalent	Nil	3.5p	7.385p
Government receive:	£	£	£
Advance Corporation Tax	Nil	12,250	25,846
Mainstream tax	52,000	39,750	26,154
Total tax	52,000	52,000	52,000

whether it distributed none, some or all of its profits after tax. However, the government also received 38.75% of the gross dividends; thus distributed profits were taxed twice: firstly in the hands of the company (which suffered Corporation Tax) and secondly in the hands of the shareholder (who suffered Income Tax at the standard rate).

The imputation system introduced in 1973

Corporation Tax was modified from 1 April 1973 by the introduction of the imputation system, the aim of which was to stop distributed profits being taxed twice, thus encouraging higher distribution and more flexibility in the reinvestment of profits. It was also claimed that the system would bring the UK tax system more into line with that in the EEC.

Under the imputation system, whenever a company pays dividends to shareholders, it is required to hand over to the Inland Revenue what is termed *Advance Corporation Tax* (ACT), which is, *in effect*, the basic rate of Income Tax (x%) that would be payable on the dividends if they were grossed up at the basic rate.

The amount of ACT payable is thus a given fraction, $x/(100 - x)$ of the dividend actually paid, where x% is the basic rate of Income Tax. For example, if the basic rate of Income Tax is 35%, ACT will be 35/65ths of the actual dividend paid. These rates of ACT and Income Tax have always coincided to date, as indeed they must do, because ACT serves two purposes:

1. It is a part payment of the company's Corporation Tax liability for the period in which the dividend is paid. (The remaining Corporation Tax payable is known as *mainstream Corporation Tax*).
2. In addition, it is "imputed" to the shareholder as a *tax credit* which exactly discharges the basic rate UK Income Tax liability on the dividend. So far as the tax inspector is concerned the shareholder's income from the company is the sum of the (net) dividend plus the tax credit. This sum of the (net) dividend plus the tax credit is usually referred to as the "gross equivalent", and it is on the gross equivalent that the dividend yield on a share is calculated.

Although the rate of Corporation Tax is much higher, the total amount of tax the government receives from a company operating mainly or solely in the United Kingdom is *normally* independent of the amount of dividends paid, as the lower part of Table 13.1 shows. Under the imputation system the company paying *no dividend* is worse off (retentions falling from £60,000 to £48,000); if rather more than half the profits after tax are distributed as dividends (centre column) both the shareholder and the company fare about the same as they did under the 1965 system, but if all the profits are distributed, *maximum dividend*, the shareholders are 23% better off (gross dividend equivalent of 7.385p per share compared with 1965's gross dividend of 6p per share).

It is ironic that the imputation system not only conflicts with policies of dividend restraint, but is also an encouragement to companies to distribute generously when the combination of inflation and historical cost accounting can well mean that a company distributing a high proportion of its reported profits is, in reality, distributing capital.

Tax years and rates of tax

The "fiscal" or Income Tax year runs from 6 April to 5 April and is referred to by stating both years, *e.g.*, Income Tax year 1976/77 is the year from 6 April 1976 to 5 April 1977.

The "financial year", (FY), runs from 1 April to 31 March and is referred to by the year in which it *starts*, *e.g.*, financial year 1976 is the year from 1 April 1976 to 31 March 1977. The rate of Corporation Tax for each financial year is usually set in the Budget at the *end* of the financial year, and tax rates since the imputation system was introduced are shown below:

Financial year (FY)	*Corporation Tax rate*	*Basic rate of Income Tax* (6 April)	*ACT as fraction of dividend*
1973	52% (Note)	30%	30/70ths
1974	52%	33%	33/67ths
1975	52%	35%	35/65ths
1976	52%	35%	35/65ths
1977	52%	34%	34/66ths

Note: Since the rate is announced at the *end* of each financial year, companies have to provide for Corporation Tax at the anticipated rate, unless their year ends on or before 31 March and their accounts are not published until after the Spring Budget. Thus if the rate is changed unexpectedly most companies have to adjust back, and this in fact had to be done in FY 1973: a Corporation Tax rate of 50% was envisaged when the imputation system was introduced, but the rate was retrospectively fixed at 52%.

If a company's accounting year falls partly in one financial year and partly in the next, the profits are divided between the two financial years on a time basis and bear Corporation Tax at the appropriate rate for each financial year. The rate of ACT, however, is the rate of ACT at the date of dividend payment (*not* the rate at the date the dividend was declared *nor* the rate in force in the period in respect of which the dividend is being paid).

CORPORATION TAX WITH NO DISTRIBUTION OF DIVIDENDS

Before we get any further involved in the complications of ACT, let us first deal with how the amount of Corporation Tax chargeable to a company is worked out, assuming that the company pays no dividends. This is the calculation of tax and after-tax earnings on what is called the "nil distribution" basis, *i.e.*, nil distribution of dividends.

Inland Revenue's assessment of Corporation Tax

The amount of Corporation Tax payable depends not on the company's pre-tax profit figure, but on the assessment made by the Inland Revenue, and there are several reasons why the tax charge shown in the profit and loss account may not be "normal", *i.e.*, may differ from the straight calculation: pre-tax profits declared x average rate of Corporation Tax during the company's accounting year. The tax charge varies because of differences that arise between the taxable profit and the profit shown in the company's accounts ("book profit"), and because of differences in the rate of tax charged. These differences fall into two categories:

1. *Permanent differences,* where expenses are disallowed or income is tax-free or taxed at less than the full rate (*see* p. 77)
2. *Timing differences,* where the company may be liable to pay the full rate of tax at some time, but not in the year being reported upon.

Easily the most important difference in most companies is the timing difference caused by depreciation (in the company's accounts) not being the same as the capital allowances applied by the tax inspector.

Depreciation and capital allowances

The amount the company shows as deducted for depreciation has nothing to do with the amount the Inland Revenue allow for wear and tear on fixed assets. In fact the tax inspector actually adds back the depreciation charge to pre-tax profits and then deducts capital allowances to arrive at the taxable profit figure.

The rules for and rates of allowances are subject to periodic change depending on government policy for encouraging capital investment. The rules in force for expenditure since 27 October 1970 divide allowances into First Year Allowances (FYA) and Writing Down Allowances (WDA), the rates for which are broadly as in Table 13.2.

Table 13.2 Capital allowance rates

	FYA	*WDA*
Plant and machinery purchased		
before 20 July 1971	60%	25% p.a.
before 22 March 1972	80%	(see Note)
after 21 March 1972	100%	
Private motor cars	Nil	25% p.a.
Industrial buildings	Nil	
Expenditure prior to 6 November 1962		2% p.a.
Expenditure after 5 November 1962		4% p.a.
Commercial buildings	Nil	Nil
New ships and scientific research	100%	

Note. A company may, if it wishes, disclaim all or part of the FYA, and doing so can sometimes be of advantage to the company (e.g., to avoid losing relief on overseas taxation).

Additional investment incentives include:

1. *Initial allowances,* (IA), currently 50% on industrial buildings and 40% on works in connection with mines and oil wells. (Unlike FYA, initial allowances are not deducted from cost in calculating the annual amount of subsequent writing down allowances, but the total of WDAs must not exceed Cost – IA).
2. *Regional development grants* on industrial buildings and plant and machinery. These grants are completely ignored in determining capital allowances.

Example of a timing difference

A company with large capital expenditure on plant and machinery will have a sub-normal amount of tax to pay for the year the expenditure is incurred due to first year allowances, but in subsequent years tax will be higher than normal unless the company has a continuing capital expenditure programme on which to claim FYAs. Example 13.3 demonstrates this.

Example 13.3 Depreciation and capital allowances

If a company invests £1 million in plant and machinery in Year 1, and uses straight line depreciation spread over an anticipated five-year life, the capital allowances and depreciation will be:

Year	*Capital allowance*	*Depreciation*
1	£1,000,000	£200,000
2	Nil	£200,000
3	Nil	£200,000
4	Nil	£200,000
5	Nil	£200,000
Total	£1,000,000	£1,000,000

Thus, in the long run, capital allowances will equal depreciation, so the effect of capital allowances is one of timing; it defers the payment of Corporation Tax rather than reduces the overall amount paid. Example 13.4, continuing the previous illustration, shows this clearly.

Deferred taxation

In order to remove the effect of timing differences from the profit and loss account, *i.e.*, to allow for deferred tax liability, many companies have in the past transferred to a Deferred Tax Account (sometimes called a Tax Equalisation Account) a sum equal to the difference between the Corporation Tax actually payable on taxable trading profits and the tax that would have been payable if the capital allowances had equalled the depreciation shown in the company's accounts.

Example 13.4 Effect of capital allowances on Corporation Tax liability

If the company in Example 13.3 made taxable trading profits of £1 million in each of the five years and we ignore all other allowances for the purpose of illustration, the Corporation Tax payable at, say, 52% would be:

Year	*Taxable profit*	*Corporation Tax liability*
1	Nil	Nil
2	£1,000,000	£520,000
3	£1,000,000	£520,000
4	£1,000,000	£520,000
5	£1,000,000	£520,000
Total	£4,000,000	£2,080,000

Had capital allowances been the same as depreciation the figures would have been:

Year	*Taxable profit*	*Corporation Tax liability*
1	£800,000	£416,000
2	£800,000	£416,000
3	£800,000	£416,000
4	£800,000	£416,000
5	£800,000	£416,000
Total	£4,000,000	£2,080,000

In Example 13.4, the deferred tax would *originate* in Year 1 and would be shown in the company's accounts for Year 1 as:

Profit and loss account

Pre-tax Profits	£800,000
Tax (see Note)	£416,000
Profits after tax	£384,000

Note

Corporation Tax payable	Nil
Transfer to deferred tax	£416,000
Total tax charge	£416,000

The deferred tax thus originated is then added to the accumulated figure for "deferred tax" in the balance sheet.

In Year 2 the Note would read:

Corporation Tax payable	£520,000
Transfer from deferred tax	£104,000
Total tax charge	£416,000

In Years 2 to 5 the effect of the timing difference would be *reversed*, in that more tax would be payable than the tax charge shown in the profit and loss account, so the transfer would be from the deferred tax account, reducing the balance in the account to zero at the end of Year 5.

Accounting for deferred taxation

SSAP 11 proposed to make it obligatory for all companies to account for deferred taxation on all material timing differences in all accounting periods beginning on or after 1 January 1976, but this met considerable opposition and, as the result of representations from the CBI and others, the implementation date was deferred by the Accounting Standards Committee pending a review of the SSAP. The results of the review were published in ED 19, together with revised proposals for a standard accounting practice, which were subsequently confirmed by SSAP 15, effective for accounting periods beginning on or after 1st January 1979.

SSAP 15 allows companies to exclude from their provisions for deferred tax "any tax effects which can be demonstrated with reasonable probability to continue for the future . . . if no liability is likely to arise as a result of reversal of timing differences for some considerable period (at least three years) ahead and that there is no indication that after this period the situation is likely to change so as to crystallise the liabilities" (SSAP 15 para 28). Where these criteria are not fully satisfied "it may be appropriate to provide only part of the full potential deferred taxation", (SSAP 15 para 30), so the scope for differences of treatment from company to company is enormous.

However, SSAP 15 does say that the "partial amount" not provided should be based on substantial calculations and assumptions which are explained in the financial statements and, in all cases, the potential amount of deferred tax for all timing differences should be disclosed by way of note, distinguishing between the various principal categories of deferred tax and showing for each category the amount that has been provided within the accounts (SSAP 15, para. 33).

Some leading companies have long opposed provision for deferred taxation. COURTAULDS, for example, in 1972 stopped making any further provision for deferred taxation in respect of UK profits, stating that:

The liability to Corporation Tax for some years to come is expected to be appreciably lower than the full rate.

The main arguments in favour of making full provision for deferred taxation are that:

(*a*) the timing of capital allowances could be changed adversely;
(*b*) a company falling on hard times can find itself with an onerous tax charge if it has to cut back heavily on capital expenditure;
(*c*) depreciation calculated on an historical cost basis can be very inadequate: providing for deferred taxation helps to produce a more realistic figure for profits after tax.

Analysts should be sceptical where after-tax profits have been increased by reducing or omitting provision for deferred taxation, unless the companies concerned have also made a realistic provision for depreciation of fixed assets (on a replacement cost basis) and have shown that stock appreciation is not available for distribution (*i.e.*, is a holding gain – *see* Chapter 22). In an inflationary period, historical cost accounts tend to overstate profits and SSAP 15 only makes matters worse.

SSAP 11 defined two permitted methods of accounting for deferred taxation:

1. *The deferral method*, where amounts taken to the deferred tax account at the rate of Corporation Tax at the time remain unchanged despite any subsequent changes, so that reversals take place at the same, original rate.
2. *The liability method*, where deferred balances are maintained at the current rate of tax, so that the balance has to be adjusted when the rate of Corporation Tax changes. Adjustments must be shown in the profit and loss account, normally as a component of the tax charge, with a note of explanation (*e.g.*, "Prior year adjustments consequent upon the increase in Corporation Tax from 50% to 52% £. . ."), although there may be occasions when such an adjustment might be regarded as an extraordinary item: for example, on a radical change in the rate of tax applied to business profits.

SSAP 11 called upon companies to state which method they were using for deferred tax in their note on accounting policies (as in BOWATER'S

1977 accounts, shown here).

BOWATER *1977 accounts*

The charge for tax equalisation represents tax on the difference between depreciation and fiscal allowances, together with other timing differences arising in the year. No adjustment is made to equalisation provided in the past years for subsequent changes in the rates of taxation.

[In other words, Bowater used the deferral method.]

SSAP 15 implies that the liability method should be used, and that major adjustments due to fundamental changes in the tax system should be treated as extraordinary items.

Other uses of the deferred taxation account

In addition to differences between investment allowances and depreciation, timing differences requiring deferred tax treatment also arise over the following items.

Stock relief
This was introduced in the Finance Act 1975 in order to stop companies being taxed on the increase in value of stocks caused by inflation. It was a stop-gap measure pending the introduction of some more permanent relief and, despite subsequent amendment, is still very crude in that it takes no account of changes in the *volume* of stock: companies are allowed, as a deduction before tax, the difference in *value* between opening and closing stocks less 15% of the trading income for the period, but the relief is recoverable to the extent of any subsequent fall in the value of the company's stock. It is, therefore, only a deferral of tax and not a permanent reduction, but SSAP 15 does not require provision for deferred taxation to be made where the tax effects can be demonstrated with reasonable probability to continue in the future. Indications from the government are that, in due course, the balance of the relief for the first two years of the scheme is likely to be written off and the scheme amended to provide for the writing off of each subsequent year's stock relief after five years.

Accruals
Certain items of expenditure or income (*e.g.*, debenture interest) are accrued in the accounts but are not included for tax purposes until paid or received (*see* the Appendix to SSAP 11 for further examples). SSAP 15 still calls for the provision for deferred taxation on these.

Revaluation of assets
Under SSAP 11, if the surplus on revaluation was written into the accounts, the additional tax that would be payable if the asset was subsequently disposed of at the revaluation value should be transferred to the deferred tax account and only the net of tax surplus should be credited to reserves, as in Example 13.5.

Example 13.5 Treatment of tax liability on revaluation surplus

Prior to revaluation a company's accounts showed:

Property at book value	£800,000
Reserves	£400,000
Deferred tax	£100,000

The property is then revalued at £1.3 million. If the property was, hypothetically, sold for £1.3 million the taxation treatment of the surplus on disposal would depend on the original cost.

For this example, let us suppose that the book value is also the original cost. The difference of £500,000 is pure gain: *i.e.*, none of it is due to depreciation or capital allowances, and it is therefore subject to an effective rate of 30% (the same rate as an individual is charged on capital gains) = £150,000 of tax, and the £500,000 surplus on revaluation would be written into the books as follows:

Property at valuation	£1,300,000
Reserves (add £350,000)	£750,000
Deferred tax (add £150,000)	£250,000

Under SSAP 11, deferred tax arising on revaluation had to be shown separately because its use to offset other timing differences in the reverse direction is restricted, so a note would be needed to explain the balance sheet entry:

Deferred taxation

Arising on trading profits, say,	£100,000
Arising on revaluation	£150,000
	£250,000

SSAP 15 points out that a taxation charge normally only arises when an asset is disposed of at a price in excess of its original cost or tax written down value and no rollover or similar relief is available, and requires provision for taxation payable on the disposal of a fixed asset to be made only when a liability is foreseen.

Balancing charges

As we have just seen, when an asset is sold, the excess of proceeds over original cost is subject to tax at the rate applicable to capital gains.

Example 13.6 No capital gain on sale of asset

Had the original cost of the property in Example 13.5 been £1.3 million, and had it attracted capital allowances to date of £550,000, the sale of the property for £1.3 million would involve no capital gain, but the capital allowances previously received would be subject to a balancing charge, *i.e.*, £550,000 would be offset against other capital allowances or, if there were none, the £550,000 would be regarded as trading income chargeable at the Corporation Tax rate (£550,000 at 52% = £286,000). Notice that, as usual, the figure in the company's accounts (*i.e.*, the book value of £800,000), has nothing to do with the tax position, which depends on the cost less capital allowances.

Where the proceeds of sale exceed the original cost and capital allowances have been taken on the asset, there is a liability for tax on the capital gain (on the amount by which the proceeds of sales exceed the original cost), and Corporation Tax is recovered on all the capital allowances previously taken.

Rollover relief

If a company disposes of an asset at a profit and purchases another asset, it can obtain what is known as "rollover relief" by electing to have the gain arising on the disposal deducted from the cost of the new asset rather than paying tax on it.

Example 13.7 Rollover relief

If freehold premises costing £200,000 were sold for £250,000, and new premises were bought for £375,000, a company could defer paying tax on the £50,000 gain by electing to deduct £50,000 from the cost of the new premises. However, if the new premises were subsequently sold for, say, £400,000, tax would be assessed on the gain of £400,000 less (£375,000 - £50,000) *i.e.*, on £75,000.

The relief is subject to a number of conditions contained in Section 33 of the Finance Act 1965, including:

(*a*) the new asset must normally be acquired in the period beginning twelve months before and ending three years after the date of disposal of the old asset;

(*b*) the assets must be fixed assets used only for the purposes of the trade being carried out, or goodwill.

Rollover relief was originally restricted to old and new assets within the same class, but this restriction was removed by the Finance Act 1971.

SSAP 15 does not normally require provision for deferred tax where advantage has been take of rollover relief.

Further reasons for "abnormal" tax charges – permanent differences

As we have mentioned, reasons why the tax charge shown in the profit and loss account may not be "normal" fall into two categories: timing differences and permanent differences.

So far, apart from Regional Development Grants, we have dealt only with timing differences, the effects of which are ironed out by the use of a deferred taxation or tax equalisation account (*i.e.*, in all company accounts where there are only *timing* differences and where provision for all these differences is made in a deferred tax account, the sum of the tax payable plus deferred tax should always equal the Corporation Tax rate percentage of the pre-tax profits).

Permanent differences, the effects of which are not of course offset by provisions for deferred tax, include the following items:

Disallowed expenses
Some items, such as the cost of entertaining UK customers, are charged by companies to their profit and loss account thus reducing pre-tax profits, but are not allowed as expenses by the Inland Revenue in calculating taxable profits. This causes the tax charge to appear higher than "normal".

Capital gains
Unless a company's capital gains are treated as an extraordinary item, the tax payable on them is included in the Corporation Tax charge, but is effectively charged at the Capital Gains Tax rate. Thus if a company's sole taxable income for the year was £100,000 of capital gains made in the normal course of business, the profit and loss account would show:

Pre-tax profits	£100,000
Taxation	£30,000
Profits after tax	£70,000

and the apparent tax rate would be 30%.

Gains and losses on loans
Gains on loans are not subject to Corporation Tax, and losses are not deductable as expenses. For example, if a company issued a loan stock at £99 per cent and subsequently bought it in for cancellation at £95 per cent, neither the £1 per cent loss on issue nor the £5 per cent gain on repurchase would be included in the calculation of the company's Corporation Tax charge.

Franked income
This is income that has already borne Corporation Tax, *i.e.*, dividends received from other UK companies, and franked income is *not* subject to Corporation Tax a second time. This means that companies receiving dividends can pass them straight through to their shareholders, together with the tax credits, without incurring any further tax. (Thus the gross value of franked income to a *company* is normally the dividend received grossed up at the Corporation Tax rate rather than at the basic rate of Income Tax).

SSAP 8 requires the sum of dividends plus tax credits to be brought in at the pre-tax level and an amount equal to the tax credits to be included in the taxation charge. For example, if a company's only taxable income was £65,000 in dividends from other companies, together with associated tax credits of £35,000, the profit and loss account would show:

Pre-tax profits	£100,000
Taxation	£35,000
Profits after tax	£65,000

and the apparent tax rate would be 35%.

Losses that cannot be offset against profits
Where a company makes a loss, it may carry that loss back for up to two years to recover Corporation Tax previously paid or, failing that, can carry the loss forward indefinitely to offset against future profits. However:

(*a*) Losses by UK subsidiaries cannot be offset against profits elsewhere in the group unless the subsidiary is at least 75% owned by the parent company. If the loss-making subsidiary is less than 75% owned, the group's tax charge will appear abnormally high, but the losses can be carried forward within the subsidiary and, if and when subsequently matched against future profits, the effect on the group's tax charge will be reversed.

(*b*) Losses by overseas subsidiaries cannot be offset against UK profits for tax purposes, but they can be carried forward as in (*a*), with the same effect.

(*c*) Capital losses, for example the loss on sale of investments, cannot be offset against trading profits.

Under- or over-provision for prior years
SSAP 6 requires that normal adjustments of estimates made in prior years should be included in the profit and loss account (*see* Chapter 14). This can have a significant effect on reported profits after tax, as is shown, for example, by the 1976 accounts of UBM, the United Kingdom's largest builders' merchants.

UBM *1976 accounts*

	£000
Profits before tax	2,933
deduct Taxation	1,092
Net profit after taxation	1,841
Earnings per ordinary share	4.6p

Their note on taxation showed that the tax charge was arrived at after deducting: "Over provisions in respect of previous years (375)". But for this, the net profit after taxation would have been only £1.466 million with Earnings per ordinary share only 3.6p and the ordinary dividends, which took £1.653 million, would have been uncovered.

Overseas earnings

1. Earnings of overseas subsidiaries are only liable to UK taxation if they are remitted to the United Kingdom. Although UK companies are normally compelled to remit two-thirds of their earnings from overseas subsidiaries, the unremitted part bears only foreign tax. The foreign tax may be at an appreciably lower rate than UK Corporation Tax, particularly in countries such as Eire, which give foreign companies several years of tax holidays to encourage them to set up subsidiaries there. In addition, some foreign countries block or restrict repatriation of earnings, thus removing or reducing any UK tax liability.
2. Any earnings remitted to the United Kingdom from certain countries, including the United States, bear a further "withholding tax" (a tax imposed by some countries on the remittance of dividends to shareholders outside the country concerned).
3. Double taxation relief (DTR) is given on overseas earnings that are remitted to the United Kingdom by overseas subsidiaries

so that they normally bear no UK tax if the foreign tax has already been borne at a rate equal to or greater than UK Corporation Tax. If the foreign tax is lower, only the difference is payable in the United Kingdom, but in both cases this is only true for foreign taxes of an income nature (taxes of a capital nature do not qualify for relief), and the relief can be reduced by the dividend distribution of the UK parent company, as we will discuss shortly. Example 13.8 illustrates the way in which double taxation relief is applied.

Example 13.8 Double taxation relief

A UK holding company which does not itself trade has one overseas subsidiary, whose profit and loss account shows:

	£000
Pre-tax profits	100
Tax paid at 40%	40
	60
Dividends	40
Retentions	20

The UK holding company's £40,000 dividends are subject to 15% withholding tax (£6,000) on remission, so the UK company actually receives £34,000.

For UK tax purposes the holding company's dividend is grossed up:

	£000
Dividend from subsidiary	40
Associated foreign tax at 40%	26.6
Gross income from subsidiary	66.6

UK tax is then calculated:

	£000
Corporation Tax at 52% on £66,600	34.7
less DTR, which is the *lesser* of (*a*) Tax paid on £34,000 net £26,600 + £6,000 = £32,600 (*b*) UK Corporation Tax liability of £34,700	32.6
Tax payable in the UK	2.1

The UK holding company's profit and loss account would show:

	£000	£000
Pre tax profits		100
UK Corporation Tax	34.7	
DTR	32.6	
	2.1	
Overseas tax	40.0	
Withholding tax	6.0	
		48.1
Profit after tax		51.9

CORPORATION TAX WITH DIVIDEND DISTRIBUTION

We have so far dealt with factors affecting the amount of tax a company pays if no dividends are paid.

The distribution of dividends may affect the company's overall tax liability if:

(*a*) the distribution is very high; *or*
(*b*) a large proportion of the company's earnings come from overseas and bear foreign tax at anything more than a very modest rate.

In the former case unrelieved ACT may increase the company's UK tax bill and in the latter the offsetting of ACT against UK tax liability on overseas earnings may reduce the relief on foreign tax. The latter is much more serious because unrelieved ACT is available for use in other years but unrelieved foreign tax is not: if relief for foreign tax is not obtained in the same year it is gone for ever.

Limitations on the use of ACT

ACT can only be set off against Corporation Tax liability on trading and on unfranked investment income, and can never reduce the mainstream Corporation Tax (referred to from now on as "mainstream tax") on income arising in the United Kingdom in any year below a minimum rate of (Corporation Tax rate minus Basic rate of Income Tax), as illustrated in Example 13.9.

Example 13.9 Use of ACT

In financial year 1975 tax rates were as follows:

Corporation Tax rate	52%
Basic rate of Income Tax	35%
So minimum rate of mainstream tax	17%

In that year, if a company operating solely in the United Kingdom had distributed considerably more than its profits after tax (perhaps to maintain its dividend in a poor year) it would have suffered unrelieved ACT as follows:

	£
Pre-tax profit	100,000
Corporation Tax (52%)	52,000
Profits after tax	48,000
Dividends paid	78,000
ACT paid (35/65ths of £78,000)	42,000
Minimum mainstream tax (17%)	17,000
ACT set-off	35,000
	52,000
Unrelieved ACT	7,000

ACT is normally set off against the Corporation Tax liability for the year in which the related dividend has been distributed, but if it cannot be used in that year, (*i.e.*, it is unrelieved) it can be carried back for two years or carried forward indefinitely.

Irrecoverable ACT

Although ACT can be carried forward indefinitely, SSAP 8 regards it as irrecoverable if its recoverability is not "reasonably certain and foreseeable", *i.e.*, the carry-forward should normally not extend beyond the next accounting period.

Alternatively, unrelieved ACT can be deducted from that proportion of the balance of deferred tax against which ACT can be set off in the future (*not* deferred tax representing future mainstream tax or tax on deferred chargeable gains). For example, with Corporation Tax at 52%, and an ACT rate of 35%, 17% must remain in charge to meet mainstream liability. Thus if a deferred tax account balance of, say, £119,000 represents tax on

Deferred chargeable gains on £50,000 at 30%	£15,000
Trading income £200,000 at 52% comprising:	
Minimum mainstream tax £200,000 at 17%	£34,000
Maximum available for ACT £200,000 at 35%	£70,000
	£119,000

then the maximum unrelieved ACT that could be set off against the deferred tax account would be £70,000.

If unrelieved ACT is set off against deferred tax it still has to be paid, but it will be debited to the deferred tax account rather than the profit and loss account, and so will *not* increase the profit and loss account figure for taxation.

Irrecoverable ACT, on the other hand, should be included as part of the tax charge, and the amount should be separately disclosed if material. In practice, because of the scope for carrying ACT forward or back and for offsetting it against deferred tax, ACT is seldom admitted to be irrecoverable.

Unrelieved foreign tax

The problem here arises because relief on foreign tax is only available against mainstream tax liability. Foreign tax cannot be used as a credit against the ACT payable when dividends are distributed. Example 13.10 is an extreme instance of this.

Example 13.10 Unrelieved overseas tax and ACT

Suppose a UK company's earnings all arise overseas and bear foreign tax (including withholding tax on remission) at the same rate as UK Corporation Tax (52%), and all earnings are remitted, then with ACT at 35%:

	Nil distribution	*Some distribution*
	£	£
Pre-tax profits	100,000	100,000
Dividends distributed	Nil	26,000
UK Corporation Tax liability	52,000	52,000
less ACT 35/65ths of dividends	None	14,000
Mainstream tax liability	52,000	38,000
less Foreign tax	52,000	52,000
Unrelieved foreign tax	None	14,000
Total tax paid	52,000	66,000
Profits after tax	48,000	34,000

Net earnings

Net earnings are the same as nil earnings unless the dividend distribution the company makes increases the company's overall tax liability.

In Example 13.10, earnings on a nil distribution basis would be £48,000, but with some dividend distribution the earnings "net" of tax would be only £34,000.

Where net earnings differ from nil, it is almost always due to unrelieved overseas tax rather than irrecoverable ACT.

"Full distribution" earnings

These are the earnings that would be attributable to ordinary shareholders if they were all distributed as dividends; they are expressed at the gross level: dividends plus associated tax credits.

As foreign tax cannot be used as a credit against ACT, the maximum distribution a company can make at gross level (dividends plus tax credits) = Pre-tax profits - minimum mainstream tax on UK earnings - Foreign tax.

In Example 13.10, "full distribution" earnings would have been £100,000 - £52,000 = £48,000, of which 65% (£31,200) would have been dividends and 35% (£16,800) tax credits.

Dividend cover

Dividend cover is the maximum dividend that a company could pay out of profits divided by the dividend actually paid.

Dividend cover with mainly UK operations

The calculation of the cover presents no difficulty when distribution of all the profits does not increase a company's overall tax liability, (*i.e.*, when overseas earnings and foreign tax are not significant and the tax charge is reasonably normal). In these cases simply divide the profits after tax, minorities and preference dividends by the ordinary dividends distributed.

Dividend cover in these cases can also be calculated by dividing earnings per share (nil basis) by the dividend per share. (Earnings per share, e.p.s., = profit attributable to ordinary shareholders ÷ number of ordinary shares in issue; *see* Chapter 14.)

Dividend cover with overseas earnings and foreign tax

Where some of the company's earnings arise overseas and bear foreign tax on which relief from UK tax is normally given, the dividend cover becomes more complicated because "full distribution" may increase the company's overall tax liability.

As we have seen, this occurs because ACT is offset against liability for UK tax before any relief is given for foreign tax and when ACT is large, as of course it will be with full distribution, some of the foreign tax may be unrelieved. The amount of foreign tax unrelieved varies with both the proportion of overseas earnings and the rate of foreign tax.

The maximum amount of dividend plus tax credit that a company can distribute out of profits (*i.e.*, the "gross" dividend under full distribution) is the *lesser* of:

(*a*) [Pre-tax earnings × (1 - CT rate) - minorities - pref. dividends] ÷ [1 - basic rate of Income Tax]

(*b*) Pre-tax earnings *minus:*
- Minimum mainstream tax on UK earnings (Note ii)
- Foreign tax (Note iii)
- Minorities (grossed up at the standard rate of Corporation Tax)
- Preference dividends (grossed up at the basic rate of Income Tax)

Notes

(i) (*a*) produces the same answer as e.p.s. ÷ dividend per share.

(ii) Minimum mainstream tax on UK earnings = UK earnings × (Corporation Tax rate - ACT rate).

(iii) The foreign tax should include the withholding tax that would be payable if all overseas earnings were to be remitted to the United Kingdom.

(iv) Franked income plus associated tax credits should be excluded from pre-tax earnings, but should be added back afterwards in both (*a*) and (*b*).

For instance, let us look at the effect on a company earning pre-tax profits of £3 million when either one-third or two-thirds of these profits arise overseas and bear foreign tax of 45%, (including withholding tax). The company has 10 million ordinary shares in issue.

Full distribution which, of course, involves full remission of overseas earnings, will be the lesser of:

	£1m overseas £2m in the UK	*£2m overseas £1m in the UK*
	£000	£000
(*a*) $\frac{£3m \times (1 - 0.52)}{0.65}$	2,215	2,215

(*b*) Total pre-tax profits	3,000	3,000
less tax of:		
(0.52 – 0.35) UK earnings	–340	–170
(0.45) Overseas earnings	–450	–900
	2,210	1,930

In both cases, full distribution increases the company's tax liability, marginally so where one-third of the profits are overseas but quite heavily when two-thirds are overseas. The detail of how this arises is shown in Example 13.11; notice that the higher the overseas element the lower the cover on £1 million dividend distribution and that the combination of high overseas earnings and a high payout makes net earnings lower than nil earnings.

Dividend cover in practice

If a company derives most of its profits from UK operations and is paying a reasonably normal tax charge, then dividend cover is obtained most simply by dividing the e.p.s. by the dividend per share.

When earnings of overseas subsidiaries are significant it may not be possible to calculate the dividend cover with precision, because:

(*a*) The company may not report the exact breakdown of pre-tax profits between UK and overseas subsidiaries (Para. 9(b) of the Listing Agreement requires a geographical analysis of trading operations outside the United Kingdom, but this may include direct exports and overseas activities of UK-based subsidiaries).

(*b*) Full distribution may cause or increase unrelieved foreign taxation.

(*c*) Full distribution will require full remission. Any increase in remission will increase any withholding tax charge.

(*d*) Foreign countries may restrict or prevent remission of earnings to the United Kingdom.

Example 13.11 Effect of overseas earnings and foreign tax

	Pre-tax profits of £3 million			
	One-third overseas		*Two-thirds overseas*	
	£000	£000	£000	£000
Dividend distribution	1,000	"Full"	1,000	"Full"
ACT Payable	538	774	538	676
UK pre-tax profits	2,000	2,000	1,000	1,000
UK CT liability (52%)	1,040	1,040	520	520
less ACT (maximum 35%)	538	700	350	350
Mainstream tax (minimum 17%)	502	340	170	170
Overseas pre-tax profits	1,000	1,000	2,000	2,000
UK CT liability (52%)	520	520	1,040	1,040
less ACT not already set off	–	74	188	326
Mainstream liability	520	446	852	714
Overseas tax	450	450	900	900
Mainstream tax *or*	70	–	–	–
Unrelieved overseas tax	–	4	48	186
Total pre-tax profits	3,000	3,000	3,000	3,000
Total taxation	1,560	1,564	1,608	1,746
"Nil" earnings	1,440	1,440	1,440	1,440
"Net" earnings	1,440	1,436	1,392	1,254
Dividends net	1,000	1,436	1,000	1,254
Tax credit	538	774	538	676
Gross dividend	1,538	2,210	1,538	1,930
"Full distribution" gross dividend	2,210	2,210	1,930	1,930
Times covered	1.437	1.0	1.255	1.0
Dividend per share	10.0p	14.36p	10.0p	12.54p
Earnings per share "Nil"	14.4p		14.4p	
"Net"	14.4p		13.9p	

A reasonable approximation of dividend cover can be made by assuming that the foreign tax rate will equal the UK rate of Corporation Tax. If a company is already reporting unrelieved overseas taxation due to dividend distribution (as required by SSAP 8), then the approximation is likely to be quite good (*see* Example 13.12).

Example 13.12 Practical calculation of dividend cover

Take a company with £7 million pre-tax profits, of which £3 million is reported or is estimated to have been earned by overseas subsidiaries. 100 million shares are in issue, the (net) dividend for the year is 1.3p, and the profit and loss account shows:

	£000
Profit before tax (*a*)	7,000
less Tax (*b*)	3,350
Profits after tax	3,650
less Dividends	1,300
Retentions	2,350

Notes give further details:

(*a*) Investment income	
Quoted	750
Unquoted	400
(*b*) Taxation	
United Kingdom	
Corporation Tax at 52%	1,600
Tax attributable to dividend income	350
Deferred taxation	1,000
Double taxation relief	(980)
	1,970
Overseas taxation	1,380
Total tax	3,350

The dividend cover is then calculated as follows:

1. Calculate the franked income plus associated tax credit:

$$350 \times \frac{100}{35} = 1{,}000$$

This is the amount included in the company's profits at the pre-tax level. (Note that this is not necessarily the same as investment income in Note (*a*), which can include unfranked income).

2. Subdivide profits and taxation, assuming that overseas profits bear *foreign* tax at the UK Corporation Tax rate, *i.e.*, overseas profits have *no* UK tax liability against which to set off ACT:

	Franked Income	*UK*	*Overseas*	*Total*
	£000	£000	£000	£000
Pre-tax profits	1,000	3,000	3,000	7,000
Taxation	350	1,560	1,560	3,470
Profits after tax	650	1,440	1,440	3,530

3. UK Corporation Tax liability against which ACT can be set off = 35/52ths of 1,560 = 1,050.
4. ACT can cover gross dividend 1,050 × 100/35 = 3,000.
5. Gross dividends of 3,000 require cash of 1,950.
6. We have assumed that there is no UK tax liability on overseas profits against which ACT can be set off, so the remaining profits after tax (3,530 − 1,950 − 650 = 930) has to be distributed *i.e.*, has to be used to pay the dividends and the ACT on them.

7.			£000	
		(1)	1,000	
	Gross distribution =	(+4)	3,000	
		(+6)	930	
			4,930	
8.	Dividends actually distributed		1,300	
	plus associated tax credit		700	(35/65ths of £1.3m)
	Gross equivalent		2,000	
9.	Dividend cover		$\frac{4,930}{2,000}$	= 2.46 times

Timing of payments of Corporation Tax

Advance Corporation Tax is payable within fourteen days of the end of the quarter in which the distribution is made, and is offset against the Corporation Tax liability for the company's accounting period in which the dividend is distributed.

The timing of payment of mainstream Corporation Tax depends on whether the company was trading before 1 April, 1965. If it was (the normal case for most listed companies), tax is payable on 1 January of the financial year following the financial year in which the company's accounting period ended, producing varying intervals:

Accounting period	*Tax payable*	*Interval*
1 May 77–30 Apr 78	1 Jan 80	20 months
1 Nov 77–30 Oct 78	1 Jan 80	14 months
1 Jan 78–31 Dec 78	1 Jan 80	12 months
1 Apr 78–31 Mar 79	1 Jan 80	9 months

These variations in the interval are a carry-over from the position before Corporation Tax was introduced.

Thus for long-established companies with years ending between April and December the Corporation Tax payable in the company's report and accounts can appear in two parts:

(*a*) Current liability: payable within twelve months – *i.e.*, previous year's liability still unpaid, less any ACT paid in the previous year.

(*b*) Deferred liability – liability for the year being reported on, less any ACT paid in the year being reported on.

In practice, a company with a year ending on 31 December and therefore having mainstream Corporation Tax to pay a year and a day later would probably show it as a current liability.

For companies which started trading after the end of March 1965, Corporation Tax is due nine months after the end of the company's accounting period.

A further complication with Corporation Tax, as we have already mentioned, is that the rate of tax is normally set retrospectively in the Spring Budget, so if the rate is altered the figure for Corporation Tax due in a company's accounting period already ended will also need adjustment, as was the case in the financial year 1973, when a rate of 50% was expected, but a rate of 52% was set retrospectively in the Finance Act 1974.

Chapter 14

PROFITS AFTER TAX, EXTRAORDINARY ITEMS, DIVIDENDS AND EARNINGS PER SHARE

PROFITS AFTER TAX

(References: SSAP 6, *Extraordinary Items and Prior Year Adjustments,* with supplement ED 16.)

The unsuspecting layman might think that, once a company had made a profit and deducted tax, all that remained to be done would be to decide how much to pay out to ordinary shareholders and how much of the profit to retain in the business. In some companies it is as simple as that, but, alas, not in many, due to the minor complications of minority and preference shareholders, the major complications of extraordinary items, prior year adjustments and transfers to/from reserves, and the legal restrictions on the distribution of profits (as well as any government dividend restraint in force at the time).

Example 14.1 shows how extraordinary items appear "below the line" in a profit and loss account – *i.e.*, below the figure for profit attributable to ordinary shareholders, on which earnings per share are calculated. The decision on whether to treat a large item as extraordinary or not can thus substantially affect the apparent profitability of the company and in some cases can actually turn a profit into a loss (or vice versa); extraordinary items are therefore the subject of considerable debate, as we will discuss shortly. The illustration also shows how any prior year adjustment should be included in a separate statement immediately following the profit and loss account (as required by SSAP 6, para.17).

Example 14.1 Extraordinary items in the profit and loss account

Profit and loss account

	£000
Profit after tax	1,231
less Minorities	68
Profit attributable to shareholders	1,163
Extraordinary items	
(less tax attributable)	247
	1,410
less Dividends	447
Retained profit	963
Earnings per share (*see* note)	11.16p
Extraordinary items per share	2.47p

Note E.p.s. based on profits of £1,163,000 less preference dividends of £47,000, and 10,000,000 ordinary shares in issue throughout the year.

Statement of retained profits/reserves

	£000	£000
Retained profit for the year:		963
Reserves at beginning of year:		
As previously reported	2,742	
Prior year adjustment	(174)	
As restated		2,568
Reserves at end of year		3,531

Minorities

As explained in detail in Chapter 15, minorities occur when a group has one or more subsidiaries which are only partially owned by the group. The other (minority) shareholders in the "partially owned" subsidiary are entitled to a share in the profit or loss of that subsidiary; their share, called "minorities" or "minority interests" has to be deducted in arriving at the profit attributable to the group's shareholders.

Preference dividends

Preference dividends, like ordinary dividends, are paid net and carry an associated tax credit. When the imputation system of taxation was introduced the basic rate of Income Tax was set at 30% and the coupons (the rates of dividend) on all UK preference shares were adjusted by statute to 70% of their former value on a once-and-for-all basis, the effects of which are shown in Example 14.2 below.

As the example shows, and incredible though it may seem, an increase in the basic rate of Income Tax under the imputation system actually *increases* the grossed up income of the preference shareholder.

Preference dividends and any arrears of cumulative preference dividends have to be met before any ordinary dividends can be declared.

Profit attributable to shareholders

Profit attributable to shareholders (sometimes called "profit attributable to the company") is what is left for the shareholders after tax and all other charges have been deducted, but *before* extraordinary items.

It is this figure of attributable profits, less any preference dividends, divided by the number of ordinary shares in issue which gives the earnings per share, *i.e.*, the amount the holder of one share would normally receive if the company distributed all its profits as dividends.

As earnings per share (e.p.s), which we will discuss in detail towards the end of this chapter, are a key measure of a company's profitability, the decision on what items should or should not be treated as extraordinary can often make a very significant difference to a company's attributable profits and thus to the e.p.s., as, for example, in the BURTON GROUP's 1975 accounts illustrated here.

BURTON GROUP *1975 accounts*

	1975	1974
	£000	£000
Profit after taxation	2,384	2,587
Minority interests	(60)	(9)
	2,324	2,578
Extraordinary items	(673)	-
Profit attributable to the holding company	1,651	2,578
Ordinary dividends	1,570	1,618
Balance added to reserves	81	960
Earnings per share	6.34p	7.03p

However, Burton's 1975 profits included £808,000 (1974: £2,993,000) arising from disposals of properties under sale and leaseback, (on which there was no tax, due to rollover relief and losses elsewhere), and 1975's extraordinary items represented provisions on unmatched foreign currency borrowings (which were not

Example 14.2 Effects of statutory adjustment on preference share coupon

A 5% £1 preference share became a 3½% £1 preference share, receiving a dividend of 3½p and a tax credit of 1½p, *i.e.*, precisely the same gross amount as before. With subsequent increases in the basic rate of Income Tax the dividend remained at 3½p but the tax credit went up:

Basic rate of Income Tax	*Preference dividend*	*Tax credit*	*Gross total*
30%	3.5p	$\frac{30}{70} = 1.5$p	5.0p
33%	3.5p	$\frac{33}{67} = 1.7239$p	5.2239p
35%	3.5p	$\frac{35}{65} = 1.8846$p	5.3846p

allowable for tax). Had the sale and leaseback transactions been treated as extraordinary, and the provision for exchange losses on borrowings been treated as a normal expense, then the adjusted figures would have halved e.p.s. in 1975 and would have put the company into loss in 1974, as shown in Example 14.3.

The treatment of currency adjustments will be dealt with in Chapter 17. Let us now proceed to a detailed discussion of extraordinary items so that the reader can judge for himself whether it was reasonable for the Burton Group to include the profit from sale and leaseback in its normal profits, *i.e.*, "above the line", or whether it should have been dealt with "below the line", *i.e.*, as an extraordinary item.

Example 14.3 Effect of treating sale and leaseback as extraordinary in BURTON GROUP *1975 accounts*

	1975	1974
	£000	£000
Profit after taxation (as reported)	2,384	2,587
Less: Profit on sale and leaseback	808	2,993
Provision for exchange losses	673	–
Adjusted profit (loss) after tax	903	(406)
Minorities	(60)	(9)
Profit (loss) attributable to the holding company	843	(415)
Ordinary dividends	1,570	1,618
	(727)	(2,033)
Extraordinary items (sale and leaseback)	808	2,993
Balance added to reserves	81	960
Earnings (loss) per share	3.24p	(1.13p)

EXTRAORDINARY ITEMS

Conflicting concepts of profit

As the general idea of accounting is many hundreds of years old, one might expect that there would be fundamental agreement among users of accounts as to the basic purpose of the profit and loss account, or income statement as it is normally termed in the United States, but there is not. There are two conflicting views of the basic purpose of the profit and loss account:

(*a*) the current operating performance concept;
(*b*) the all-inclusive concept.

Current operating performance concept
Those who advocate the current operating performance concept believe that the profit and loss account should be designed to disclose the earnings of the business which arise from the normal operating activities during the period being reported upon. If this was followed to the extreme, the profit and loss account would include only the ordinary activities of the business during the reporting period; anything extraordinary or relating to prior years, and the effects of accounting changes, would be excluded. A profit and loss account prepared in this way facilitates comparison both with those of the same business for earlier periods and with those of other companies for the current period.

All-inclusive concept
Advocates of the all-inclusive concept, on the other hand, believe that the profit and loss account should include all transactions which bring about a net increase or decrease in net tangible assets during the current period, apart from dividend distributions (which appear in the appropriation section) and transactions such as the issue of shares. The aggregate income shown by such income statements over the life of an enterprise then constitutes a complete historical summary of net income. Advocates of the all-inclusive concept warn that if extraordinary items, the effect of accounting changes and prior period adjustments are charged or credited directly to retained earnings, as they are under the current operating performance concept, there is a danger that they will be overlooked in a review of operating results of several periods.

There has been a shift of opinion towards the all-inclusive concept during the past few years, not only in the United Kingdom but also in the United States and Canada, although none of these countries adopts a pure all-inclusive basis.

SSAP 6 definition of extraordinary items

SSAP 6 uses two confusingly similar terms: extraordinary items and exceptional items. Extraordinary items are defined as:

"Those items which derive from events or transactions outside the ordinary activities of the business and which are both material and expected not to recur frequently or regularly. They do not include items which, though exceptional on account of size and incidence (and which may therefore require separate disclosure), derive from the ordinary activities of the business. Neither do they include prior year items merely because they relate to a prior year."

The classification of items as extraordinary depends on the nature of the business. For example, most companies would regard the sale of land as an extraordinary item, but REDLAND, whose business involves the continual acquisition and disposal of land (*e.g.*, gravel pits, sold off when worked out), states specifically in its accounts that "profits from sales of land and property surplus to operating requirements are not considered to be extraordinary items, and are included in profits before tax."

Presentation of extraordinary items

Extraordinary items (less attributable taxation) should be shown separately in the profit and loss account for the year, below the results derived from ordinary activities, and their nature and size disclosed. If there are extraordinary items, the profit and loss account for the year should include the following elements:

(*a*) profit before extraordinary items;
(*b*) extraordinary items (less taxation attributable);
(*c*) profit after extraordinary items.

Importance of extraordinary items

Extraordinary items should be studied carefully for the following reasons:

(*a*) Treatment of ordinary items as extraordinary (or vice versa) can make a very significant difference to earnings per share.
(*b*) They may signal important changes in the nature of the business.
(*c*) They may also give important clues to the quality of management and to the future profitability of the company.

For example, terminal losses written off may indicate:

(*a*) the capacity of the management to admit their mistakes and/or to face up to changed economic circumstances, and their ability to take action to correct the situation once and for all, rather than devoting a disproportionate amount of management time and other resources into trying to revive dying ducks;
(*b*) the likelihood of higher future profits as the result of cutting out a loss-maker.

At the same time, the chairman's or directors' report and other sources of information (*e.g.*, press reports), should be checked to get a full picture of what lies behind an extraordinary item. For example WHEATSHEAF, primarily a food distributor, explained in some detail in the 1975 chairman's statement that they had decided to cut their losses on diversifying into leisure activities because the reduction in disposable incomes of the middle income residents of urban and suburban areas had very much reduced the potential profitability of the amenity service the company had hoped to provide in the 1970s.

It is worth emphasising that one of the main limitations of many companies is the availability of first class management: if a large proportion of it is devoted to "salvage operations" the rest of the business is less likely to be run to maximum advantage.

Exceptional items

Items of abnormal size and incidence which derive from the ordinary activities of the business are sometimes called *exceptional items* (a term used but not defined by SSAP 6), and should be separately disclosed above the line (SSAP 6, para. 14). Examples of items which might be exceptional items are: a material profit (or loss) on disposal of a fixed asset and provisions for pension scheme deficits and for plant obsolescence.

Prior year items

Prior year items are items which relate to an earlier year or years. Those which represent the normal recurring corrections and adjustments of accounting estimates made in prior years should be included in the normal calculation of pre-tax profits and, if material, their size should be stated in the published accounts.

Prior year adjustments
Only those prior year items which are the result of:

(*a*) changes in accounting policies, *or*
(*b*) the correction of fundamental errors,

and are material, are treated as "prior year adjustments" for the purpose of SSAP 6. Prior year adjustments should not appear in the profit and loss account for the year being reported on, but in the statement of retained profits/reserves immediately following the profit and loss account for the year.

Restatement of accounts
Prior year adjustments (less attributable taxation) should be accounted for by "restating prior years", adjusting the opening balance of retained profits accordingly. Where practicable, the effect of the change should be disclosed by showing separately in the restatement of the previous year the amount involved, but restatement in any real sense is comparatively rare. The analyst should therefore ensure that prior year adjustments are applied to the figures for the prior year or years concerned to obtain a true comparison of the company's results from year to year.

Examples of items needing special treatment (if material) (*see also* Fig. 14.4 overleaf)

Prior year adjustments
(*a*) Change in accounting policy (*e.g.*, change from a method of computing the cost of stock and work in progress including no overheads to one including all production overheads).
(*b*) Correction of fundamental errors (*e.g.*, a major error in adding up stock figures); these are comparatively rare.

Extraordinary items
(*a*) Discontinuance of a significant part of a business.
(*b*) Sale of an investment not acquired with the intention of resale.
(*c*) Writing-off of goodwill or other intangibles because of unusual events or developments during the period.
(*d*) Expropriation of assets.

Charge in current year – disclose separately as exceptional
(*a*) Abnormal charges for bad debts.
(*b*) Abnormal write-offs of stocks and work in progress.
(*c*) Abnormal expenditure on research and development.
(*d*) Abnormal losses on long-term contracts.
(*e*) Most adjustments of prior year tax provisions.
(*f*) Exchange differences (unless connected with an extraordinary item).
(*g*) Profit or loss on disposal of a fixed asset (unless the transaction itself is extraordinary for SSAP 6 purposes).

DIVIDENDS

Distribution of dividends

In deciding what profits to distribute the directors of a company should have in mind:

(*a*) what is prudent in cash terms;
(*b*) what is prudent from an accounting viewpoint;
(*c*) what is legally permissible.

Ideally, directors should choose the lowest of these three figures.

In deciding what is prudent in cash terms, directors should weigh up the cost of raising capital in various ways. Is it, for instance, better to borrow (*i.e.*, increase the gearing), rather than ask equity shareholders to contribute more towards the net assets of the company? And, if equity shareholders are to be called upon to provide more, should they be asked to do so by means of a rights issue, in which case each shareholder has the choice of whether to take up, or sell, his rights; or should profits be "retained", in which case the individual shareholder has no choice?

Unfortunately, the picture is confused by inflation and the present, historical cost, method of accounting. With no inflation (or an inflation accounting system recognised for tax purposes) a company would, in theory, be able to distribute all its profits and maintain its assets in real terms. With inflation running at 10–15% most companies need to retain at least half their earnings as calculated by historical cost accounting in order to main their assets in real terms (but more of that in Chapter 22).

Having decided how much it is necessary to retain in order to continue the existing scale of operations, and how much should be retained in order to expand, out of profits, the scale of operations, the directors should look at what remains.

Ideally, a company should pay a regular, but somewhat increasing, dividend. For example, from a market point of view, it is preferable to

Fig. 14.4 Flowchart of decisions on extraordinary items, exceptional items and prior year adjustments

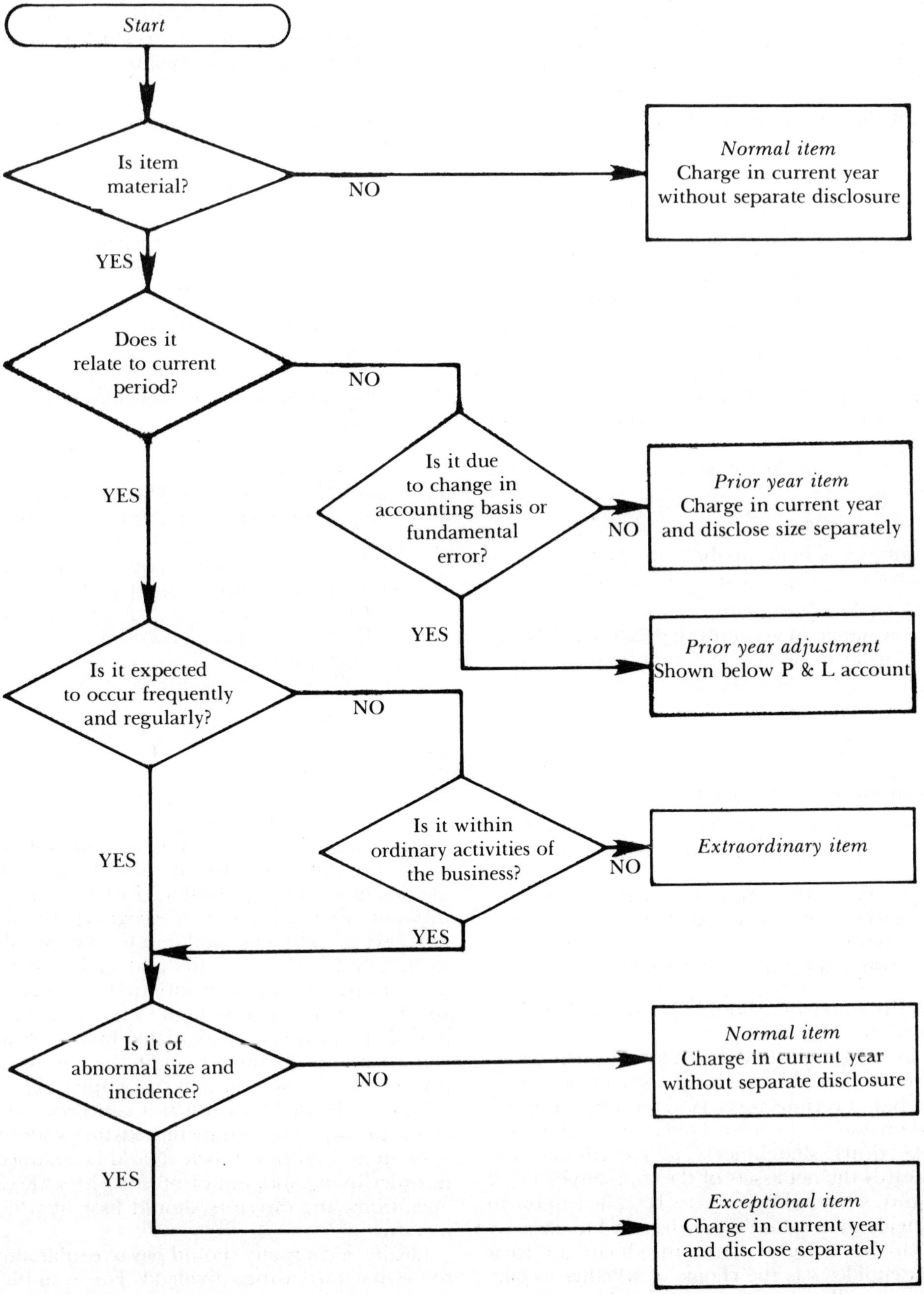

pay: 8.0p; 9.0p; 9.0p; 9.0p; 9.5p; 10.0p; rather than 8.0p; 12.0p; 10.5p; 4.0p; 10.0p; 10.0p; though both represent the same total sum in dividends over the six years, because investors who need steady income will avoid erratic dividend payers, and because a cut in dividend undermines confidence in the company's future. In other words, the directors of a company should think twice before paying a dividend this year which they may not be able to maintain, or setting a pattern of growth in the rate of dividend which could not reasonably be continued for the foreseeable future. For if they do either of these things, they are liable to disappoint shareholder expectations, to damage their market rating and to see their share price slashed if their dividend has to be cut.

Legal restrictions on dividend distribution

There is case law authority for the following propositions:

1. Dividends cannot be paid out of capital. (Where dividends are paid out of capital, the directors responsible are jointly and severally liable to the company).
2. Dividends may only be paid out of profits. The definition of profits has never been free from doubt; indeed it can never be free from doubt so long as directors have a choice on whether to capitalise expenditure (*i.e.*, to show it in the balance sheet) or to charge it against revenue (*i.e.*, in the profit and loss account). Two items over which there might, for instance, be dispute are (i) legal expenses on the purchase of a freehold property: some accountants would write these off as expenses, others would treat them as part of the purchase price of the property; (ii) expenditure on promotion, which could not conceivably have benefited that year, might be carried forward as deferred revenue expenditure to be charged in the following period, but many accountants would write it off immediately.
3. Losses of "fixed" capital need not be made good.
4. Losses of "circulating capital" (*i.e.*, current items such as stock in trade) during the year must be made good.
5. Revenue losses of previous years need not necessarily be made good.
6. Uncapitalised profits of earlier years may always be distributed.
7. A realised surplus on capital may be distributed as a profit.
8. It is possible that even an unrealised surplus arising on a *bona fide* revaluation may be distributable.

A modern accounting view on dividend distribution

An attempt was made in the Companies Bill 1973 to define profits available for dividend. The Bill never became law, but Section 72 made it clear that:

1. Profits available for dividend are, so far as they have not already been distributed, the combined total of revenue profits and realised capital profits for all earlier years, after the deduction of revenue losses and realised capital losses of those years. Any losses brought forward into the accounts must thus first be absorbed.
2. Even then, profits should only be distributed if the directors are satisfied that the remaining capital assets (*i.e.*, assets other than current assets), are at least equal to book value.
3. Unrealised capital profits may be used (only) for the purpose of paying up new bonus shares. They cannot be paid out in the form of dividends, nor used to write off past losses.

In addition, most companies lay down their own rules for dividend distribution in their Articles by adopting Articles 114 to 116 of Table A (the model set of Company Articles given in the First Schedule to the Companies Act 1948); these Articles say:

"114. The company in general meeting may declare dividends, but no dividend shall exceed the amount recommended by the directors.

115. The directors may from time to time pay to the members such interim dividends as appear to the directors to be justified by the profits of the company.

116. No dividend shall be paid otherwise than out of profits."

Here the word "profits" is unfortunately undefined, and so could include unrealised profit, but any company found distributing profit before realisation should be viewed with the deepest possible suspicion.

Declaration of dividends

(Reference: CA 1967, Sch. 1, paras 114–122.)

Any dividends the directors recommend are required to be shown:

(*a*) In the profit and loss account, together with any interim dividend already paid (CA 1967, Sch. 2, para. 12(1)(h)).

(*b*) In the balance sheet as a current liability (CA 1967, Sch. 2, para. 8(1)(e)).

Interim dividends can be declared by the directors without reference to the shareholders, but by convention they do not normally exceed half the anticipated total for the year. They appear in the profit and loss account as a distribution but only in the balance sheet if the company has not paid the interim dividend by the end of the accounting period.

EARNINGS PER SHARE

(Reference: SSAP 3, *Earnings per Share.*)

Earnings per share (e.p.s.) are the amount of profit, after tax and all other charges, that has been earned for each ordinary share and, as such, are a much better measure of the company's performance than profits, which can be boosted by acquisitions paid for by the issue of new shares and are not diluted by rights issues.

The e.p.s. depend, rather obviously, on the amount of attributable profits and the number of shares in issue, thus:

$$\text{e.p.s.} = \frac{\text{Profit attributable to ordinary shareholders}}{\text{Number of ordinary shares in issue}}$$

What is a little less obvious is that a company's profits may rise without a corresponding rise in earnings per share, because of changes in the issued share capital, as Example 14.5 shows.

The issued share capital of BOOTS remained unchanged from 1972 to 1975. In the same period CHLORIDE made some small acquisitions for paper (*i.e.*, issued new shares as consideration rather than paying cash) and made a 1-for-4 rights issue in December 1974, so that although profits in the year to 31 March 1975 rose more than 30% the growth in earnings per share was not nearly so marked. In fact, because the rights issue did not occur until well over halfway through the company's year, the full effect was not felt until 1976, when e.p.s. fell to 10.6p despite profits rising a further 19% in that year. Finally, UBM made no rights issues during the period, but did increase its issued share capital by 41% between 1972 and 1975, partly in acquisitions and partly by the issue of shares on conversion of loan stock.

The effect of acquisitions on earnings per share

The fact that an acquisition for paper makes e.p.s. grow at a slower rate than profits does not mean that acquisitions for paper are bad for e.p.s. It all depends on whether the e.p.s. are higher with the acquisition than they would have been without it (Example 14.6).

Earnings growth by acquisition

Buying earnings cheaply enables a company to boost its e.p.s. when its own earnings are static, or even when they are falling. Suppose in our previous example that the attributable profits of the company were expected to fall the following year to £912,000, despite the recently acquired business performing satisfactorily. The company finds another victim (Example 14.7).

"But", you may say, "how did the company in the example manage to get the shareholders of the second acquisition to accept 2.4 million

Example 14.5 Comparison of growth in profits and e.p.s.

	Year ending in				% Growth p.a.
	1972*	1973*	1974	1975	1972–1975
BOOTS (Year end 31 March)					
Attributable profits £m	16.4	27.2	30.7	31.4	+ 24% p.a.
Earnings per share	9.2p	15.2p	17.3p	17.6p	+ 24% p.a.
CHLORIDE (Year end 31 March)					
Attributable profits £m	4.5	5.5	6.5	8.5	+ 24% p.a.
Earnings per share	7.0p	8.3p	9.7p	10.8p	+ 16% p.a.
UBM (Year end 28 February)					
Attributable profits £m	1.8	3.1	3.9	2.4	+ 9% p.a.
Earnings per share	5.7p	8.2p	10.1p	6.1p	+ 2% p.a.

*Figures adjusted to allow for change in tax system

Example 14.6 Acquisition for paper

	Existing company	*Acquisition*	*Company post-acquisition*
Attributable profits (£000)	800	200	1,000
Issued equity (000 shares)	8,000		
Vendor consideration (000 shares)		1,600	
Resulting equity (000 shares)			9,600
e.p.s.	10p		10.4p

In this case 1.6 million shares are issued for a company bringing in £200,000 at the attributable profit level, or 12.5p for each new share, which is higher than the e.p.s. of the existing company, so the e.p.s. of the company, post-acquisition, are improved. Had the acquiring company paid more than 2 million shares for the acquisition, its earnings per share would have fallen.

Example 14.7 Further acquisition

	Present company	*Second acquisition*	*Resulting company*
Attributable profits (£000)	912	468	1,380
Issued equity (000 shares)	9,600		
Vendor consideration (000 shares)		2,400	
Resulting equity (000 shares)			12,000
e.p.s.	9.5p		11.5p

shares for attributable earnings of £468,000, which is 19.5p per share, far higher than the e.p.s. of the acquiring company?" And well may you ask – the secret is in "market rating".

Market rating – the PER

The measure of a company's market rating is its Price/Earnings Ratio (P/E ratio or PER), which is the market price of the ordinary share divided by the earnings per share.

PER Share price ÷ e.p.s.

The PER depends mainly on three things: the overall level of the stock market, the industry in which the company operates and the company's record. In an average market the PER of the average company in an average sector might be around 7 or 8, with high quality "blue chips" like BOOTS or MARKS & SPENCER standing on twice the average P/E ratio, while a small company in an unfashionable sector might be lucky to be on a 4 or 5 times multiple, perhaps less if the shares have a restricted market (*e.g.*, large family holdings are closely held), or even lower if the shares are unquoted.

A useful guide to the current rating of different industries is shown daily (except on Mondays) in the *Financial Times* in its table of "FT Actuaries Share Indices", which gives the PER of each sector of the market and also the PER of the 500 Share Index, on both a "net" and a "nil" basis. These PERs are *historic*, which means that they are calculated on the figures given in the latest published report of each company. Most analysts estimate a company's profits and e.p.s. for the current year and will quote a *prospective* PER (P/PER) as well as an historic one (*see* Example 14.8):

Prospective PER

$$= \frac{\text{Ordinary share price}}{\text{Estimated e.p.s. for current year}}$$

Example 14.8 Historic and prospective PER

Suppose a company's latest report and accounts, usually published two to three months after the year has ended, gives earnings per share of 8.0p. The analyst is expecting profits to rise by about 27% in the current year, the tax charge to stay about the same (as a percentage of pre-tax profits), and for there to be a proportionately higher charge for minorities (because one partly owned subsidiary is making a hefty contribution to the improved profits). He therefore estimates that e.p.s. will rise a little less than profits, to about 10.0p. The current share price is 56p, so

Last year's e.p.s.	= 8p	Historic PER	= 7.0
Current year e.p.s.	= 10p	Prospective PER	= 5.6

"Wonder growth" by acquisition

There is nothing fundamentally wrong with improving a company's earnings per share by acquisition, and it can be beneficial all round if there is some industrial or commercial logic involved, *i.e.*, if the acquired company's business fits in with the acquiring company's existing activities or employs common skills and technology, or if the acquirer can provide improved management and financial resources. However, the practice is open to abuse, especially in bull markets.

Enter the "whizz-kid" (known as a "gunslinger" on the other side of the Atlantic), who might proceed as follows:

1. Acquire control of a company that has a listing on the stock exchange, but little else, *e.g.*, the "DEMISED TEA COMPANY", known in whizz-kid jargon as a "shell".
2. Reverse your shell into an unlisted company, thus giving your victim the benefit of a ready market for his shares and yourself the benefit of a company with real assets.
3. Sell off some of the assets, particularly property that is ripe for development. Don't lose any sleep over the fact that closing a factory throws 200 people out of work, as the office block that will replace it will house twice that number of civil servants in the Department recently set up to encourage investment in industry; this "asset-stripping" process is essential to provide the cash to gain control of your next victim.
4. By now the earnings per share of the Demised Tea Company since renamed "ANGLO-TRIUMPH ASSETS", have shown remarkable growth, albeit from a very low base (it's very easy to double profits of next-to-nothing), the bull market has conveniently started and the Press have noticed you. You project a suitable image of dynamic young management, talking to them earnestly about the need for British Industry to obtain a fair return on assets, and your photograph appears in the financial sections of the Sunday papers. You have arrived.
5. Your share price responds to Press comment, putting your "go-go" company on a PER of 10 or 12; you continue to acquire companies, but now use shares rather than cash, thus continually boosting your e.p.s., as we have shown.
6. Following Press adulation, you broaden out into TV financial panels, seminar platforms, and after-dinner speeches; the bull market is now raging; Anglo-Triumph features regularly as an "up stock" in the price changes table on the front page of the *FT* as the PER climbs towards 20. Deals follow apace, and Anglo-Triumph thrusts ahead, acquiring a huge conglomeration of businesses in an ever-widening range of mainly unrelated activities – it may be shoes, or ships or sealing-wax, but it's certainly Alice in Wonderland.
7. The moment of truth. The bull market, after a final glorious wave of euphoria, tops out. Profits in Anglo-Triumph's businesses turn down as little or nothing has been done to improve their management. Asset-stripping becomes politically unacceptable, and the word "conglomerate" is coined to describe hotch-potch outfits like Anglo-Triumph. Down goes Anglo-Triumph's share price, and with it the market rating; without a high PER the company can no longer boost profits by acquisition, and the game is up.

Whether the whole edifice of Anglo-Triumph collapses completely or becomes just another lowly rated ex-glamour stock depends on the financial structure of the company. If it has geared up (*i.e.*, has built up debt, on which interest has to be paid), and hasn't the cash to service these debts, the company will probably be forced into liquidation unless some sympathetic banker (possibly embarrassed by the prospect of incurring a huge loss if the company goes under), decides to tide things over until "hopefully" better times.

We must now return to earnings per share, but for further reading on "fly operators" we would refer readers to Michael Brett's hilariously true-to-life articles in the *Investors Chronicle* on the activities of whizz-kid Mr Rudyard Sharpe, ace of the asset strip and darling of the Sunday share tipsters (*Investors Chronicle* 14 and 21 February 1975) and, in the same vein, fringe banker Mr Cyril Buck of "FASTBUCK FINANCE" (*IC* 22 February and 29 November 1974) and property developers Messrs Oliver and Arthur Fact (*IC* 17 and 24 January 1975 and *IC* Property Survey of 4 April 1975).

Adjustments to earnings per share – SSAP 3

If a company issues new shares during the year, the e.p.s. for *that year* have to be calculated using the time-weighted average number of shares in issue during the year, and the e.p.s. of *previous years* have to be adjusted to allow for any bonus element in the share issue. SSAP 3 describes in detail the method of adjustment to be used by companies for each type of issue, which are briefly described here.

Scrip (Bonus) issue or share split
Use the year-end figure for number of shares, and apply a factor to previous years' e.p.s. to put them on a comparable basis. For a scrip issue of y shares for every x shares held, the factor is $x \div (x + y)$ and for a split of 1 old share into z new shares it is $1 \div z$ (Example 14.9).

Shares issued in an acquisition
The shares are assumed to have been issued at market price (even if the shares issued, the "vendor consideration", have been placed at a discount at the time). The weighted average number of shares in issue during the year is calculated and used for working out the e.p.s. (Example 14.10).

Example 14.9 Scrip issue and e.p.s.

Let us suppose that "UNIVERSAL TRADERS LTD" is a company whose year ends on 31 December. At the end of 1975 the issued share capital was £4,000,000, of which £1,000,000 was in 3½% preference shares and £3,000,000 was the equity share capital of 12,000,000 ordinary shares of 25p each. No new shares were issued in 1976 and e.p.s. reported in 1976 were 8p: see tabulated accounts below, showing adjustments to previous years' e.p.s. required by the issue of new shares in this and ensuing examples.

In 1977 the company made a 1-for-3 scrip issue and profits after tax increased from £1.255m to £1.525m. Earnings per share were 7.5p which, at first sight, appear to be down on the previous year, but 1976's figure of 8p has to be adjusted by a factor of $3 \div (3 + 1)$ to make it comparable with 1977: ¾ of 8p = 6p.

"UNIVERSAL TRADERS LTD" *Accounts*

Year end 31 December	1976	1977 *Scrip issue*	1978 *Acquisition*	1979 *Rights issue*
	£000	£000	£000	£000
Profit after tax	1,255	1,525	1,745	2,165
less Minorities	260	290	310	420
	995	1,235	1,435	1,745
less Preference dividends	35	35	35	35
Attributable profits	960	1,200	1,400	1,710
add Convertible interest (net)				72
Fully diluted attributable				1,782
Ordinary shares in issue	12m	16m	18m	22.5m
1978 weighted average			17.5m	
1979 fully diluted				23.75m
e.p.s. reported in 1976	8p	–	–	–
e.p.s. in 1977 and 1978 with 1976 adjusted	6p	7.5p	8.0p	–
e.p.s. in 1979 with prior years adjusted	5.76p	7.2p	7.68p	7.6p
Fully diluted e.p.s.	–	–	–	7.5p

Example 14.10 Acquisition issue and e.p.s.

To continue Example 14.9, on 1 April 1978 Universal Traders acquired another company and issued 2 million new ordinary fully paid 25p ordinary shares in payment (an acquisition "for paper").

At the year end, the profits of the new subsidiary for the period 1 April to 31 December 1978 were included in Universal Traders' consolidated profit and loss account and the weighted average number of shares in issue during the year was calculated:

$$\frac{\text{16m for 3 months plus 18m for 9 months}}{\text{12 months}} = \text{17.5m on weighted average}$$

Profits at the attributable level came out at £1,400,000 to give earnings per share of 8.0p.

Rights issue
A rights issue is regarded as being partly an issue at the market price and partly a scrip issue (the bonus element); the e.p.s. of previous years are adjusted by the factor appropriate to the bonus element in the same way as a scrip issue (Example 14.11).

Example 14.11 Rights issue (on first day of company's year) and e.p.s.

Let us suppose Universal Traders made a rights issue on 1 January 1979 on the basis of one new share for every 4 shares held at a price of 80p per share, against a market price of 100p on the last day the old shares were quoted cum-rights. The issue would have the same effect as a 1-for-5 at 100p, followed by a 1-for-24 scrip issue. The factor for adjusting the e.p.s. for previous years is thus 24 ÷ (1 + 24), which can be calculated in more complicated cases by the formula:

Theoretical ex-rights (xr) price ÷ actual cum-rights (cr) price on the last day of quotation cum-rights

where the Theoretical xr price is, in this case, 1 share at 80p plus 4 old shares at 100p each = 5 shares for 480p = 96p, and 96/100 = 24/25.

If, instead of being made on the first day of the company's year (as in Example 14.11), a rights issue is made during the company's year, the calculation of the bonus element and the factor for adjusting previous years' e.p.s. is just the same but, in addition, the weighted average number of shares in issue during the year has to be calculated.

Example 14.12 Rights issue (during company's year) and e.p.s.

If Universal Traders had made their 1-for-4 rights issue on 1 September 1979, then the number of shares at the beginning of the year is adjusted by the reciprocal of the e.p.s. factor and the calculation to find the weighted average is:

$$\left[18\text{m} \times \frac{25}{24} \times \frac{8}{12}\right] + \left[22.5\text{m} \times \frac{4}{12}\right] = 20\text{m shares}$$

which would give e.p.s. of 8.55p rather than 7.6p for 1979.

Adjusting the number of shares in issue during the first 8 months of 1979 by 25/24 allows for the bonus element of the rights issue, *i.e.*, it puts the shares in issue at the beginning of the year on the same basis as the shares in issue at the end of the year.

Fully diluted earnings per share
Where a company has in issue any form of security that does not, at present, rank for ordinary dividends but may do so in the future, *e.g.*, convertibles, deferred or partly paid shares, warrants or options granted, the effect on earnings per share of these securities becoming entitled to dividends is called "full dilution", and SSAP 3 requires companies to show fully diluted earnings per share if dilution reduces the basic e.p.s. by 5% or more.

Example 14.13 Full dilution of e.p.s.

Suppose that Universal Traders had made a £2 million issue of 7½% convertible unsecured loan stock (CULS) during 1979, entitling holders to convert into ordinary shares on the basis of 62½ ordinary shares per £100 nominal of CULS at any time between 1981 and 1986. The calculation of fully diluted e.p.s. allows for the extra 1.25 million shares that would be issued if all the CULS holders converted, and for the annual interest of £150,000 the company would save at the pre-tax level, which has to bear Corporation Tax before being attributable to shareholders. In our example, with Corporation Tax at 52%, fully diluted e.p.s.:

$$\frac{£1.71\text{m} + (£0.15\text{m} \times 0.48)}{22.5\text{m} + 1.25\text{m}} = 7.5\text{p}$$

7.5p, in Example 14.13, is less than a 5% drop on the basic e.p.s. of 7.6p and so it does not have to be shown in the accounts, though some companies show fully diluted e.p.s. even if dilution actually increases the e.p.s., *e.g.*, AARONSON BROS LTD, as shown here.

AARONSON BROS LTD *Earnings per share*

	1975	1974
Earnings per share:		
basic	4.44p	4.14p
fully diluted	4.61p	4.33p

Note 5 Earnings per Share
The calculation of basic earnings per share has been based on earnings of £862,447 (1974 – £803,780) and on the 19,422,665 Ordinary Shares of 10p each in issue at 30 September 1975.

The fully diluted earnings per share has been based on 21,204,843 Ordinary Shares taken as in issue, calculated as follows:

Ordinary Shares in issue as at 30 September 1975	19,422,665
Maximum number of Ordinary Shares into which the 2,700,000 4.25 per cent Cumulative Redeemable Preference Shares of £1 each become convertible between 31 May 1975 and 31 May 1981	1,782,178
	21,204,843

Where full dilution involves payments to the company, *e.g.*, warrant holders exercising their right to subscribe for shares at a given price (the exercise price), the calculation of fully diluted e.p.s. assumes that the company would invest the proceeds of subscription in 2½% Consols.

Adjustments for additional depreciation

Some companies depress their earnings per share by charging additional depreciation on a replacement cost basis in calculating their trading profit; in these cases the analyst needs to add back the additional depreciation charge to put the profits and earnings per share on a basis comparable with other companies (Example 14.14).

Replacement cost accounting is discussed further in Chapter 22.

Net and nil basis

SSAP 3 requires companies to show net earnings per share in the profit and loss account and to state the amount of the earnings and the number of shares used in the calculation, which is usually done in an accompanying note. Where there is a material difference between earnings per share calculated on the net basis and on the nil distribution basis, because the distribution of dividends has increased the company's tax charge (*i.e.*, has incurred irrecoverable ACT or has caused overseas tax to be unrelieved, as we described in Chapter 13), the e.p.s. calculated on the nil distribution basis should also be shown on the face of the profit and loss account.

Earnings on more than one class of share

Where there is more than one class of equity share or where some shares are only partly paid, the earnings should be attributed to the different classes of share in accordance with their dividend rights or profit participation.

Example 14.14 Adjusting e.p.s. for additional depreciation: ASSOCIATED PORTLAND CEMENT

ASSOCIATED PORTLAND CEMENT (now BLUE CIRCLE) in 1977 reported profit after taxation and minorities of £21.8 million to give e.p.s. of 27.0p, but had included an additional depreciation charge of £10 million in calculating their trading profit. As the additional depreciation charge is not an allowable expense for Corporation Tax purposes, it can be added back at the after-tax level:

	As reported £m	*Adjusted* £m
Profit after taxation	24.7	24.7
Add back additional depreciation		10.0
Adjusted profit after taxation		34.7
Interest of minority shareholders *see* Note (i)	2.9	4.1
Profit attributable to ordinary stockholders	21.8	30.6
Earnings per £1 ordinary stock unit	27.0p	37.8p

Notes

(i) Minority interests are adjusted pro rata to the increase in profits after tax unless the amount of additional depreciation attributable to minorities happens to be known, which is unlikely.

(ii) If adjustments have been made to "normalise" the tax charge (*see* Chapter 24), the additional depreciation should be added back at the pre-tax level and the standard tax charge should then be recalculated.

MOVEMENTS IN RESERVES

As well as the requirements of the Companies Act 1967, (*see* p. 16), SSAP 6 requires that a statement of retained profits/reserves should immediately follow the profit and loss account for the year. The ICI example overleaf illustrates this.

ICI *Statement of retained profits/reserves*

Reserves applicable to parent company	1976	1977
	£ million	£ million
At beginning of year	949	1,264
Profit retained for year	162	133
Amounts taken direct to reserves (Note 8)	153	(16)
At end of year	1,264	1,381

Note 8

Reserves	1976	1977
	£ million	£ million
At beginning of year	949	1,264
Profit retained for year:		
By parent company	24	129
By subsidiaries	126	3
In principal associated companies	12	1
Amounts taken direct to reserves:		
Share premiums, less expenses	141	12
Exchange adjustments:		
Book value of overseas subsidiaries	–	–
Fixed assets	101	(51)
Loans	(110)	42
Investments and other items	20	(21)
Other movements	1	2
At end of year	1,264	1,381

Chapter 15

SUBSIDIARIES AND GROUP ACCOUNTS

(Reference: SSAP 14)

HOLDING COMPANIES, SUBSIDIARIES AND GROUPS

Definitions

(Reference: CA 1948, S. 154.)

A *holding company* is a company which exercises control over another company, its subsidiary company, and is often referred to as the *parent* company.

A *subsidiary company* is a company, control over which is exercised by a holding company by virtue of the fact that the holding company either:

(*a*) is a member of it and controls the composition of its board of directors; *or*

(*b*) holds more than half in nominal value of its equity share capital.

For this purpose *equity share capital* comprises any part of the issued share capital which carries the right to participate beyond a specified amount in either a capital or a revenue distribution. It will include not just the ordinary share capital but all share capital other than non-participating preference shares.

Control involves the power to appoint all or a majority of the board without the consent or concurrence of some other person. (It arises from rights conferred by the Articles, or from voting rights.)

A *group* is a holding company, together with its subsidiary company or companies.

A *wholly-owned subsidiary* is one in which all the share capital is owned either by the holding company or by other wholly-owned subsidiaries.

A *partially-owned subsidiary* is one in which some of the share capital is owned outside the group. The outside shareholdings are called minority interests.

For an illustration of the use of these terms, *see* Example 15.1.

Example 15.1 Partially and wholly owned subsidiaries

H is the holding company of a group of companies, and is incorporated in Great Britain.

H holds	100,000 of the	100,000 ordinary shares of	S
H holds	7,500 of the	10,000 ordinary shares of	T
S holds	5,100 of the	10,000 ordinary shares of	U
T holds	1,000 of the	1,000 ordinary shares of	V

The H group may be depicted thus:

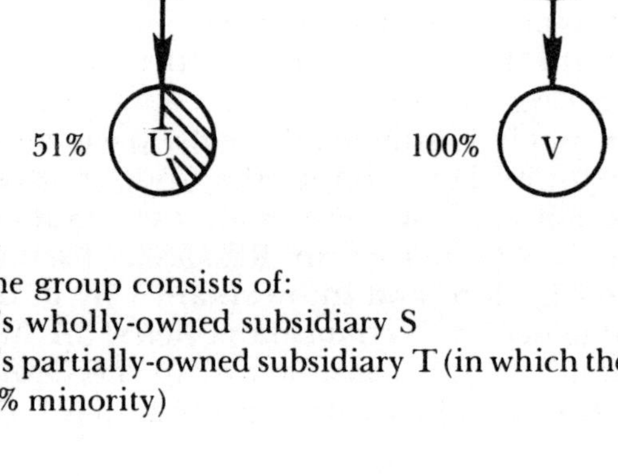

The group consists of:
H's wholly-owned subsidiary S
H's partially-owned subsidiary T (in which there is a 25% minority)

T's wholly-owned subsidiary V (which in law is also a subsidiary of H, but colloquially a partially-owned sub-subsidiary of H)
S's partially-owned subsidiary U (in which there is a 49% minority).

Statutory requirements for group accounts

Where at the end of its financial year a company has subsidiaries, "group accounts" must be laid before the company in general meeting together with the company's own balance sheet and profit and loss account (CA 1948, S. 150). Group accounts for this purpose normally comprise:

(*a*) a consolidated balance sheet dealing with the state of affairs of the company and all the subsidiaries to be dealt with in group accounts; *and*

(*b*) a consolidated profit and loss account dealing with the profit or loss of the company and those subsidiaries;

but, as we shall discuss, alternative methods of presentation are allowed.

Exceptions to consolidation of subsidiaries

Under Section 150(2)(b) of the Companies Act 1948, group accounts need not deal with a subsidiary if the holding company's directors are of the opinion that:

1. It is impracticable or would be of no real value to members, in view of the insignificant amounts involved, or would involve expense or delay out of proportion to the value to members of the company. For example, for several years the accounts of BAT INDUSTRIES (British American Tobacco) stated, quite simply "BAT Zaire SARL not consolidated owing to lack of information".
2. The result would be misleading, or harmful to the business of the company or any of its subsidiaries. The inclusion of a material foreign subsidiary in consolidated accounts could be misleading if there are severe restrictions on the remittance of its currency, for shareholders and creditors might draw incorrect inferences as to the earnings and liquid resources of the group available for dividends or the payment of creditors. For example, the group accounts of BOC do not consolidate the results of BOC's subsidiaries in Rhodesia, Uganda and Ceylon, and they explain why in the statement of accounting policies: "A subsidiary is not consolidated in the Group accounts where, in the opinion of the directors, effective control can no longer be exercised due to intervention by Government such that the inclusion of its results in the Group accounts would be misleading." A somewhat similar situation arises where civil war is raging or a subsidiary operates in enemy-occupied territory during wartime.
3. The business of the holding company and that of the subsidiary are so different that they cannot reasonably be treated as a single undertaking. If the directors are of such an opinion about each of the company's subsidiaries, group accounts are not by law required at all. (S. 150(2)(b)). In practice many groups are so diversified that the business of the holding company and its various subsidiaries are so different that they would be a rather odd single undertaking, but few groups claim exemption on this ground.

Group accounts are not required where the company is at the end of its financial year the wholly owned subsidiary of another body corporate incorporated in Great Britain. (S. 150(2)(a)). In Example 15.1, S would not need to produce consolidated accounts, but T would.

Alternative methods of presentation

Group accounts need not take the form of consolidated accounts for the entire group if the holding company's directors are of the opinion that the same or equivalent information can be better presented to the company's members in some other form, for instance by showing the accounts of a subsidiary separately (CA 1948, S. 151(2)).

The holding company's own profit and loss account

The holding company's profit and loss account need not be presented if the consolidated profit and loss account shows how much of the consolidated profit or loss for the financial year is dealt with in the holding company's own accounts and, in practice, one seldom sees the holding company's own profit and loss account.

The company's financial (accounting) year end

Under Section 153 of the Companies Act 1948 a holding company's directors must ensure that the financial year of each of its subsidiaries coincides with the holding company's own financial year, unless in their opinion there are good reasons against it. If the financial year of a subsidiary does *not* coincide with that of the holding company the group accounts must, unless the Department of Trade otherwise directs, deal with the subsidiary's state of affairs at the end of its financial year immediately preceding that of its holding company and with its profit or loss for that financial year (CA 1948, S. 152(2)).

Unfortunately, the Companies Act uses the term "financial year" here to mean the company's accounting year; the term is normally used to describe the Corporation Tax year, which runs from 1 April to 31 March, as described in Chapter 13. Many companies nowadays arrange for their overseas subsidiaries to end their accounting year, say, three months before that of the holding company, in order to make the task of preparing group accounts easier.

Interests in another company

If a company, A, wishes to obtain an interest in the activities of another company, B, it may do so in three ways:

(*a*) by buying some or all of the assets of company B;
(*b*) by buying some shares in company B;
(*c*) by making a bid for company B.

Buying assets of company B
If company A only wishes to acquire some or all of the assets of company B, it may do so either by paying cash or by paying in shares of company A; the latter is an example of a vendor consideration issue of shares described in Chapter 4. Example 15.2 illustrates the process.

Example 15.2 Acquisition of assets by share issue

Let us suppose that, at 31 December 1977, the balance sheets of A and B were:

	A	B		A	B
	£	£		£	£
Ordinary share capital	60,000	20,000	Net assets	90,000	32,000
Reserves	30,000	12,000			
	90,000	32,000		90,000	32,000

Suppose A purchases the net assets of B by the issue to company B of 40,000 £1 ordinary shares (valued at par at the time), then company A's balance sheet would become:

	£		£
Ordinary share capital	100,000	Net assets	122,000
Reserves	30,000	(£90,000 + 32,000)	
		Goodwill	8,000
		(£40,000 − 32,000)	
	130,000		130,000

Goodwill represents the *excess* of the purchase consideration (*i.e.*, the value of the shares A issued to B) over the book value of the net assets purchased.

After A's purchase B's balance sheet would show:

	£		£
Ordinary share capital	20,000	Investment at cost	40,000
Reserves (£12,000 + 8,000 profit on realisation of net assets)	20,000		
	40,000		40,000

B would not automatically cease to exist; it would become an investment holding company.

Had A's shares been listed and had they been standing at say 200p at the time, A would only have needed to issue, say, 20,000 £1 ordinary shares, and A's balance sheet after the purchase would have been:

	£		£
Ordinary share capital	80,000	Net assets	122,000
Share premium a/c	20,000	Goodwill	8,000
Other reserves	30,000		
	130,000		130,000

Where goodwill does arise, many companies write it off against reserves (and it is standard practice for analysts to do so in their calculations even when the holding companies do not).

Buying some shares in company B

(*a*) If A acquires 5% or less of the equity of B, A's balance sheet would show the purchase as an *investment* (*see* Chapter 7).

(*b*) If A acquires more than 5% of the equity of B, the purchaser would still show the purchase as an *investment*, but would be obliged by Section 4 of the Companies Act 1967, as amended by the Companies Act 1976, to declare its interest (*see* p. 38).

(*c*) If A acquires 20% or more of the equity of B, and is allowed by B to participate in the major policy decisions of B, usually by holding a seat on B's board, then A should treat B as an *associated company* (*see* Chapter 16).

(*d*) If A acquires 30% or more of the voting rights of B, or if A in any period of twelve months adds more than 2% to an existing holding of between 30% and 50% in B, then Rule 34 of the Takeover Code obliges A to make a bid for the remainder of the equity of B at a price not less than the highest price A paid for any B shares in the previous twelve months.

Making a takeover bid for company B

Company A may offer the shareholders of B either cash or "paper" (*i.e.*, shares and/or loan stock and/or warrants of A). If A has already gone over the 30% limit or has added more than 2% in twelve months to a holding of 30–50%, the offer must be in cash or be accompanied by a cash alternative. If the bid results in A acquiring 90% or more of the shares of B that it did not already own, A may force the remaining B shareholders to accept the bid using the procedure laid down in Section 209 of the Companies Act 1948.

Capital reserve on consolidation

In Example 15.3, had the net assets acquired exceeded the purchase consideration (the market value of the shares issued), the difference would have been termed "capital reserve on consolidation" or "surplus arising on consolidation" and would have been shown separately among reserves. Alternatively, had any capital reserve on consolidation existed in respect of another of A's subsidiaries, the goodwill cost of control would normally have been set off against it.

Example 15.3 Acquisition of the entire share capital

Let us suppose that A made a successful bid of 2 shares in A for each share of B (with no cash alternative or with the cash alternative underwritten to ensure that A did not have to provide any cash). Thus A acquires the entire share capital of B by the issue of 40,000 £1 ordinary shares in A to the *shareholders* of B, and the balance sheet of A will become:

	£		£
Ordinary share capital	100,000	Net assets	90,000
Reserves	30,000	Shares in subsidiary at cost	40,000
	130,000		130,000

The balance sheet of A does not disclose the underlying net assets of B, simply A's investment in B but, to comply with the provisions of the Companies Act 1948 described earlier in this chapter, company A must also present consolidated accounts. The *consolidated balance sheet of the group* (A and its subsidiary B) simply substitutes the net assets of B for the asset "Investment in B":

	£		£
Ordinary share capital	100,000	Net assets	122,000
Reserves	30,000	Goodwill on consolidation	
		(£40,000 – 32,000)	8,000
	130,000		130,000

Goodwill on consolidation (or "cost of control") represents the excess of the purchase price over the net assets acquired. Clearly, had the market value of shares issued exactly equalled the net assets there would have been no goodwill, and in practice many companies write off any difference against reserves in the year of acquisition of subsidiaries.

Where a capital reserve on consolidation arises (*i.e.*, when a holding company has paid less than book value for an acquisition), one might well ask whether the assets of the new subsidiary have been overstated, *i.e.*, whether provisions need to be made against stocks or debtors, or further depreciation provided on fixed assets.

There are, however, circumstances where assets, or even cash, can be acquired at below book value; take, for instance, the case of a private company with an issued share capital of £100,000, still held by the handful of shareholders who originally subscribed at par; the company has sold off all its assets piecemeal, leaving £1.1 million in cash; the shareholders might well decide to sell out for £1 million payable in shares of a listed company in order to avoid any immediate Capital Gains Tax liability.

CONSOLIDATED ACCOUNTS

The consolidated balance sheet

In simple terms a consolidated balance sheet shows all the assets and all the liabilities of all group companies whether wholly owned or partially owned. Where a partially owned subsidiary exists, its shareholders' funds are provided partly by the holding company and partly by the minority interests.

To illustrate the basic principles of consolidated accounts let us take the case of a holding company, "H LTD", with a partially-owned subsidiary, "S LTD", and imagine that we wish to prepare the consolidated balance sheet for the H Group at 31 December 1977. H paid £340,000 cash for 200,000 of the 250,000 £1 ordinary shares of S Ltd on 1 January 1974, when the balance sheet of S was as shown overleaf.

There are six steps to consolidating the two companies' balance sheets at 31 December 1977, which are also shown overleaf.

1. *Ascertain the goodwill cost of control* by comparing the cost to H Ltd of its investment in S Ltd with H Ltd's share of the equity shareholders' funds of S Ltd at the date of acquisition. The goodwill cost of control will be:

	£000	£000
Purchase consideration		340
Holding company's share of ordinary shareholders' funds at date of acquisition:		
4/5ths of Ordinary share capital	200	
4/5ths of Reserves	68	268
Goodwill cost of control		72

Note that:

(*a*) Any *pre-acquisition profits* of S Ltd which have not already been distributed will form part of that company's reserves, and are thus represented by equity shareholders' funds taken into account in computing goodwill cost of control.

(*b*) Any distribution by S Ltd after it is acquired by H Ltd which is made out of pre-acquisition profits (*i.e.*, reserves existing at acquisition) must be credited not to the profit and loss account of H Ltd as income, but to the asset account "Investment in S Ltd" as a reduction of the purchase price of that investment. The goodwill cost of control does not change.

2. *Compute the holding company's share of the undistributed post-acquisition profits of the subsidiary.* This equals the holding company's proportion of the change in reserves since the date of acquisition:

$$\frac{200,000}{250,000} \times (£150,000 - 85,000)$$
$$= (£120,000 - £68,000)$$
$$= £52,000$$

This, added to the holding company's own reserves, represents the reserves of the group which will appear in the consolidated balance sheet:

£52,000 + £480,000 = £532,000

3. *Compute minority interests in the net assets of S Ltd:*

Minority interests =

Minority proportion × Net assets (capital + reserves) of S Ltd at balance sheet date

The minority interest in the equity shareholders' funds of S Ltd is:

Minority proportion × Equity shareholders' funds of S Ltd at balance sheet date (31 December 1977)

$$= \frac{50,000}{250,000} \times £400,000 = £80,000$$

"S LTD" *Balance sheet at 1 January 1974*

	£000		£000
Ordinary share capital	250	Fixed assets:	
Reserves	85	Freehold land and buildings	120
		Plant and machinery	146
Ordinary shareholders' funds	335		266
7% Debenture	100		
		Net current assets	169
	435		435

"H LTD" *and* "S LTD" *Balance sheets at 31 December 1977*

	H Ltd £000	*S Ltd* £000		*H Ltd* £000	*S Ltd* £000
Ordinary share capital	500	250	Fixed assets:		
Reserves	480	150	Freehold land and buildings	150	120
Ordinary shareholders' funds	980	400	Plant and machinery	250	180
				400	300
10% unsecured loan stock	120	–	Shares in S Ltd	340	–
7% Debenture	–	100	Net current assets	360	200
	1,100	500		1,100	500

"H GROUP" *Consolidated balance sheet at 31 December 1977*

	£000		£000
Ordinary share capital	500	Fixed assets:	
Reserves	532	Freehold land and buildings	270
		Plant and machinery	430
Ordinary shareholders' funds	1,032		700
Minority interests	80		
H Ltd's 10% ULS	120	Net current assets	560
S Ltd's 7% Debenture	100	Goodwill – cost of control	72
	1,332		1,332

4. *Draw up the consolidated balance sheet:*
   (*a*) insert as share capital the share capital of the holding company;
   (*b*) insert the figures already computed for (i) goodwill (cost of control) (*see* 1 above) and (ii) minority interests (*see* 3 above);
   (*c*) show as "reserves" the total of the reserves of the holding company and the post-acquisition reserves of the subsidiary applicable to the holding company (*see* 2 above).

5. *Cancel out any inter-company balances:* the aim of the consolidated balance sheet is to show a true and fair view of the state of affairs of the group as a whole. Inter-company balances (where an item represents an asset of one group company and a liability of another) must be cancelled out since they do not concern outsiders. Thus, if S Ltd owes H Ltd on current account £10,000, this £10,000 will appear as an asset in H Ltd's own balance sheet, and as a liability in that of S Ltd, but it will not appear at all in the consolidated balance sheet.

6. *Consolidate:* add together like items (*e.g.*, add freehold land and buildings of the holding company and freehold land and buildings of the subsidiary) and show the group totals in the consolidated balance sheet. Omit, in so doing, the share capital of the subsidiary, reserves, and the investment in the subsidiary, which have already been taken into account in steps 1 to 3.

It will be seen that only the share capital of the holding company appears in the consolidated balance sheet. The share capital of the subsidiary has disappeared, one-fifth of it becoming part of "minority interests" while the other four-fifths (£200,000), together with H's share of S's reserves on acquisition (£68,000) and the "goodwill – cost of control" (£72,000) balance out the removal of H's balance sheet item "shares in S Ltd" (£340,000).

The consolidated profit and loss account

As explained on p. 100 most holding companies avoid the need to publish their own profit and loss accounts by showing the amount of profit or loss they deal with in the group consolidated profit and loss accounts.

Consolidated profit and loss accounts follow the same pattern as the one we described for single companies at the beginning of Chapter 12, except that if the group contains partially owned subsidiaries, the minority interests in the profits of those subsidiaries have to be deducted at the after-tax level.

Continuing with our example of H Ltd owning four-fifths of the £250,000 ordinary share capital of S Ltd, let us suppose that at the beginning of 1978 S Ltd issued 30,000 £1 7% preference shares to a third party as part-payment for an acquisition, and that the pre-tax profits and tax charges of H Ltd and S Ltd for that year were:

	H Ltd	*S Ltd*	*Total*
	£	£	£
Profit before tax	90,000	64,000	154,000
Corporation Tax at 52%	46,800	33,280	80,080
Profit after tax	43,200	30,720	73,920

The combined pre-tax profit, tax and profit after tax will be shown in the group's consolidated profit and loss account.

Calculation of minority interests
The minority interests in the profits after tax of S Ltd will then be computed as follows:

	S Ltd	*Minority interests*
	£	£
Profit before tax	64,000	
less Corporation Tax	33,280	
Profit after tax	30,720	
less Preference dividends	2,100	2,100
Attributable to ordinary shareholders	28,620 × $\frac{1}{5}$ =	5,724
Minority interests total		7,824

It is this sum of £7,824 which will be deducted as "minority interests" from the profit after tax in the consolidated profit and loss account.

Appropriations of the subsidiary
Suppose, for instance, that S Ltd proposed a single ordinary dividend of 4p for 1978. Then the profit attributable to S Ltd's ordinary shareholders would be appropriated as follows:

	Total	*Minorities*	*H Ltd*
	£	£	£
Attributable	28,620	5,724	22,896
Proposed dividend of 4.0p per share	10,000	2,000	8,000
Retentions	18,620	3,724	14,896

H Ltd's share of the proposed dividend (£8,000) would also appear, as dividends receivable, in the holding company's accounts, and the two figures would cancel out on consolidation. The dividends payable to minority shareholders (£2,000) would be charged (behind the scenes) against the minority interests deducted on consolidation, and the minorities' share of the retentions (£7,824 – £2,100 preference dividends – £2,000 ordinary dividends = £3,724), added to the consolidated *balance sheet* item "minority interests".

The group profit and loss account
Suppose H Group declared dividends of £25,000 for the year. The group profit and loss account would then show:

	£
Profit before tax	154,000
less Tax	80,080
Profit after tax	73,920
less Minority interests	7,824
	66,096
less Dividends	25,000
Retentions	41,096

Retained profit

The group's retained profit of £41,096 would be carried forward partly in the holding company's accounts:

	£
H Ltd profit after tax	43,200
H Ltd's dividends from S Ltd	8,000
less Dividends paid by H Group	25,000
	26,200

The remainder, £14,896, would be carried forward in S Ltd's accounts, being H Ltd's share of S Ltd's retentions.

Some company accounts, such as those of HEPWORTH CERAMIC HOLDINGS (illustrated below), show where the retained profits of the group are being carried forward.

Alternatively, this information may be given in a note to the accounts. Note, *en passant*, that Hepworth Ceramic has written off goodwill as a prior year adjustment, *i.e.*, as the result of a change in accounting policy.

Unrealised profits on stocks

One group company frequently supplies another company within the group with goods in the ordinary course of trade; indeed, this sort of trading link may often be at the very heart of the existence of the group in the first place. But where one group company has made a profit on the supply of goods to another group company and those goods, or some of them, remain in stock at the end of the accounting year, a problem arises and, although nothing can normally be gleaned from the accounts, the procedure for consolidation is designed to prevent a group's profits being artificially inflated by sales within the group.

Subsidiary acquired during the accounting period

Where a subsidiary is acquired during the accounting period, any pre-acquisition profits of that subsidiary must be excluded from the group's results. The holding company's share of pre-acquisition profits is, of course, reflected in the net assets of the subsidiary at the date of acquisition, and is taken into account in computing the goodwill cost of control (or the capital reserve on consolidation).

There are two ways of treating this in the consolidated profit and loss account:

1. The pre-acquisition profits of the subsidiary (and its turnover and expenses for the period prior to acquisition) may be excluded completely from the consolidated profit and loss account, and only the post-acquisition profits, turnover and expenses of the subsidiary included; for example, WHITBREAD, in their 1976 accounts, simply stated in their note on accounting policies: "Basis of consolidation: the consolidated accounts incorporate the accounts of the company and each of its subsidiaries for the year ended 28 February 1976, and also the group's share of seven months' post-acquisition profits of Long John International Limited and its subsidiaries" although Long John (the whisky distiller) had cost Whitbread £18½ million in convertible stock and cash, and might have merited separate treatment.

2. The whole of the subsidiary's pre-tax profit for the year, including the pre-acquisition portion (and the whole year's turnover and expenses), may be included.

HEPWORTH CERAMIC HOLDINGS *Statement of retained profits*

	1975 £000	1974 £000
Retained profit of the year:		
Holding company	3,307	8
Subsidiaries	822	909
Associated companies	34	11
	4,163	928
Retained profits at beginning of year:		
As previously reported	17,518	16,590
Goodwill written off as a prior year adjustment	9,729	–
	7,789	16,590
Retained profits at end of year	11,952	17,518

In this case the holding company's share of the pre-acquisition profits of the subsidiary must subsequently be deducted (*e.g.*, S. PEARSON & SON LTD, shown below).

The second of these two methods is more helpful, since it shows a whole year's turnover and profits, which may then fairly be compared with the assets employed at the end of the accounting period. Furthermore, it provides some indication of the future level of profits of the group as a whole, but it is unfortunately less frequently used than method 1.

A further variation, used occasionally when a group makes a substantial acquisition, is to present the results of the new subsidiary in a separate profit and loss account within the group's accounts at the end of the year of acquisition, and this is how DIXONS PHOTOGRAPHIC treated WESTON PHARMACEUTICAL when they acquired it in 1976, shortly before Dixons' accounting year ended.

Further statutory requirements in consolidated accounts

The following requirements have to be satisfied only in relation to the *holding company*, not to the group:

(*a*) Remuneration of directors (CA 1948, S. 196). Only the remuneration of the directors of the holding company need be shown, but all their remuneration from the group should be included (*e.g.*, fees they may receive for being directors of subsidiaries).

(*b*) Particulars of loans to officers (CA 1948, S. 197). (Loans to directors are not normally allowed – CA 1948, S. 190.)

(*c*) Employees' emoluments in excess of £10,000 per annum (CA 1967, S. 8).

However, all these requirements have to be met by each subsidiary in its own accounts, which are not normally available but do have to be filed eventually at Companies House.

S. PEARSON & SON LTD *Treatment of pre-acquisition profits*

	1975		1974
	£	£	£
Profit of the group before taxation		25,018,673	20,426,693
Deduct proportions attributable to:			
Minority interests	6,242,723		6,126,089
Periods prior to acquisition	1,949		13,074
		6,244,672	6,139,163
Profit before taxation attributable to S. Pearson & Son Ltd		18,774,001	14,287,530

THE INTERPRETATION OF CONSOLIDATED ACCOUNTS

Profitability of subsidiaries

There are companies (ANGLO-AMERICAN CORPORATION OF SOUTH AFRICA LTD is one of them) which offer to provide shareholders of the holding company with the full report and accounts of all subsidiaries. This is very useful, especially to the analyst, but it is also very rare. Most listed companies are not particularly forthcoming about the profitability of the various component parts of their organisation, and many do not file the reports and accounts of their subsidiaries at Companies House at the same time as they publish their consolidated accounts.

Thus, while in theory it is possible to deconsolidate strategic parts of the group in order to find out just where the profits are being made, this may not be easy, nor may it be possible at the time the report and accounts of the holding company become available; but the effort involved can be very rewarding, as Example 15.4 shows.

Example 15.4 Analysing subsidiaries' performance: KLEINWORT BENSON

The 1974 accounts of the merchant bank KLEINWORT BENSON showed:

	1973 £000	1974 £000
Banking group profits after tax and after transfer to reserves	3,964	3,581

but an alert analyst, aware that these figures included bullion dealing profits of wholly owned subsidiary SHARPS PIXLEY, obtained the following figures from Companies House:

	1973 £000	1974 £000
Sharps Pixley profits after tax	723	2,248

indicating that, but for the very substantial contribution of bullion dealing, banking group profits would have taken a nasty tumble in 1974. It is not, however, possible to quantify the level to which they would have fallen simply by netting out the bullion dealing profits, because the undisclosed transfer to reserves would probably have been reduced in those circumstances.

Leaving aside the possibilities of devilling at Companies House, the analyst should look carefully at the group's published accounts to see if there are any clues as to the spread of profitability (in addition to those already gleaned from the geographical analysis required by the Listing Agreement, which we discussed in Chapter 12). Worthy of special note are the figures for pre-acquisition profits and minority interests.

Pre-acquisition profits
When a subsidiary is acquired on a known date, and its profits for the whole year are included in the holding company's consolidated profit and loss account and the pre-acquisition profits are subsequently deducted, the apportionment of the pre-acquisition share of the profits is almost always done on a time apportionment basis. It should therefore be possible to compute the profitability of that subsidiary for the year, and to compare it with any forecast made at the time of the acquisition, and with profits it earned in earlier years.

Minority interests
Where most of a group is wholly owned, a clue to the profitability of the partially owned part of the group will be given by minority interests. The figure is of particular significance where the minority interest in the profits varies sharply, as in Example 15.5.

Example 15.5 Subsidiary performance indicated by minority interests: OWEN OWEN

The Liverpool-based department store company OWEN OWEN's 1976 profit and loss account reported:

	1976 £000	1975 £000
Profit after taxation	1,300	1,063
Profit attributable to minority interests	207	112

while information on subsidiaries showed all except one to be wholly owned, and the partially-owned one, G. W. ROBINSON, to be incorporated in Canada. The chairman's report confirmed that the Canadian subsidiary had done very well in 1976, helped by the weakness of sterling.

A swing in minorities from profit to loss is especially interesting, for although the chairman's or directors' report will doubtless draw attention to a lossmaker that has been turned round, it may be more reticent about a partially owned subsidiary running into loss.

Transfer prices
A further hazard we should mention in assessing the profitability of individual subsidiaries is that of "transfer pricing". When two subsidiaries of a holding company trade substantially with each other or with the holding company (*e.g.*, a manufacturing subsidiary wholesaling through a trading subsidiary) the transfer prices may not always be arm's length prices, and thus the profitability of the business transacted may be slanted towards one subsidiary at the expense of the other. This may be done deliberately to minimise taxation generally, to maximise profits in currencies the group most needs (*e.g.*, for the servicing and repayment of foreign loans and to increase overseas investment without paying the dollar premium), and possibly to hide highly lucrative activities from the jealous eyes of potential competitors.

Subsidiary's holding of holding company's shares

With certain minor exceptions a subsidiary cannot be a member of its holding company (*i.e.*, cannot hold shares in its holding company, either directly or through a nominee), and any allotment or transfer of shares in a company to its subsidiary is void (CA 1948, S. 27(1)).

The Act does not indicate what should be done when a company, B, holding shares in another company, A, becomes a subsidiary of A, but it is generally accepted that B has an obligation to dispose of them to a new holder, or to procure the holding company to cancel them as part of a reduction of capital.

Information to be given on subsidiaries

Sections 3 and 4 of the Companies Act 1967 require that where a company has a subsidiary, its accounts must show:

(*a*) the subsidiary's name;
(*b*) if incorporated in Great Britain, the subsidiary's country of registration (England or Scotland) if different from that of the holding company; if incorporated outside Great Britain, the subsidiary's country of incorporation;
(*c*) the proportion of the nominal value of each class of the subsidiary's share capital held by the holding company.

But information about a subsidiary either incorporated, or carrying on business, outside the United Kingdom, which would be harmful to the business of the company or any of its subsidiaries if made public, need not be disclosed if the Department of Trade agrees.

Where the required information would be of excessive length, details need be given only of subsidiaries principally affecting the profits or losses and the assets of the group, but in this case full particulars must be annexed to the annual return.

Holdings in subsidiaries held directly by the holding company must be distinguished from those held by another subsidiary.

Chapter 16

ASSOCIATED COMPANIES

(Reference: SSAP 1, *Accounting for the Results of Associated Companies.*)

Accounting definition

Although loosely used in other contexts, the term "associated company" is defined for accountancy purposes in SSAP 1:

"A company (not being a subsidiary of the investing group or company) is an associated company of the investing group or company if:

(*a*) the investing group or company's interest in the associated company is effectively that of a partner in a joint venture or consortium; *or*

(*b*) the investing group or company's interest in the associated company is for the long term and is substantial (*i.e.*, not less than 20% of the equity voting rights), and, having regard to the disposition of the other shareholdings, the investing company or group is in a position to exercise a significant influence over the associated company."

In each case it is essential that the investing group or company participates in commercial and financial policy decisions of the associated company, including the distribution of profits, and this is usually achieved by representation on the board of the associated company.

It is thus possible for a holding of less than 20% to rank as an associated company (if the investing group's interest is effectively that of a partner if, say, there are six equal partners in the consortium); or for an interest of, say, 40% not to be an associated company (if the investing group plays no significant part in the commercial and financial decision making and is not represented on the board).

Substantial holdings

Both the Companies Act 1967 and the Stock Exchange Listing Agreement require companies to disclose certain information on substantial investments in other companies but these other companies need not necessarily be "associated companies" for accounting purposes. These disclosure requirements for "substantial holdings" are given in Chapter 7 (*see* p. 38).

Where a company has a holding of 20% or more in another company, but does not treat it as an associated company, a good set of accounts will explain why, *e.g.*, JONES, STROUD.

JONES, STROUD *1976 accounts: Note on investments*

Investments include a 36.2% holding in Fothergill & Harvey Limited and a 39% holding in J. & J. Cash Limited. Only dividends received of £147,975 have been included in the Consolidated Group Profit as it is considered that the Group did not exercise a significant influence over either company's affairs during the year.

Summary of accounting treatment of associated companies

Consolidated profit and loss account

Turnover: nothing included from associates.

Pre-tax profit: share of associates, shown separately.

Tax: share of associates, shown separately.

Extraordinary items: share of associates, included in the group figure unless material.
Net Profit Retained: share of associates, shown separately.

Consolidated balance sheet
Unless shown at valuation, the investing group's interest should be shown at *cost,* less amounts written off, plus share of the associated companies' subsequent *retained profits and reserves.* Some companies show just a single figure, others break it down into components, including loans made by the group to associated companies – ARTHUR GUINNESS, for example, illustrated below.

Value of investments in associated companies

It is easy to see why SSAP 1 calls for more information about associated companies. Before the SSAP was introduced it was not uncommon to find a major trade investment carried at its cost of many years earlier, although it was yielding a substantial income and worth vastly more than its balance sheet value.

For example, in the extracts from STOCKLAKE HOLDINGS' accounts (p. 113), the *company's* balance sheet shows an investment in an associated company [D] at a mere £70,000, although the share of profit of the associated company [A] was £187,736, suggesting that the investment was worth much more than its cost. Only in the consolidated balance sheet is the investment shown at cost *plus* the investing company's share of post-acquisition reserves [E], a figure of £459,488.

(If any associated companies are held through subsidiaries, the difference between the item "associated companies" in the holding company's balance sheet and in the consolidated balance sheet will represent the holding company's share of post-acquisition reserves, plus the book value, normally cost, of investments in associated companies held through subsidiaries.)

Presentation of information on associated companies

Stocklake Holdings' accounts show a fairly typical treatment of associated companies. The share of profits appears on the face of the consolidated profit and loss account as a separate item [A], but the share of the tax charge appears only in a note [C]. Had there been any extraordinary items relating to associated companies it is probable that these too, if material, would have appeared in the notes.

It is worth noting that, whereas in consolidated accounts the tax charge which appears, [B], includes the entire tax charge of the holding company and all its subsidiaries, the amount included for associated companies is only the holding company's share of tax of associated companies. Similarly, the profit before tax of the group is the entire profit of the holding company and its subsidiaries, but *only the holding company's share* of profit of associated companies is shown.

The consolidated profit and loss account of Stocklake Holdings, together with Note 10, shows that the investing group's share of the profit after tax of the associated company was £118,141 (£187,736 less £69,595 tax), compared with £99,943 (£162,298 less £62,355 tax), in 1972. But it is clear that losses were made by the associated company in earlier years, for Note 4 shows the investing company's share of a debit balance on profit and loss account of £26,096 [G] at the end of 1972. The suggestion is that the associated company is just recovering from an unhappy period; as profits after tax in 1972 were £99,943, the deficit brought forward from 1971 must have been £126,039, confirming the recovery situation in the associated company.

Further study of Note 4 in the extracts shows that there has been a sharp rise in the capital reserve attributable to the group's shareholding [F], and this is explained in Note 6 as being due to a revaluation of fixed assets [H].

ARTHUR GUINNESS *Note to the consolidated accounts*

Associated companies	1976 £000	1975 £000
Shares at cost:		
Unquoted – Directors' valuation £15.1 million (£11.9 million)	3,382	3,248
Quoted – On UK Stock Exchange: Market value £0.1 million (£0.1 million)	384	384
– Overseas: Market value £7.1 million (£6.6 million)	1,350	557
Share of post-acquisition reserves	13,543	10,366
Loans	6,199	6,794
	24,858	21,349

Associated company dividends

Where a company follows SSAP 1, the dividends paid by, and received from, its associated companies are not necessarily shown in the accounts. They can be calculated by preparing a summary profit and loss statement in respect of the associate(s), when the difference between the balance one would expect to have been carried forward, and that actually carried forward, represents the dividends paid by the associate(s) to the investing group, as in Example 16.1 for Stocklake Holdings' associate in 1973.

Example 16.1 Calculation of associate's dividend: STOCKLAKE HOLDINGS

		£
Share of associate's profit	[A]	187,736
less Share of associate's tax	[C]	69,595
		118,141
Balance brought forward	[G]	(26,096)
		92,045
Balance carried forward	[G]	64,045
Dividends paid by the associated company to the investing group		28,000

STOCKLAKE HOLDINGS LTD *Extracts from 1973 accounts*

Consolidated profit and loss account	[Text ref.]	1973	1972
		£	£
Group sales for year		25,263,955	26,186,966
Group profit before taxation		1,403,742	1,253,257
Share of profit of associated company	[A]	187,736	162,298
		1,591,478	1,415,555
Taxation (Note 10)	[B]	699,127	706,874
Group profit after taxation		892,351	708,581
Note to the consolidated profit and loss account			
Note 10: taxation charged in the accounts			
Share of taxation of associated company	[C]	69,595	62,355
Company's balance sheet			
Investments . . .			
Associated company (Note 4) at cost	[D]	70,000	99,040
Group consolidated balance sheet			
Investments . . .			
Associated company (Note 4)	[E]	459,488	202,791

Notes to the balance sheets

Note 4: Associated company

The company has a 40% (1972 – 40%) interest in the issued share capital of £1,000 of Northern Shipbuilding & Industrial Holdings Ltd, incorporated in England. A holding of £29,040 in 8% unsecured loan stock was repaid during the year.

The company's interest is:		1973	1972
		£	£
Shares at cost		70,000	70,000
Reserves attributable to company's holding			
Capital reserve (Note 6)	[F]	325,443	129,847
Profit and loss account (1972 deficit) after net dividend of £28,000	[G]	64,045	(26,096)
		459,488	173,751
8% Unsecured loan stock		–	29,040
		459,488	202,791

Note 6: Capital reserve

		£
Revaluation of associated company's fixed assets after provision for deferred Capital Gains Tax of £84,000	[H]	195,596

Chapter 17

FOREIGN EXCHANGE DIFFERENCES

(Reference: ED 21, *Accounting for Foreign Currency Transactions.*)

The problem of variable exchange rates

Until relatively recently, companies with overseas subsidiaries or associates had little difficulty in producing group accounts: most exchange rates were fixed and, although minor differences arose due to the cost of *conversion* (the process of exchanging money in one currency into money in another currency), the adjustments were trifling and *translation* (the process of expressing accounts kept in one currency in terms of another currency) for the purpose of consolidation was simple, except where major devaluations occurred.

With the advent of floating exchange rates, the treatment of overseas accounts has become a major problem, in particular over the rate of exchange to be used for the translation of balance sheet items, where the choice lies between:

(*a*) the *closing rate* (the rate of exchange at the balance sheet date) *and*

(*b*) the *historical rate* (the rate of exchange prevailing at the time of each transaction – *e.g.*, at the date of purchase of a fixed asset),

while hybrid methods of translation use a combination of the two rates.

The development of a UK accounting standard

A UK accounting standard is being developed on the subject of foreign currency transactions and translations, and practice is already being influenced by the exposure draft, ED 21. Meanwhile, SSAP 6, *Extraordinary Items and Prior Year Adjustments,* recommends that, pending the issue of a standard, the accounting policies adopted by companies on currencies should be disclosed and explained in accordance with SSAP 2, *Disclosure of Accounting Policies.*

The proposals of ED 21

ED 21 proposes to allow companies to use either of two methods for dealing with the accounts of foreign operations, the closing rate method or the temporal method, which operate as follows.

In the profit and loss account

1. *Closing rate method.* The profit for the year should be translated either at the closing or at the average rate. The choice between the two rates can make a considerable difference to the reported profit; for example, if a German subsidiary made a profit of DM10 million during a year in which the rate of exchange fell from DM5.4 = £1 at the beginning of the year to DM4 = £1 at the end, averaging DM5 = £1 because most of the fall occurred in the last three months, on an average basis the group accounts would include German profits of £2 million; on a closing rate basis they would include £2.5 million.

2. *Temporal method.* Revenues and expenses are translated at the actual rate of exchange ruling at the time of each transaction (*i.e.*, the historical rate). With this method the profit shown in the foreign subsidiary's accounts is not itself translated: the sterling profit included in the group accounts is the accumulation of all credit and debit transactions translated into sterling at the time each one occurs, and in the case of

depreciation depends on the rate of exchange when each asset was acquired.

In the consolidated balance sheet

1. *Closing rate method.* All items are translated at year end exchange rates. If the rate of exchange has changed since the previous balance sheet date (or since the date on which any subsequent transaction was recorded) there will be an exchange difference.

   Exchange differences should normally be dealt with as follows:
   (*a*) on fixed assets – deal with through reserves (but any uncovered deficits should be dealt with in the profit and loss account, as should the recovery of previously uncovered deficits);
   (*b*) on foreign currency net borrowings – offset deficits against gains on translating fixed assets, with any residue being dealt with in the profit and loss account;
   (*c*) all other translation differences should be reported in the profit and loss account.

   Under ED 21 translation differences from these three sources should be dealt with in the profit and loss account, being shown separately as "Exchange gain (loss)" after profit after tax: *i.e.*, they do not affect the earnings per share.

2. *Temporal method.* Fixed assets are translated at the historical rate (the rate prevailing at the original transaction or at subsequent revaluation), but items carried at current values, including long-term borrowings, are translated at the closing rate. All translation differences should be reported as part of the profit for the year, but they do not have to be shown separately and they *do* affect earnings per share.

Comment on the two proposed methods

The arguments in favour of the temporal method are firstly that, in translating items shown at historical cost, it is consistent to use historical rates of exchange, and secondly that it is in line with the translation method laid down in the United States by FAS 8 (the US Financial Accounting Standards Board Statement No. 8).

The main difficulty that arises with the temporal method is that, unlike the closing rate method, it creates no surpluses on the translation of overseas fixed assets to balance deficits on the translation of foreign currency borrowings (even though the borrowings may have been to finance the overseas fixed assets). Also, the closing rate method is much simpler to operate.

Current UK practice

In the United Kingdom 90% of major companies use the closing rate method, which is out of step with the practice in much of the rest of the world, and in particular with the United States, where only the temporal method is permitted. A cynic might suggest that this may have something to do with the fact that in recent years sterling has tended to fall in relation to most other major currencies and that the employment by UK companies of the closing rate method has ensured that unrealised gains have been recorded on currency translation. Against this it has frequently been necessary to set heavy provisions in respect of overseas borrowings repayable at rates vastly different from those at which they were incurred. It would hardly be fair to translate overseas debt at the closing rate and not do the same to overseas assets purchased with the amounts borrowed.

Realised differences

Most companies deal with realised differences above the line, but some treat major losses as extraordinary items. The WEIR GROUP, for instance, borrowed DM55 million against two promissory notes in April 1970 and used the proceeds (£6.3 million) mainly for investment in the United Kingdom. Then, as the pound fell year by year, the company made a series of provisions to cover the increase in the sterling equivalent of the debt, treating the provisions as extraordinary items (*i.e.*, below the line) and, when in 1975 the loan was repaid early, WEIR also treated the terminal loss as an extraordinary item. As the figures from the accounts (overleaf) show, the sums involved were significant in relation to pre-tax profits.

The overall loss of around £3.6 million on a £6.3 million loan was even more significant because it was not allowable for Corporation Tax purposes.

Weir presumably borrowed Deutsche Marks at 7¼% because interest rates were lower in Europe, but although the company may have been extraordinarily unlucky with the weakness of sterling, the borrowings were made in the normal course of the company's business, and so the treatment of the losses as extraordinary items is open to question. However, Weir did realise how vulnerable the unmatched loan made them, and negotiated early repayment in 1975 instead of 1979: as the sterling/DM rate subsequently fell to less than half that of 1970,

WEIR GROUP *Treatment of losses on foreign currency borrowings*

Year end Dec	*7¼% DM Loan Value in balance sheet*	*Extraordinary item on loans P & L account*	*Reported pre-tax profit*
	£	£	£
1970	6,301,919	–	1,652,161
1971	6,588,799	(273,364)	2,320,727
1972	7,323,569	(751,278)	2,549,492
1973	8,814,103	(1,530,671)	2,957,302
1974	9,717,314	(903,211)	3,023,816
1975	–	(167,786)	6,205,402

early repayment saved the company from a further loss of at least £3 million.

Unrealised differences
The majority of UK companies translate their fixed assets at the closing rate and deal with the unrealised surpluses and unrealised deficits direct to reserves, some showing what they are doing in a statement immediately following the profit and loss account, with the note on fixed assets showing how some of the difference occurs.

A typical example of companies using the closing rate method is BRITISH-AMERICAN TOBACCO (BAT), whose accounting policy reads:

"Differences on Exchange. Exchange differences arising on the retranslation to sterling (using rates of exchange ruling at the end of the year) of net assets at the beginning of the year are taken direct to reserves and shown in the Statement of Total Gains. Other exchange differences are reflected in profits for the year."

BAT's profit and loss account did not disclose the extent of "other exchange differences", but the "Statement of Total Gains" appeared at the foot of the profit and loss account and is shown here.

BRITISH-AMERICAN TOBACCO *Statement of total gains*

	1977	1976
	£m	£m
Net profit	210	170
Increase (decrease) in sterling value of opening overseas net assets due to exchange movements	(49)	147

The same information was shown in the "Statement of Funds Provided and Applied" and, in addition, the note on fixed assets showed a net decrease on fixed assets of £26 million due to differences on exchange (as in the second extract, opposite). No other information is given on exchange differences, so it is impossible to say where the remaining decrease of £23 million occurred.

TRAFALGAR HOUSE, on the other hand, gives a breakdown in a note, also shown here.

TRAFALGAR HOUSE *Note on foreign exchange*

Foreign currencies
All assets and liabilities expressed in foreign currencies have been converted at the rates of exchange ruling at 30 September 1977. The net surplus of £6,280,000 (1976 – deficiency of £15,988,000) arising from such conversion has been credited to reserves.

	1977	1976
	£000	£000
This surplus arises in relation to:		
Long term borrowings	7,081	(17,299)
Other net liabilities	783	(3,477)
Fixed assets	(1,584)	4,788
	6,280	(15,988)

Quarterly and half-yearly figures
As mentioned earlier, most companies use year-end rates in translating profit and loss account items, but doing so creates a problem in quarterly and half-yearly figures, since the closing rate cannot be known until the year is over, and the quarterly and half-yearly profits have to be retranslated later. UNILEVER's sales for the first quarter of 1975 were originally reported to be £1,478 million on the basis of the first quarter's closing rate. Translated at the closing rate for the year they became £1,589 million, 7.5% more.

Taxation
The position with regard to overseas activities is

BRITISH-AMERICAN TOBACCO *Note on fixed assets*

	Land and buildings £m	*Plant, machinery and equipment* £m	*Total* £m
Cost . . .			
Differences on exchange	(16)	(17)	(33)
Depreciation . . .			
Differences on exchange	(4)	(3)	(7)

complicated by the problems of taxation. Unless a profit or loss item falls within the scope of a tax schedule dealing with income subject to Corporation Tax, or arises from the disposal of an asset in such a way as to be within the computation of a capital gain, then the profit is not taxable, and no relief is available in respect of any loss.

In particular, losses on repayment of foreign borrowings are not allowable for tax purposes, although the matter is under review. Some companies, including ICI, have overcome this difficulty by channelling foreign currency borrowings through a separate finance company subsidiary; there is no distinction between capital and revenue losses in a banking-type operation so foreign exchange losses show up as revenue losses and qualify for full tax relief.

What the analyst should study

Because of the variety of ways in which UK companies may treat foreign exchange differences, the accounts of companies with substantial foreign interests or overseas borrowings need careful study.

A suggested sequence to follow is to start with the statement of accounting policies, to see what method the company uses to deal with foreign exchange differences, and then check:

1. The profit and loss account and reserves, to see what differences have been taken below the line (either separately or as extraordinary items) and what have been taken direct to reserves. In addition the amount due to exchange differences taken above the line may sometimes be disclosed.
2. Loans – to establish the extent of overseas borrowings, their change in value in sterling terms, and the degree to which they match the countries in which overseas operations are conducted. Where operations are in politically risky areas, local borrowings may help avoid the company being left with debts that still have to be honoured elsewhere in the event of the assets they financed being confiscated.
3. Fixed assets, to see what exchange differences have been credited or debited.
4. Current assets, to look for large amounts of cash. These may indicate:
   (*a*) profits from overseas operations which the company cannot transfer out of the country of origin because of local exchange control regulations, *or*
   (*b*) profits earned in low-tax areas and held there to avoid the UK tax that would be payable on remission, *and/or*
   (*c*) overseas profits being held overseas for further investment outside the United Kingdom.

Finally, one should keep an eye open for mention of foreign currency in the chairman's statement, the directors' report and elsewhere.

Unmatched overseas borrowings

By far the most dramatic impact that currency fluctuations have had on the profitability of UK companies in recent years has been the effect of unmatched borrowings (borrowings in one country's currency to invest in another country). Companies have sometimes had little choice in the matter – for example with capital investment in France, where the French have insisted that foreign capital should finance foreign investment in their country – but in most cases unmatched borrowings have been entered into voluntarily by companies that have sought the lower interest rates prevailing in stronger currency countries. As the lower interest rates (broadly reflecting the lower expectations of inflation) benefit the borrower's profitability in the short run then it seems only reasonable, when the difference catches up in the form of a provision for or loss on repayment, that it too should be reflected in the profit and loss account, but this is seldom the case.

WEIR GROUP, which we described earlier in this chapter, provides a good example of the costliness of borrowing in a strong currency to finance operations in a weak-currency country, but the effect can eliminate profits altogether and even eat into shareholders' funds. For example, the 1975/76 accounts of J. LYONS showed after-tax profits of £2.6 million compared with £7.9 million debited direct to group reserves on account of foreign exchange fluctuations, which a note to the accounts explained in helpful detail.

J. LYONS *Note to 1975/76 accounts*

	The Group	
Foreign exchange fluctuations	£000	£000
Provision for unrealised exchange differences on borrowings at 26 March 1976 –		
Debentures and loans of United Kingdom companies	15,994	
Less provisions no longer required in respect of loans repaid	604	
	15,390	
Loans repayable within one year	1,778	
		17,168
Increase in sterling equivalent value of overseas subsidiary companies' borrowings due to decline in value of sterling		6,187
		23,355
Unrealised exchange differences arising on consolidation of balance of overseas companies' net assets		15,440
		7,915

Chapter 18

SOURCE AND APPLICATION OF FUNDS STATEMENTS

(Reference: SSAP 10, *Statements of Source and Application of Funds.*)

Purpose

Traditionally, published accounts have comprised:

(*a*) a balance sheet providing a statement of the financial position at the end of a company's accounting year, together with "corresponding figures" showing the position at the end of the previous year (which is, of course, the same as the position at the beginning of the year being reported upon);

(*b*) a profit and loss account showing, in particular, the amount of profit retained in the business from that year.

It is today widely accepted that, apart from share capital issued or redeemed and any revaluation of fixed assets, the profit and loss account should explain all changes in shareholders' funds between one balance sheet date and the next (*i.e.*, retentions, including extraordinary items). It thus provides a link between successive balance sheets.

The profit and loss account does not, however, bridge the gap between each item in successive balance sheets, which can only be done by a note on the individual item (*e.g.*, fixed assets) or by a source and application of funds statement, sometimes called a funds flow statement or more simply a funds statement. In the United States such a statement is called a statement of changes in financial position, which is precisely what it is: a statement explaining the balance sheet changes which occurred during the period.

Current practice

Source and application statements have for some years been prepared externally by investors and analysts seeking a more detailed understanding of company reports and accounts. During the 1960s there was a strong trend in the United States and Canada towards the inclusion of funds statements as part of the annual accounts, and this is today general practice there.

In the United Kingdom the practice of including funds statements in reports and accounts has grown steadily during the past decade, and is now mandatory for most companies under SSAP 10.

At this stage we should perhaps point out that where a company itself prepares a funds statement it *may* make use of facts and figures not otherwise available to the external analyst. Indeed, it is often this additional information which makes the funds statement so valuable to an analyst. For example, in MARLEY's 1976 accounts the note on fixed assets showed "Additions" in the normal form, but the funds statement distinguished between the cost of replacing existing assets and the purchase of further assets (*see* illustration).

MARLEY *Funds statement*

	1976	1975
Application	£m	£m
Expenditure on fixed assets:		
(i) replacements necessary to maintain the business	3.1	1.1
(ii) additional assets to expand the business	8.0	7.1
	11.1	8.2

In this chapter we will look at two separate aspects of funds statements:

(*a*) the requirements of SSAP 10;
(*b*) the interpretation of source and application statements, including how to estimate the likely requirements for funds in the future.

The requirements of SSAP 10

Companies with a turnover of £25,000 or more per annum, producing audited financial accounts for periods beginning on or after 1 January 1976, must include a statement of source and application of funds both for the period under review and for the corresponding previous period.

Normal layout
No standard form of statement is prescribed, but the appendix to SSAP 10 gives examples in the following format:

Sources Funds generated from operations; Funds from other sources
Applications Dividends, tax, fixed assets; Increase/decrease in working capital.

This format is broadly followed by most companies, though with many variations, particularly over where to start. "Retained earnings" used to be the traditional starting point before SSAP 10, but as funds statements now have to include dividends paid, the latest point at which a statement can start is "Profits after tax" (as adopted in the example from ICI's well presented accounts, opposite). The examples given in the appendix to SSAP 10 suggest including both dividends and tax by starting with "Pre-tax profits", while a few companies, CARRINGTON VIYELLA for example, start right back at "Trading profit" and thus include interest payments too, so this is the first point to check when studying a funds statement: where does it start?

Treatment of minorities
Where the accounts are those of a group, SSAP 10 requires the funds statement to be "so framed as to reflect the operations of the group". The examples in SSAP 10 achieve this by beginning with the item:

Profit before tax and extraordinary items, *less* minority interests	£xxx

and then adding back

Minority interests in the retained profits of the year	£xxx

ICI, on the other hand, do not deduct minority interests in the funds statement in their 1976 accounts (*see* extract), but show:

Dividends:	
Subsidiaries to minority shareholders	£14m

but the net effect is just the same: the retentions on the part of minorities are left in as a source of funds. (Note that ICI's last source of funds in 1976, "Increased investment of minorities in subsidiaries £10 million", is *not* minorities' share of retentions of partially-owned subsidiaries, but their contribution to a rights issue made by a partially owned subsidiary during 1976.)

Associated companies
Associated companies are an entirely different matter. The holding company does not control the funds of associated companies, so they are not treated as part of the holding company's funds. However, the profit and loss account of the holding company does include its share of the profit of associated companies as part of the profit before tax; some of this may have been remitted by way of dividends paid to the holding company (and thus is a source), and some may have been retained by the associates. This latter part has to be deducted as an adjustment not involving the movement of funds:

Profit retained in associated companies	£xxx

"Netting off"
SSAP 10 recommends (though does not specifically require) that there should be a minimum of "netting off", since netting off tends to mask the significance of individually important figures.

There is, for instance, a vast difference between A and B in the following:

	Company A	*Company B*
Purchases of long-term investments	£56,000	£488,000
less Sales of long-term investments	£4,200	£436,200
	£51,800	£51,800

if the portfolio of long-term investments at the beginning of the period was £468,100. For A the movement during the period represents a minor increase in the portfolio, whereas B suggests almost a 100% change. But both would appear on a "netting off" basis as an application of £51,800.

Book cost
The accounting standard does not require the proceeds of sale of an asset to be shown. Many

ICI *Statement of Source and Application of Funds, 1976*

	Group	
	1975	*1976*
	£ million	*£ million*
Source of funds		
Profit after taxation and grants	196	326
Depreciation provision	182	205
Temporary use of amounts set aside for taxation	7	126
Miscellaneous items	20	18
Total generated from operations	405	675
Funds from other sources	114	354
Issues of ICI Ordinary Stock	15	206
Issues of Loan Stocks (less repayments)		
United Kingdom	3	(2)
Overseas	96	114
Deferred liabilities – advance payments for oil sales	–	20
Increased investment of minorities in subsidiaries	–	10
Total funds obtained	519	1,029
Application of funds		
Dividends	70	97
Parent company	59	83
Subsidiaries to minority shareholders	11	14
Investment	450	659
Purchase of new fixed assets	332	438
New investment in subsidiaries and trade investments	47	66
Additional working capital		
Stocks	67	159
Debtors	58	206
Creditors	(54)	(210)
Total funds applied	520	756
Increase/decrease in net liquid resources	(1)	273

companies show the book amount of the asset sold, and the profit/loss on sale, in two separate places, so the true cash flow of the transaction is not visible.

For example, if a surplus piece of freehold land stands in the books at £54,000, but is sold for £230,000, the transaction in reality is a source of funds of £230,000. But some companies would bury £176,000 (the profit on sale) among the extraordinary items (or worse still as part of the trading income for the year), and show only "Fixed asset disposals, at book value, £54,000" in their funds statement, or, worse still, describe it as "Sale of freehold land, £54,000", with no clue as to it being only the book value.

Purchase or disposal of a subsidiary

Under SSAP 10, a source and application statement may reflect the purchase or disposal of a subsidiary either as a single item, or reflect the effect in each item in the statement. A helpful method adopted by some companies is to provide a breakdown of the figure for Acquisitions at the bottom of the source and application of funds statement, for example,

ENGLISH CHINA CLAYS' 1977 accounts, illustrated here.

ENGLISH CHINA CLAYS *Source and applications statement, 1977*

Analysis of acquisitions

	£000		£000
Net assets acquired		**Discharged by**	
Fixed assets	5,064	Shares issued	4,364
Stocks	537	Cash paid	1,317
Debtors	2,568		
Creditors	(3,138)		
	5,031		
Goodwill	650		
	5,681		5,681

The interpretation of source and application statements

A funds statement may be useful to a chairman at an annual general meeting, or to an analyst when confronted by an investor asking embarrassing questions such as:

Where did all the profits go?
If those are the profits, why wasn't it possible to pay a larger dividend?
How come, when there has been a loss, that a dividend can still be paid?
What happened to the proceeds of the recent rights issue?
What happened to the proceeds of disposal of a major fixed asset (*e.g.*, freehold property)?
In the case of a group growing rapidly by takeovers for paper (shares or loan stock), how did the company pay for these new subsidiaries?

However, a funds statement, or a series of funds statements, may also be of use to an analyst trying to trace movements over several years, to identify the trends in liquidity and to estimate the likely need for funds in the future.

Interpreting an imaginary funds statement

Example 18.1 shows the funds statement from an imaginary set of accounts for 1978, together with a projected statement for the year ending 31 December 1979. Each line is numbered for ease of reference (S for source, A for application, while the line numbers in the table on "Other information" at the bottom refer to other pro formas in Chapter 24).

Let us look at this information in conjunction with comments gleaned from the chairman's report.

Changes in net liquid funds (Line A 12)
The improvement in 1977 was due mainly to the sale of a subsidiary (Line S 12) and to the low tax paid (Line A 1).

In 1978 the fall in net liquid assets was due mainly to the purchase of a subsidiary for £4 million in February 1978 (Line A 5) being paid for in cash (no new shares were issued, Line S 15), only part of which was financed by an increase in loans of £3 million (Line S 17), the remainder being funded by deferred tax and an increase in overdraft.

Chairman's comments as an aid to forecasting liquidity
IEC's turnover went up by more than £10 million in 1978, but pre-tax profits only increased by £377,000. The chairman commented in his report that turnover in the first three months of the current year was 27% up on the corresponding period in 1978 but that, although all divisions are currently trading profitably, increased costs and the effect of price controls are continuing to put pressure on margins. Despite currently adverse trading conditions, the board of IEC has every confidence in the future prosperity of the company, and is continuing the capital investment programme initiated in 1977 so as to be ready to take maximum advantage of the economic upturn when it comes. In addition, the chairman announced that, since the year end, a further acquisition had been made, the consideration being £500,000 in cash.

Using last year's figures, current trading conditions and anything we can glean from the chairman's comments on this year's prospects, let us now try to project 1979's sources and applications for the Imaginary Engineering Company. Of course, any attempt to project the future financial position of a company without the detailed and up-to-date information available within that company is bound to be rough and ready, but it will indicate whether the company is growing healthily, remaining static or heading for cash problems.

IEC's projected funds statement for 1979

Line S 1 1978's improvement included eleven months contribution from the £4m acquisition; as margins are still under pressure there is little scope for further improvement, say £7.0m at most for 1979.

Example 18.1 Funds statement "IMAGINARY ENGINEERING COMPANY" ("IEC")

Line*	*Year ending 31 December*	1977	1978	1979 *Projected*
	Source	£000	£000	£000
S 1	Profit before tax *less* minorities	6,247	6,624	7,000
S 2	Extraordinary items	(203)	-	
S 4	Depreciation	3,650	3,741	3,800
S 6	Minority retentions	298	327	330
S 11	Disposal of fixed assets	802	758	775
S 12	Sale of subsidiaries	740	-	
S 14	**Generated from operations**	11,534	11,450	11,905
S 15	Issue of shares	-	-	
S 17	Increase in Loans	-	3,000	
S 18	(Decrease in Loans)	-	-	(650)
S 23	**Source total**	11,534	14,450	11,255
	Application			
A 1	Tax paid	1,947	2,927	3,100
A 2	Dividends	1,780	1,958	2,154
A 4	Purchase of fixed assets	4,890	3,880	4,380
A 5	Purchase of subsidiary	-	4,000	500
A 11	Increase (Decrease) in Working Capital	1,277	2,263	2,545
A 12	Increase (Decrease) in Net Liquid Funds	1,640	(578)	(1,424)
	Application total	11,534	14,450	11,255
	Other information			
112	Debt/Equity ratio	64.1%	82.8%	
106	Acid test	0.82	0.61	
1	Turnover (£000)	32,705	42,857	
110	Working capital ratio	21.7%	22.3%	
	Capital commitments:			
	Authorised (£000)	5,186	5,801	
	Contracted (£000)	1,296	1,480	

*For an explanation of the line numbers, see the pro-forma analysis charts in Chapter 24.

Lines S 4, 6 and 11 No evidence of marked change.
Line S 17 High Debt/Equity ratio (line 112) leaves little scope for further borrowing.
Line S 18 £650,000 convertible unsecured loan stock remaining unconverted at last date for conversion 31 Dec 78, is due for redemption on 31 Dec 1979.
Line A 1 Assuming tax paid in 1978 represented tax at 46.8% on 1977's profits, and that tax paid in 1979 will be at a similar rate on 1978's profits.
Line A 2 The company is likely to increase dividends by the maximum allowed, *i.e.*, 10% under present dividend restraint policies.
Line A 4 The expenditure on fixed assets in past years has been roughly equal to the capital commitment that has been let to contract plus half the authorised expenditure. The chairman has said that the investment programme is continuing, so using the same lead time £1.48m plus ½ × £5.801m = £4.380m.
Line A 5 The cost of the current year acquisition announced by the chairman.
Line A 11 A 27% increase in turnover and a normal working capital ratio of 22% will mean an increase in working capital in 1977 of 0.27 × £42.857m × 0.22 = £2.545m.

These figures require a balancing item of £1.424 million in Line A 12 to make the 1979 Application total equal the Source total, meaning that the company is likely to have a decrease in net liquid funds in 1979 of around £1.4 million – £1.5 million on the present evidence.

However, as the "Acid test" ratio (Line 106) has already fallen to a very low level, a further increase in the overdraft looks undesirable. The most likely solution, to restore the imbalance caused by the £4 million acquisition made for cash in 1978, aggravated by substantial increases in the working capital requirement, is for IEC to make a rights issue (Line S 15) in 1979, and one might well ask why part of the consideration for the £4 million acquisition was not made in paper.

Limitations of funds statements

A source and application statement is a record of historical facts. It will record expenditure upon additional plant and machinery, but can express no opinion upon whether the expenditure was necessary, or will be profitable. Similarly, it may show an expansion of stocks (or debtors), but it will not tell us whether this was due to:

(*a*) poor stock or production control;
(*b*) inability to sell the finished product; *or*
(*c*) a deliberate act of policy, because of a feared shortage of supply, a potential price rise, or the need to build up stocks of a new model (or product) before it is launched.

And, in the case of increased debtors, it will not tell us whether it is the debtors who are slow to pay, or the credit policy which has changed; or whether they merely represent the expansion of turnover. It will show how new capital was raised, but not whether it was raised in the best way, nor indeed whether it really needed to have been raised at all or if it could have been avoided by better asset control.

Source and application of funds statements do not usually tell us:

(*a*) Where the money is. In the case of a multinational group, exchange controls or the tax situation may make it impossible or undesirable to remit some funds to the United Kingdom.
(*b*) How much more the company can borrow from its bankers. A fall in liquidity may be perfectly in order where a company has made arrangements with its bankers to cover just that eventuality. On the other hand, a company compelled by its bankers to reduce the scale of its operations may show a satisfactory improvement in liquidity, while being crippled by its inability to expand, or possibly being unable to maintain its existing plant properly.

As we have seen in our example of estimating the future fund requirements of the Imaginary Engineering Company, we had to draw on other information from the chairman's statement and from the accounts, and to use ratios (which we will describe more fully in Chapter 23) in order to help us interpret and project the company's flow of funds and so, although a source and application statement is often very handy for giving quick answers to questions about where the money came from and where it went, it is most useful when read in conjunction with all the other information available.

Chapter 19

HISTORICAL SUMMARIES

Variations in form and content

Although an historical summary of the salient features of company accounts is not a requirement of the Stock Exchange's Listing Agreement for companies, it was requested by the Chairman of the Stock Exchange, London, in a letter to companies in 1964, and over 90% of top companies now provide some form of historical summary. Most companies choose either a five- or ten-year period, but there is no uniformity of content. DALGETY, for example, show only four basic items in their "Ten-year survey" (illustrated below).

DALGETY *Ten-year survey*

	Group profit before tax *£million*	*Profit after tax attributable to Members of Dalgety Limited* *£million*	*Basic earnings per ordinary share* *Pence*	*Dividend per ordinary share* *Pence*
1968	3.5	1.8	12.4	6.776
1969	4.4	2.4	13.7	7.33744
1970	4.4	2.4	13.6	7.33744
1971	3.6	1.4	7.3	5.64344
1972	5.8	2.7	14.7	6.88248
1973	15.3	6.9	28.9	7.33744
1974	19.2	9.0	37.2	7.37413
1975	6.8	1.3	4.3	7.86936
1976	15.6	10.0	38.0	8.65629
1977	**17.1**	**9.4**	**33.3**	**11.6769**

Notes

1. Earnings and dividends have been calculated after allowing for the 1 for 5 scrip issue in 1972, and the bonus element in the rights issue in 1977.
2. Dividends per Ordinary Share are shown at the amount received by the Ordinary Shareholders. In the years 1968 to 1972 inclusive dividends were declared gross and the tax deducted therefrom by the Company paid over to the tax authorities.
3. The profit after tax and earnings per share for 1976 and 1977 reflect the revised accounting policy for deferred taxation described in the notes on the accounts.

Many companies go much further than this; BUNZL PAPER, for instance, provide 24 different items, filling a whole page of the accounts (*see* opposite, while others like ALLIED BREWERIES give as much as two or three pages of comparative figures.

Unlike Bunzl, most companies present their summaries with columns chronologically from left to right, which makes studying them much easier, except possibly for Arab investors.

Difficulties of interpretation

Among the difficulties facing the shareholder or analyst who tries to interpret a five- or ten-year summary are the following.

Inflation
Whereas pre-war it was reasonable in Britain to suppose that a pound today was the same as a pound last year and would be the same as a pound next year, rapid inflation has made this concept of a stable currency (referred to in the United States as the "uniform dollar concept") unsustainable. A pound in 1979 is not the same as a pound in 1978, 1977, 1976 or 1969. To read a ten-year record as though it is, is to obtain a false picture, and can be just as misleading as the company chairman who makes much of yet another year of record profits when they have advanced a mere 5% compared with a 15% or 20% rate of inflation. On the other hand, to try to allow for the changing pace of inflation over a ten-year period is very difficult, as we will discuss in Chapter 22.

Changes in accounting bases
Although changes in accounting bases are comparatively uncommon, most companies change their accounting ideas, either expressly or unknowingly, over a long period. Unless the figures for earlier years are revised, or a note drawing attention to the change in basis is included in the five- or ten-year statistical summary, readers may be misled. Thus, a company may until 1972 have operated on the basis that research and development expenditure should be capitalised, *i.e.*, carried forward as an asset whenever the benefits of the expenditure could reasonably be foreseen, but may now write it all off in the year in which it was incurred. Clearly, neither the figures in the profit and loss account up to 1972, nor those in the balance sheet, are comparable with the figures of later years.

Changes in basis may arise without any positive decision having to be made on the part of the company. For instance, during the last few years there have been several changes in the Corporation Tax system, one result of which is that dividends per share which were formerly shown gross may now be shown net and/or gross. In BUNZL's summary on the facing page, dividends are shown falling from £1.074 million in 1972 to £0.888 million in 1973, while the next line shows that dividends including ACT (*i.e.*, the gross equivalent dividends under the new system) did, in fact, rise. Similarly, the comparability of turnover for some companies has been affected by the change from Purchase Tax to VAT, while others have been affected by changes in the rate of Excise Duty.

Changes in the composition of the group
Where a group either grows or contracts, comparability is bound to be affected. Most groups do not strip out the effect of companies no longer being part of the group, nor do they include additions to the group for the whole period, but only from the date of acquisition.

Use of ratios

Thus, while a five- or ten-year summary can be very helpful, its limitations in the present inflationary climate and the adjustments which need to be made because of changes in accounting bases and in the composition of the group means that it should be treated with caution. However, as we have said, some companies do go to considerable trouble to make the figures as comparable as possible, and explain adjustments in footnotes, as Dalgety did in the extract reproduced at the beginning of this chapter.

It is sometimes possible to avoid some of these difficulties by using ratios; the current ratio and quick ratio and the collection period (Debtors/turnover), are comparable year by year, for example. But this is not true of all ratios. For instance, profit margin (Trading profit to sales ratio), is affected in historical cost accounts by stockholding gains and by the charging of depreciation only on the basis of historical cost, while Earnings per share are, of course, directly affected by inflation, since earnings are expressed from year to year in pounds of different vintages, while the number of shares in issue is unaffected by inflation

The key ratios

Despite all the difficulties we have discussed, the company's own historical summary does provide a readily accessible picture of the company's progress over past years, and should therefore be used when the analyst cannot afford the time and effort involved in preparing the detailed summary we advocate in Chapter 24, and the two key ratios to look at are Earnings per share and Shareholders' funds per share.

BUNZL PULP & PAPER *Group five-year summary*

	1976	1975	1974	1973	1972
	£000	£000	£000	£000	£000
Turnover	197,234	154,092	150,143	94,530	72,763
Trading surplus	11,917	11,607	13,897	8,145	6,631
Share of associates' surplus	2,155	2,041	1,733	1,271	1,010
Interest and dividends receivable	1,339	1,037	599	774	620
Interest payable	*2,235*	*2,438*	*2,162*	*1,612*	*1,147*
Group surplus before taxation	13,176	12,247	14,067	8,578	7,114
Taxation	*6,345*	*5,763*	*7,502*	*4,320*	*3,017*
Group surplus after taxation	6,831	6,484	6,565	4,258	4,097
Minority interests	*981*	*932*	*991*	*512*	*367*
Earnings for shareholders	5,850	5,552	5,574	3,746	3,730
Extraordinary items	1,855	1,006	337	935	324
Earnings after extraordinary items	7,705	6,558	5,911	4,681	4,054
Dividends	1,158	1,039	961	888	1,074
(total including Advance Corporation Tax)	1,759	1,599	1,453	1,292	1,231
Dividends per share	4.442p	3.969p	3.672p	3.391p	4.10p
(total including Advance Corporation Tax)	6.716p	6.106p	5.551p	4.935p	4.70p
Earnings per share					
Before extraordinary items	22.3p	21.2p	21.3p	14.3p	14.2p
After extraordinary items	29.4p	25.0p	22.6p	17.9p	15.5p
Shareholders' funds per share	165.2p	140.2p	119.1p	100.4p	86.1p
Net assets employed					
Fixed assets	38,385	32,366	27,780	23,817	19,393
Associated companies	6,944	5,870	4,793	4,116	3,519
Net current assets	30,860	25,031	23,625	16,506	13,546
	76,189	63,267	56,198	44,439	36,458
Financed by					
Shareholders' funds	43,260	36,713	31,194	26,294	22,551
External sources and deferments	32,929	26,554	25,004	18,145	13,907
	76,189	63,267	56,198	44,439	36,458

Figures in italics represent deductions

Earnings per share

E.p.s. are of prime interest to the investor and a crude adjustment can quite easily be made to allow for the effect of inflation by the use of the Retail Price Index (*see* Appendix 3). The method is as follows:

(*a*) Give the base value of 100 to the first earnings per share and scale the remaining e.p.s. figures in the series being adjusted.

(*b*) Place the **RPI** for the month of each balance sheet date below each e.p.s. figure (using base January 1962, if starting before January 1974).

(*c*) Give the base value of 100 to the first **RPI** figure and scale the remaining **RPI** figures in the series.

(*d*) Divide (*a*) by (*c*) and multiply by 100 to obtain an inflation-corrected series of the e.p.s. growth (or decline) from base 100.

Example 19.1 below shows this method in practice, based on figures from the BUNZL summary illustrated on the previous page.

Thus, an apparently maintained e.p.s. in 1973 was, in real terms, almost a 10% decline, an almost 50% advance in 1974 was really only about 14% up on 1972, and apparently static e.p.s. in 1975 and 1976 were declines.

The halving of the value of the pound in the five years between 1971 and 1976 has had a diabolical effect on e.p.s.: not only are profits each year overstated due to the historical cost method of accounting, but the resulting series of e.p.s. can rise in a comforting upward trend when in real terms they are falling.

Shareholders' funds per share

As shown in the Bunzl example, or what we call net asset value per share (n.a.v.).

The progression over the years shows how much profit is being ploughed back into the company to help earnings grow, and is a much better indicator than overall figures for assets employed or for shareholders' funds, which can be boosted by acquisitions for paper. The n.a.v. can, of course, be boosted by upward revaluation of assets, particularly of property, which is usually the cause of any sharp jump in n.a.v. that is larger than the year's e.p.s. less the dividend per share, *i.e.*, is larger than any change that could be caused by retained earnings.

Example 19.1 Adjustment of e.p.s. for inflation: BUNZL PULP & PAPER

	Year ending 31 December				
	1972	1973	1974	1975	1976
Earnings per share before extraordinary items	14.2p	14.3p	21.3p	21.2p	22.3p
(*a*) E.p.s. to base 100 in 1972	100	100.7	150.0	149.3	157.0
(*b*) Retail Price Index for December	170.2	188.2	224.2	280.0	322.2
(*c*) RPI to base 100 in 1972	100	110.6	131.7	164.5	189.3
(*d*) Real growth in e.p.s. $= \frac{(a)}{(c)}$	100	91.0	113.9	90.7	82.9

Chapter 20

THE DIRECTORS', CHAIRMAN'S AND AUDITORS' REPORTS

THE DIRECTORS' REPORT

Contents

The contents of the directors' report fall broadly into three categories:

1. *Information required by law* – the statutory requirements – a mass of information some of which is obvious from the accounts anyway, some of which is of comparatively little interest to the analyst (but appears to have been motivated by political considerations, *e.g.*, contributions for political purposes), but some of which may be of vital interest and importance to anyone interpreting the accounts.
2. *Information required by the Stock Exchange's Listing Agreement,* which we described in Chapter 3, some of which overlaps the statutory requirements.
3. *Voluntary information,* the information and commentary which the company wants to include about the events of the past year, about current trading and about plans and prospects for the future.

The voluntary information is normally contained mainly or wholly in the chairman's report, leaving the directors' report chiefly a catalogue of compulsory information, but if there is no chairman's report, and there is no compulsion for a chairman to report separately from his board of directors, any voluntary information will be included in the directors' report. In this chapter we will assume that there is a chairman's report, and we will deal with voluntary information under that heading, later in this chapter.

Statutory requirements

Under Section 157(1) of the Companies Act 1948, and Sections 16–20 of the Companies Act 1967, a directors' report must give the following information:

(*a*) the *principal activities* of the company and its subsidiaries, and any significant changes during the year;
(*b*) recommended *dividend* and proposed transfers to reserve;
(*c*) the names of the *directors* and details of their interests;
(*d*) particulars of significant changes in *fixed assets*;
(*e*) the reason for and details of any *issue of shares or debentures* made during the year;
(*f*) where the business has carried on two or more classes of business which, in the opinion of the directors, differ substantially from each other, an analysis of *turnover and pre-tax profits of each class of business*;
(*g*) *employees* – if 100 or more are employed in the United Kingdom, the average number employed and their aggregate remuneration (disregarding persons working wholly or mainly outside the United Kingdom);
(*h*) details of *political or charitable contributions,* if over £50 in the year;
(*i*) value of *goods exported* from the United Kingdom, or a statement that no goods have been exported during the year;
(*j*) *any other matters.* This is an omnibus clause obliging directors to disclose "particulars of any matters so far as they are

material for the appreciation of the state of the company's affairs" providing disclosure would not, in the opinion of the directors, be harmful to the company.

The Listing Agreement

As described in Chapter 3, the Listing Agreement requires companies to circulate certain information with the annual report; this information is usually contained in the directors' report, but may appear separately or in notes to the accounts. Items of particular interest are:

(*a*) the geographical analysis of turnover and trading results of any operations outside the United Kingdom;
(*b*) holdings, other than by directors, of 5% or more of any class of voting capital;
(*c*) whether or not the company is a "close company".

Control of the company

It is always worth checking whether a small company has any "bid prospects", such as a substantial holding by another, acquisition-minded, company, as this can explain why the company's share is looking overrated or "expensive" in comparison with other similar companies.

On the other hand, if the company is a close company (*i.e.*, under the control of its directors or of five or fewer persons – *see* Chapter 2), or if the directors' interests are substantial although not controlling, the dividend policy is likely to be conservative, because dividends paid to the directors or controlling shareholders will be heavily taxed in their hands. In addition, growth will probably be limited to ploughing back profits, because directors or the controlling shareholders are unlikely to be in a position to take up their entitlement in a rights issue, and because acquisitions for paper would also dilute their control.

However, if the principal director shareholder is nearing retirement, with no obvious successor (check list of shareholders for family names of the next generation, and remember that new issue prospectuses give directors' ages), then an agreed bid could well be in store.

The board of directors

Although many companies are built up primarily through the efforts of a single person, a one-man band is a potentially dangerous situation. He's going to present a succession problem in due course, and what would happen if he had a heart attack tomorrow? And if he's egocentric, he may surround himself with yes-men and come an awful cropper with his company.

We would therefore prefer a top management team: it is, for example, preferable not to combine the posts of chairman and managing director, and to have a separate finance director, and to have at least five board members. We would be unhappy, for instance, with a recent statement by one chairman/MD: "Apart from overall control of the Group's affairs, I shall have particular responsibility for financial control, and investigating possible acquisitions by the company."

We like the inclusion of a few non-executive directors, providing they are of a healthily independent disposition, devote sufficient time to the company to have a good grasp of its affairs (*i.e.*, they must know what's going on), are prepared to make a stand/resign if they disagree on important issues and bring some relevant experience to the boardroom.

Having checked the composition of the board and the management structure, let us now have a look at the chairman's statement, not only for what it says but also for what we can read between the lines.

THE CHAIRMAN'S REPORT

Sequence of study

It is difficult to lay down a set of rules as to the best order in which to study a report and accounts, and each individual will develop his own method (one stockbroker tells us he always goes straight to the directors' holdings to see if they are reducing their holdings!), but we think it is useful to start by glancing at the chairman's and the directors' report to see whether anything has occurred which would invalidate a straight forward comparison between one year and another. If, for instance, a major acquisition took place at the beginning of the year under review, almost all operating and financial ratios are likely to have been affected. This does not mean that the ratios are useless: simply that the analyst must bear in mind the change in composition of the group every time he compares one ratio with another.

Having then studied the accounts (a process we will discuss in detail in Chapters 23 and 24) and having examined any analysis given of turnover and pre-tax profits between classes of business and any geographical analysis of turnover and trading results outside the United Kingdom, the reader will now have a good idea of how the company has fared in the past year, but little idea why (except in the context of happening to know that it was a good, average or bad year for the industry or industries in which the company operates), and little idea of how the company is likely to do in the current year and beyond. It is to the chairman's report that we should look for this information.

Contents

In companies which believe in keeping shareholders well informed, the chairman's report will usually contain comment on:

(*a*) overall trading conditions during the period, current climate and general outlook;
(*b*) the performance achieved by each activity, current trading and future prospects;
(*c*) special items of interest (*e.g.*, closures and new ventures);
(*d*) company strategy and plans for the future.

We find it's useful to read through the whole report underlining key phrases and points of interest as we go, before getting down to any detailed analysis.

Estimating current year profits

A rough estimate of profits for the current year can be constructed (by each activity separately reported) by quantifying the chairman's comments, bearing in mind prevailing conditions and prospects for the industry concerned; for example, "POLYGON HOLDING COMPANY LTD" (Example 20.1).

The chairman may also give some overall view, *e.g.*, Polygon Holding's turnover in the first three months of the current year has been 22% higher than the same period last year, the paper division's order book is now four months, compared with one month last year, and, despite constant pressure on margins and the increasing ineptitude of government, the outlook for the group is encouraging. "Outlook encouraging" sounds to us like a 20–25% increase in pre-tax profits, *i.e.*, to £4.3–£4.5 million, pointing to the middle of the range we constructed division by division.

Other points to bear in mind in making a profits estimate are these:

1. Lossmakers discontinued will not only eliminate the loss but should, in addition, improve liquidity (and thus reduce interest charges, assuming there is an overdraft). But have all terminal losses been taken?
2. Most new ventures, branches, factories, depots, etc., are doing well if they break even in their second year of operation.
3. What is the chairman's previous record? Has he been accurate – cautious – unduly optimistic – erratic? Have past assurances of better times ahead been unfulfilled?
4. Remember, too, that one of the chairman's most important jobs is to maintain general confidence in the company, so he is likely to concentrate on the good points and only dwell briefly or remain silent on the weaker

Example 20.1 Estimating current year profits: "POLYGON HOLDING COMPANY LTD"

Activity	*Industrial climate*	*Chairman's remarks*	*Previous year* £m	*Reported year* £m	*Estimate of current year* £m
Building	Continued recession	"Further decline inevitable"	1.0	0.8	0.5–0.6
Paper	Cyclical upturn	"Marked improvement"	2.2	1.8	2.4–2.8
Bookmaking	One of the UK's few growth industries	"Continued progress"	1.0	1.2	1.4–1.5
Plastic extrusions	Demand flat	"Market share increasing but lower margins"	0.6	0.75	0.6–0.8
Interest charges	Rates down 2%	"Improvement in liquidity likely"	−0.8	−1.0	−0.8
		Pre-tax total	4.0	3.55	4.1–4.9

aspects of the company. Here it is a good idea to jot down questions, even if the analyst or shareholder is unlikely to have the opportunity of putting them to the company, because it helps to establish what the chairman hasn't revealed and whether any unexplained area is likely to be significant. A good question to ask oneself is "What are the company's main problems, and what is being done about them?"

5. Beware of vague statements, such as:
   (*a*) "Turnover in the first ten weeks of the current year has exceeded the corresponding figure for last year." It may be 1% ahead in value because of inflation, but a 12% drop has occurrred in volume.
   (*b*) "Unforeseen difficulties have occurred in . . . and a provision of £1.3 million has been made." Unless there is some indication of the likely overall cost of overcoming these difficulties, or of abandoning the activity altogether, the company should be assumed to have an open-ended lossmaker on its hands.

Longer-term prospects

The chairman of a company should be continually looking to the future and, unless he and his board have good sound ideas on where the future growth in profits is likely to come from, and are steering the company in that direction, then above average profits growth is unlikely. Although there must, of course, be some restrictions on what a chairman discloses about plans for the future, because of competition, he will usually include some indication of where he thinks the company is going in his annual report.

A good past growth record is clearly encouraging (a no-growth company is likely to stay a no-growth company unless the management or the management's attitude changes), but what indications are there of future growth? Possibilities to look for are:

1. *Better margins on existing business.* This is an unreliable source of growth unless the company *either*
   (*a*) has some very strong competitive advantage, such as patents or lucrative long-term contracts, *or*
   (*b*) has spent large sums of money building up brand images and carving out market share, and is now beginning to reap the benefits,

   and even then the profits growth will only last until the patents expire, the long-term contracts run out and the brand images tarnish.
2. *Further expansion of existing activities within the United Kingdom.* Is there any scope for this, or is the company in a position like BOOTS or MARKS & SPENCER, with a store in every town of any size, or like PILKINGTON, with 90% of the UK glass market?
3. *Diversification within the United Kingdom.* This was BOOTS' answer to their saturation problem with chemist shops: they widened the range of goods sold to include records and tapes, hi-fi, cameras, binoculars, even sandals. Boots were using their remarkable retailing expertise in wider product ranges, rather than going into some totally unrelated activity, and there does need to be some logic in diversifications or they can come very badly unstuck.
4. *Acquisition within the United Kingdom.* Has the company got a successful record of acquisitions, or would this method of growth be new to them (and therefore more risky)? This was part of PILKINGTON's solution for further growth; they diversified through fibreglass into insulation, boosting the process by acquisition.
5. *Exports.* Is the product suitable for export, or would transport costs make competitiveness overseas unlikely or impossible (*e.g.*, bricks)? Does the company export already, is it a significant amount, and is it growing? The chairman may report that "exports are 80% up on last year", but if this is an increase from 0.1% to 0.18% of turnover, this is hardly thrilling, and one should be wary of the chairman whose efforts to paint a rosy picture involve misleading statements like that, which should in honesty be qualified by some phrase like "albeit from a very low base".
6. *Are there opportunities for overseas growth*, like MARKS & SPENCER opening stores in Europe, or PILKINGTON putting down float glass plants overseas, either on its own, or in joint ventures, or by licensing the process to foreign glass manufacturers? There are, however, a good many hazards in opening up operations abroad, apart from the initial expense and the restrictions on exporting capital from the United Kingdom: different business ethics and practices, language, law, accounting and

tax systems and so on. For manufacturing abroad, cost levels may change over time, so that what today looks a good investment may prove otherwise in years to come if the cost of living rises faster in that country than elsewhere.

7. *Is the company spending money on, and attaching importance to, developing new products?* This is particularly important for pharmaceutical companies; BEECHAM, for instance, in 1976 reported £15.3 million spent on research and development, representing about 7% of the pharmaceutical product group's turnover.

   It is equally important for companies with substantial income from patents, which must eventually expire. PILKINGTON, for example, are developing a new glass-based concrete reinforcement called "Cemfil", using their world supremacy in glass technology to expand into building materials.
8. *Is the company ploughing profits back?* Profits in most industries cannot expand beyond a given point unless the asset base (needed to support the trading needed to generate the profits) is also expanded. There is a limit to gearing up, while acquisitions and rights issues don't necessarily enhance e.p.s.: only steady ploughback gives scope for steady growth in e.p.s.

In the context of future growth, it is also worth checking press cuttings for stories on the company, which often contain glimpses of the company's thoughts on the future (*see* Chapter 21 on McCarthy's press cutting service).

Information on the quality of management

Returning to the business of assessing the strength of the management, perhaps the most encouraging facet is when the chairman admits to a mistake or to being caught wrong-footed, and reports what is being or has been done about it. A somewhat extreme example comes from the "rag trade": the chairman's statement for WEARWELL in 1976, a year in which trading results had fallen from £1 million profit to £28,000 loss on turnover down from £7.1 million to £6.2 million and with over £½ million in terminal losses, contained the following comments.

WEARWELL *Extracts from chairman's report, 1976*

. . . in 1973 we operated what was basically a cash and carry operation. [In 1974 and 1975 the company made two acquisitions for cash and we] found ourselves in the business of building up stock and financing customers for considerable periods . . . sales not as buoyant as expected . . . liquidity difficulties in the opening weeks of 1976 . . . instituted immediate measures, namely:

1. Closure of the mail order supply business which had required the financing of substantial stocks.
2. Cutting out much of the credit business with chain stores.
3. The waiver by directors of a substantial part of their salary entitlement together with a waiver of between 94.0% and 99.9% of their total entitlement to the interim dividend.
4. Strenuous efforts were made to liquidate stocks.

. . . your company operates now only in the cash and carry type business which is where your management has proved its expertise.

We are glad to say that WEARWELL is still in business, although we weren't very keen on the change the company made in its treatment of deferred tax in the 1976 accounts, which we will describe in more detail when we come to auditors' reports later in this chapter.

In contrast, the chairman of a housebuilding company reported proudly in 1974 that "notwithstanding all these problems [the three-day week, the shortage of mortgage funds, rising interest rates and increases in building costs] your company increased its turnover to a new record level". The turnover had risen from £25.4 million to almost £44 million on an equity base of less than £2 million net of goodwill and after writing £8.7 million off the value of the land bank, now in the books at a mere £24.4 million plus £23.4 million work in progress. Apart from the feeling that the chairman was steering his company straight for the eye of a financial typhoon, and his avoidance of mentioning the year's pre-tax loss of £6.3 million in his statement, there were a number of fairly conspicuous danger signals scattered around the report:

(*a*) The notice of the AGM included a resolution to appoint a top London firm of accountants to be joint auditors with the existing provincial firm of auditors.

(*b*) The directors' report contained a little paragraph on "financial arrangements", which revealed that the group's bankers had agreed to "roll up" interest on group borrowings.

But perhaps the most telling fact was an omission: the group's habit of including an historical summary (which in the 1973 accounts had shown turnover since 1966 advance from £½ million to £23.7 million and pre-tax profits progressing over the same period (£000): 142 - 259 - 427 - 621 - 1,020 - 1,538 - 2,844 - 7,002) had been discontinued! The fall into loss in 1974 was too painful to face. Liquidation followed quite shortly afterwards.

In this context, John Argenti's book *Corporate Collapse* demonstrates that any company that goes on doubling its profits year after year will, in all probability, eventually meet disaster. An underlying reason for this is that a company producing such meteoric profits is probably very highly geared, and is thus highly vulnerable to any marked downturn.

THE AUDITORS' REPORT

(Reference: Companies Act 1948, Section 162.)

Appointment of auditors

Every company is required to appoint at each annual general meeting an auditor or auditors to hold office from the conclusion of that meeting until the conclusion of the next AGM. Until recently a retiring auditor was normally reappointed automatically, unless he did not wish to be, but it is now necessary to pass a resolution to re-appoint auditors to hold office.

Auditors' access to information

Under the Companies Act 1976 it has become an offence for a director or company secretary to give false or misleading information to auditors, and auditors of holding companies have the right to obtain information about subsidiary companies which they themselves do not audit.

The auditor has a right of access at all times to the books and accounts and vouchers of the company and to require from the officers of the company such information and explanations as he thinks necessary for the performance of his duty. He has the right to attend any general meeting, and to be heard thereat on any part of the business of the meeting which concerns him as auditor.

Scope of the report

The auditors are required to report to the members (*i.e.*, to the shareholders) whether in their opinion the profit and loss account and the balance sheet, and any group accounts, have been properly prepared in accordance with the Companies Acts, and give a true and fair view of the profit and state of affairs of the company or group.

If they are of the opinion that proper accounting records have not been kept, or that the accounts are not in agreement with the books, or if they are unable to obtain all the information and explanations necessary for their audit, they must state the fact in their report.

Qualified report

Any auditors' report which is not "clean", that is, which contains an element of reservation, is referred to as a "qualified report". It should not, however, be thought that if a report is qualified the financial integrity of the company's directors is necessarily called into question, although in some cases there may well be considerable doubt as to their integrity or to their judgement or to both; it is the analyst's job to read between the lines and discern what the auditor is trying to tell you within the limitation of the tact and diplomacy he needs to exercise to keep his client.

Of course, if the auditors qualify the report *and do not seek re-election,* then all warning systems should be set to "red alert", unless ample and convincing evidence is found to prove that all is well with the company.

Types of qualification

In trying to assess what the auditors really think (*i.e.*, what an indiscreet auditor, if such a fellow existed, might tell you in confidence over a glass of beer), it may help to divide qualifications into two categories, "accounting treatment" and "unsatisfactory information".

Accounting treatment

The directors may feel that a current accounting practice (*i.e.*, a requirement of an SSAP) is "inappropriate" for their type of business in their particular circumstances.

A point to check in these cases is whether there has been a *change in the company's accounting practice in a year of falling profits,* and if so, did the change reduce or increase the fall? (Hint: we've never known the latter to occur.) Take, for example, WEARWELL, which we discussed earlier in this chapter; in a year when trading profit fell from £1,007,005 to a loss of £28,945, the company decided not only to change the treatment of deferred taxation (long before the principles embodied in SSAP 15 became acceptable) but also to transfer part of the existing provision for deferred tax to bolster dwindling reserves, and got the qualification they deserved:

WEARWELL *Qualification to auditors' report*

To the Members of WEARWELL LIMITED.

We have examined the accounts set out on pages 8 to 16. As stated in note 1 these accounts have been prepared under the historical cost convention, including the revaluation of a freehold property.

In our opinion the accounts under that convention give, subject to the accounting policy for deferred taxation set out in note 1, a true and fair view of the state of affairs of the company and of the group at 30 April 1976 and of the result of the group for the period ended on that date and comply with the Companies Acts 1948 and 1967.
STOY, HAYWARD & CO.,
Chartered Accountants

1. Accounting policies
Deferred taxation
In previous years full provision has been made for the contingent liability for deferred taxation. In view of the probability that the major part of this provision will not be required it is now the group's policy only to consider the estimated liability that might arise under the current stock appreciation relief legislation. The provision in this respect was £393,400 at 2 May 1975 and the Directors consider this amount to be adequate for this purpose, and consequently no further provision is necessary. The unrequired balance of the provision at 2 May 1975 has therefore been added to reserves or deducted from goodwill arising on consolidation as appropriate. Full details of the contingent liabilities at 30 April 1976 are given in note 17.

Variations from standard accounting practices are not always a matter of expediency; in fact some companies, like PILKINGTON, substantially reduce their reported profits by depreciating plant on a regularly revalued basis (rather than historical cost) in a very sensible effort to provide for replacement rather than merely writing off the historical cost over the life of the asset. Their auditors draw attention to this in their report:

PILKINGTON *Extract from auditors' report*

We report on the accounts and the group summary of the source and use of funds which are together set out on pages 12 to 23. These have been prepared under the historical cost convention including the revaluation of fixed assets as explained in the statement of accounting policies set out on pages 12 and 13. In our opinion, the accounts and summary together give, under the accounting convention stated above, a true and fair view of the state of affairs at 31 March 1976 and of the profit and the source and use of funds for the year ended on that date and comply with the Companies Acts 1948 and 1967.

Unsatisfactory information
In our next example, J. B. EASTWOOD's auditors not only point out an unusual accounting policy, but politely disagree with it and comment that "it has not been practicable from the records available . . .", which we would take to mean that the auditors also do not like the way the books are kept.

J. B. EASTWOOD *Extract from qualified auditors' report*

The statement of accounting policies discloses that no depreciation is provided in respect of freehold and long leasehold properties and certain equipment relating thereto. Expenditure on maintenance of buildings and on part renewals of equipment is fully written off as incurred and it has not been practicable from the records available to segregate expenditure on renewals from that on repairs and maintenance.

Notwithstanding that the lives of the relevant assets may be extended as a result of such expenditure, in our opinion the fixed assets concerned (other than land) depreciate by reason of use coupled with the effluxion of time and provision should therefore be made for such depreciation in arriving at the profit of the Group.

This all sounds a bit ominous, but a check on reports from earlier years reveals that Eastwood have at least been consistent. Their policy appears to be to spend more money on renewing their chicken houses, etc., in good years than in bad ones, as a way of helping to smooth out their very volatile profit record:

	1974	1975	1976
Reported pre-tax profits/losses (£000)	6,033	(544)	7,002

The shareholder is left to guess how much *more* volatile they would have been with normal depreciation: the effect of Eastwood's unusual accounting practice is not quantified. This, we feel, is not at all satisfactory, but at least the auditors have made it quite clear to anybody who takes the trouble to read their report.

A rather more alarming example comes from PEACHEY PROPERTY CORPORATION's accounts for the year to June 1976:

PEACHEY PROPERTY CORPORATION LTD *Qualified auditors' report*

TO THE MEMBERS OF PEACHEY PROPERTY CORPORATION LIMITED

In our report on the accounts for the year ended 24 June 1975 we drew attention to the fact that we had not been able to corroborate the information given to us about amounts totalling £282,000. As stated in Note 4, the directors have deemed it prudent to make provision against these amounts pending the results of enquiries they are making. We have still not been able to corroborate the information given to us about these amounts nor consequently to establish that the expenditure was properly incurred on the business of the group. In addition we have not been able to corroborate the information given to us about the assets of £90,000 and the expenditure of £54,832 also referred to in Note 4.

As stated in Note 11 the directors are unable to estimate the value of certain land purchased in 1974 and held in partnership with another party which is indebted to the company in the sum of £825,000 plus interest. These items are reflected in the accounts in Interest in Partnerships in the sum of £2,800,000. In the circumstances set out in the note we are unable to judge whether or not any provision is required in relation to this amount.

Subject to the foregoing, in our opinion the accounts on pages 10 to 19 which have been prepared under the historic cost convention (with the exception that certain properties have been included at the amount of their valuation in 1965) give, under that convention, a true and fair view of the state of affairs of the company and of the group at 24 June 1976 and of the profit and the source and application of funds of the group for the year then ended and comply with the Companies Acts 1948 and 1967.

PRICE WATERHOUSE & CO.
Chartered Accountants

It is also of note that the publication of Peachey's report and accounts and the holding of the AGM had become later in recent years:

Year end 24 June	*Directors' report dated*	*AGM held on*
1972	28 February 1973	23 March 1973
1973	24 January 1974	15 February 1974
1974	24 July 1975	15 August 1975
1975	6 May 1976	28 May 1976
1976	18 April 1977	13 May 1977

For the year ending 24 June 1974 the company was in breach of the Companies Act 1948 requirement that the balance sheet and profit and loss account be made up not earlier than nine months before the meeting (twelve months where there are overseas interests). Delay in publishing the annual report and accounts is usually a bad sign; the Stock Exchange likes to see them issued within six months of a company's year end, and failure to do so is comparatively rare among listed companies (*see* p. 140 for details of the period currently allowed by the Companies Act 1976 for laying and delivering accounts.)

Chapter 21

OTHER SOURCES OF INFORMATION

Investors and analysts should recognise that the annual report and accounts of a company represent only a part, albeit a key part, of the total information available to them, and they should not neglect other sources. For convenience the other sources can be divided into:

(*a*) information the company provides, *and*
(*b*) external information.

INFORMATION PROVIDED BY THE COMPANY

The main sources of information from the company itself, apart from the annual report and accounts, are:

(*a*) half-yearly (and in a few cases quarterly) reports;
(*b*) prospectuses;
(*c*) circulars;
(*d*) company newsletters and magazines;
(*e*) catalogues and sales information literature;
(*f*) annual meetings;
(*g*) company visits.

Half-yearly reports and quarterly reports

Although there is no statutory provision for interim reports nor, as yet, any SSAP on them, companies whose securities are listed on the London Stock Exchange are required by the Listing Agreement to produce them (*see* Chapter 3).

In addition to providing information on the first six months, interim figures can and should be used subsequently in conjunction with the full year's figures to detect changes in trends in the second half (*see* Chapter 23).

Interim statements are not audited and it is possible that the stringent look which is given to the balance sheet at the end of the year, and the consequent making of adequate provisions, does not occur at the half-year. This tends to mean that exceptional and extraordinary items are somewhat more likely to be included in the second half of a year than in the first half.

Prospectuses

When a company offers shares or debentures for sale to the general public it is obliged in law to issue a prospectus; the Fourth Schedule to the Companies Act 1948 lays down the items which a prospectus must contain, and the main requirements are expanded in the Schedule II to the Stock Exchange's *Admission of Securities to Listing* - the Yellow Book.

When a company "goes public" - that is, when its shares gain a listing on the Stock Exchange (*see* Chapter 3) - the prospectus requirements are heavier than if the company already has its securities listed, and the prospectus is about the most comprehensive document the company ever produces about itself. The normal layout followed is:

1. Details of the offer, share capital and indebtedness.
2. Details of the company's directors, secretary, auditors, financial advisers, solicitors, bankers and stockbrokers.
3. The chairman's letter giving:
   (*a*) brief history of the company;

(*b*) a comprehensive description of its business;
(*c*) information on the management and staff;
(*d*) details of the company's premises;
(*e*) use of the proceeds of the issue (where any new shares are being issued);
(*f*) the earnings record, with a forecast for the current year's profits and intended dividends;
(*g*) the company's plans and prospects for the future.

4. The accountants' report containing a table of the last five years' profit and loss accounts and balance sheets.
5. Various statutory and general information on share capital and options, on the Articles of Association, on subsidiary and associated companies, directors' interests and service agreements, taxation clearances, material contracts, and any pending litigation.

On other occasions of shares being offered to the general public either directly, as in a secondary offer for sale of existing shares already listed (*e.g.*, the government's £550 million sale of BP shares in June 1977), or indirectly, as in a rights issue of new shares of a company whose existing securities are already listed, much less information is required, but nevertheless the prospectus of a secondary offer or the circular letter to shareholders produced for a rights issue can be useful sources of up-to-date information on a company.

Circulars on acquisitions and realisations

Chapter 4 of the Yellow Book divides transactions into four classes, as shown in Table 21.1.

When a listed company makes a Class 1 transaction (*i.e.*, equivalent to 15% or more of the existing company), shareholders have to be sent a circular giving full details; alternatively, if the company is making a takeover bid, they can be sent a copy of the offer document, providing the offer document includes all the information required for circulars on acquisitions (as contained in Part B of Schedule II to the Yellow Book). In either case the information provides the analyst with useful details of any major additions to or realisations of the company's assets.

Circulars also have to be sent to shareholders for Class 4 transactions (those involving a director or substantial shareholder, past or present); these can be of considerable interest if the transactions are large and/or if there is any question of sharp practice, but the majority are fairly mundane, produced mainly to ensure that

Table 21.1 Criteria for classification of transactions

Class	*Size of acquisition or disposal*	*in relation to*	*The acquiring or disposing company*	*Stock Exchange requirements*
1	Value of assets *or* Net profit before tax *or* Consideration given *or* Equity capital issued	15% or more of 15% or more of 15% or more of 15% or more of	Company's assets Company's net profit before tax Company's assets Equity capital previously in issue	Company must give particulars to the Quotations Department and to the Press *and* send circular to shareholders
2	Not Class 1 but bigger than Class 3			Company must give particulars to the Quotations Department and to the Press
3	Value of assets *or* Net profit before tax *or* Consideration given	less than 5% of less than 5% of less than 5% of	Company's assets Company's net profit before tax Company's assets	No announcement required unless Listing is being sought for securities given in consideration
4	Transactions involving a director, past director, substantial shareholder or past substantial shareholder			Quotations Department must be consulted beforehand. A circular to shareholders and their approval in general meeting normally required unless transaction is very small.

shareholders' interests are scrupulously protected.

Documents issued in a contested bid

When the management of a company defend a bid they have to make the best possible case for the company's continued independence and, in doing so, they will often be rather more forthcoming about the company's future plans and prospects than they normally are in the annual report. Analysts may therefore find it worth reading any documents that a company has issued in successfully contesting a bid. It is also interesting to see whether a company subsequently lives up to any rosy picture it may have painted of its future at the time of the bid.

Company newsletters and magazines

An increasing number of companies now produce a house magazine or newsletter for employees, and many produce a "report to employees" summarising the company's results for the year, often presenting the information in charts or diagrams. These publications can be very helpful in giving the analyst (as well as the employee) a better feel for the company, and they may contain information that is *not* included in the accounts.

Companies producing an annual newsletter or report to employees may also send copies to shareholders to ensure that information given to employees is also made available to the shareholders, but where newsletters are published more frequently or where a large group has several subsidiaries, each of which has its own separate newsletter, they are unlikely to be distributed to investors. If the analyst can lay his hands on them he may gain a better insight into the various activities of the company and pick up facts that are not generally available.

Catalogues and sales information literature

The shareholder or analyst who really wants to know a company should study its catalogues and sales literature for evidence of pricing policy, marketing ability, changes in product range, quality or design.

Failure to adapt to changing circumstances is an early sign of sleepy management. Innovation may be essential if the company is to keep moving - but not every management is capable of thinking up new ideas and of putting them into practice. Promotional literature on new products can sometimes indicate the potential for success.

Annual General Meeting

When all is going well, annual meetings tend to be sparsely attended. This is a pity, because they provide an opportunity for shareholders to seek and obtain further information about their company.

The usual business of an AGM is:

1. to receive the report and accounts;
2. to declare a dividend;
3. to elect directors;
4. to appoint auditors;
5. to transact any other ordinary business.

Any ordinary shareholder may attend the AGM and speak. Normally his best opportunity to obtain information is upon the motion considering the accounts. If the information he seeks is reasonable (*e.g.*, not of a confidential nature or likely to be of more value to the competition than to members) and he does not obtain a satisfactory answer, he should press the point; and state publicly his dissatisfaction. He may find he has more support than he expects.

Generally, directors are prepared to answer all reasonable questions when times are good, but become guarded when the situation is unsatisfactory. If this occurs, the individual shareholder may find that he can obtain the information during informal discussion after the meeting.

Company visits

Companies differ widely in their attitude to company visits by analysts and/or shareholders. Most major companies welcome the interest of both and arrange from time to time group visits at which plans and prospects are discussed in depth, and those interested are able to seek further information.

Those actually making visits should ask themselves:

(*a*) Is there any evidence of cut-back, of falling sales and growing stocks or of maintenance delayed to save cash?
(*b*) Is the work force contented - or are labour relations uneasy?
(*c*) Do they look efficient - or is there a general atmosphere of chaos?
(*d*) Do they appear forthcoming, or are they hiding something?

It is also worth asking management whether they are experiencing any difficulties: good management are usually prepared to talk about the problems facing their company, and to explain the action they are taking to overcome them.

Finally, always ask about the competition: the replies will help to show whether the management have a practical and realistic attitude to the business environment in which they operate, and may well provide the analyst with useful information about other companies in the industry. We well remember on one company visit, in reply to a question about a competitor, the chairman simply remarked "that company is structured for disaster". The competitor went bust a year later.

EXTERNAL INFORMATION

There is a vast range of external information useful to the analyst who wishes to make a study in depth of a particular company, group or industrial sector. Useful sources include:

(*a*) the Registrar of Companies;
(*b*) Extel;
(*c*) McCarthy Information services;
(*d*) dataSTREAM;
(*e*) government statistical publications;
(*f*) specialist and trade publications.

The Registrar of Companies

The Registration Department of the Department of Trade has offices at Companies House, 55 City Road, London EC1Y 1BB, and at Crown Way, Maindy, Cardiff CF4 3UZ and, for Scotland, at Exchequer Chambers, 102 George Street, Edinburgh.

Rules for filing accounts
Section 6 of the Companies Act 1976 requires a company to lay accounts before its members in general meeting and to deliver them to the Registrar of Companies within certain time limits fixed by reference to its accounting year-end. The limit for a UK public company is seven months, which can be extended by three months if the company has interests outside the United Kingdom.

Other information to be filed
Companies are also required to file with the Registrar:

(*a*) copies of their Memorandum and Articles of Association, and details of any subsequent changes;
(*b*) address of the registered office, and the place at which the company's registers are kept, if not at the registered office;
(*c*) details of the company's share capital and debentures;
(*d*) details of each mortgage and charge on the assets of the company;
(*e*) a list of the directors and secretary and any changes.

In addition, Sections 124–126 of the Companies Act 1948 require a company to file an *annual return,* which contains a summary of (*b*) to (*e*) above and a list of past and present members. Every third year the list must be a complete list of persons holding shares or stock in the company; in the intervening years only changes need be given, but in each year the return must show anyone whose name has appeared on the register as holding shares or stock in the company at any time since the last return. It is therefore possible to find out from Companies House if anyone has been a registered shareholder at any time, however short the period of ownership, although nominee names may hide the beneficial owner.

Inspecting a company's files
Companies' files are now maintained at Cardiff where they can, if required, be inspected on payment of a 5p search fee. The normal method of working is, however, to inspect a microfiche of the file (on payment of the same search fee). Copies of any microfiche may be obtained for a fee, and the copy microfiche belongs to and may be taken away by the searcher. So anyone with suitable microfiche equipment can consult the file at leisure in his own office.

No postal search facilities are currently available through the Registrar, but there are a number of search agents who will provide the service on payment of a suitable fee, for example Jordan & Sons Ltd, Jordan House, 47 Brunswick Place, London N1 6EE.

The microfiche facilities available at City Road, London and at Cardiff are virtually identical, and there is no significant time difference in the recording of information at the two offices. For instance, information on charges registered in London is available on the microfiche file in Cardiff within the hour.

Analysing a group
Most group accounts contain a general breakdown of their activities, but much more detail can often be obtained by examining the accounts which each subsidiary and associated company has to file at Companies House.

Extel Cards

Since Moodies ceased trading in 1976, Extel (Extel Statistical Services Ltd, 37–45 Paul Street, London EC2A 4PB), is now the only company in the United Kingdom which publishes cards on information from company accounts. Extel's services include:

1. The *British Company* service, covering almost every company listed on the British and Irish Stock Exchanges. Two individual cards are issued for each company:
   (*a*) An Annual Card, which summarises the company's activities and lists its subsidiaries and associated companies, its board members, its share and its loan capital (with history). Tables are given of profit and loss items for the last ten years and dividend payments for the last five years, together with the latest balance sheet, a summary of the chairman's most recent statement and a whole host of other information ranging from the company's registered number to its net asset value.
   (*b*) A Cumulative News Card, issued as and when dividends are announced and when other major items of news justify.
2. The *Analyst's* service, which complements the British Company service and covers about 1,500 companies, giving a ten-year record (analysed and adjusted) of capital changes, balance sheets, profit and loss accounts, share prices, dividends, etc.
3. The *Unquoted Companies* service, which is an extension of the British Company service. It contains similar information about unquoted companies, on the same system of continuous updating year after year.

The British Company service, which is an essential part of any stockbroker's or professional investor's office, costs several hundred pounds a year, takes up about eight cubic feet of filing cabinets and needs two or three hours' clerical effort per week to cope with the steady stream of new cards.

A less expensive and more condensed form of information on companies is provided by Extel's *Handbook of Market Leaders*, which is published twice a year. It covers only the companies in the *FT* Actuaries Index but does include a share price graph as well as other information covering a five-year period.

McCarthy Information services

The Press provides a major source of news and information on companies, but keeping track of what appears on any particular company is a time-consuming and somewhat hit-and-miss affair. Fortunately McCarthy's (McCarthy Information Ltd, The Manor House, Ash Walk, Warminster, Wiltshire BA12 8PY) provide an excellent service covering, in the United Kingdom:

Financial Times	*Evening News*
The Times	*Irish Times*
Daily Telegraph	*Irish Independent*
The Guardian	*Sunday Times*
Daily Mail	*The Observer*
Daily Express	*Sunday Telegraph*
The Scotsman	*Sunday Express*
Yorkshire Post	*The Economist*
Evening Standard	*Investor's Chronicle*

All relevant news, comment and articles on a company are cut out and reproduced on information sheets and a new sheet is circulated to subscribers, on a daily basis for the Quoted Company service and on a weekly basis for McCarthy's range of other services, which includes services on Australian, North American and European companies, on UK unquoted companies, and on industries, banking and property.

dataSTREAM

"dataSTREAM" is a brilliantly conceived computer-based system which provides detailed information both on individual companies and on companies within a specified sector of the market. Analysis of individual company accounts can be obtained on a five-year basis, covering profit and loss account, balance sheet and financing table, together with key accounting ratios, while the same information for a single year can be displayed on up to five companies at a time.

The system is accessed from remote visual display units (VDUs) situated in subscribers' offices and, once the initial programme has been selected, a series of questions is displayed on the VDU to enable the user to specify exactly what he requires. The information is then displayed on the VDU and can be printed out on a dataSTREAM teleprinter if hard copy is required.

dataSTREAM also provides a chart plotting facility, macro-economic data, price monitoring and performance measurement, a portfolio performance program and a news channel.

The dataSTREAM system, pioneered by stockbrokers Hoare & Co. Govett, is now run as an independent company (dataSTREAM International Ltd, 9–12 King Street, London EC2V 8DU), and over 250 remote terminals serve financial and investment institutions both in the United Kingdom and in Europe. The annual subscription for a single terminal (VDU and keyboard) is several thousand pounds.

Government statistical publications

Although the Department of Trade and Industry does produce a weekly magazine, *Trade and Industry*, containing the latest information on a variety of statistics, the best overall presentation of the huge range of statistics prepared by government departments is given in the *Monthly Digest of Statistics*, published by the Central Statistical Office of the Government Statistical Service.

Other CSO publications include:

Financial Statistics (monthly) - gives the key financial and monetary statistics of the United Kingdom.

Economic Trends (monthly) - commentary and a selection of tables and charts providing a broad background to trends in the UK economy.

Annual Abstract of Statistics - contains many more series than the monthly digest and provides a longer run of years.

National Income and Expenditure - known as the "Blue Book", which is published annually and gives detailed estimates of the national accounts including consumers' expenditure over the previous ten years.

A useful booklet *Government Statistics - a brief guide to sources* is available free from the Central Statistical Office, CO:CSO Section, Great George Street, London SW1P 3AQ.

Specialist and trade publications

Trade magazines published by trade associations may contain useful statistical information compiled from the association's own members, as well as general news about the industry, while independent specialist magazines provide useful background information in their particular sphere. Some independent magazines are published on a private subscription-only basis, for example *Tattersall's Trade Review*, a specialist periodical for the textile industry.

Government departments also produce a wide range of publications on individual industries, in particular National Economic Development Committee reports from the National Economic Development Office, NEDO. All NEDO publications are listed in a free booklet *Nedo in Print*, obtainable from NEDO Books, 1 Steel House, 11 Tothill Street, London SW1H 9LJ.

Finally, on a broader note, an independent view and forecasts on the UK and world economy are contained in the *National Institute Economic Review*, published by the National Institute of Economic and Social Research, NIESR. The NIESR, 2 Dean Trench Street, Smith Square, London SW1P 3HE, is an independent non-profit-making body, which conducts research by its own staff and in co-operation with the universities and other academic bodies.

Chapter 22

INFLATION ACCOUNTING

SUMMARY

In attempting to present a true and fair view of a company's affairs, accounting systems have two principal enemies: inflation and subjective judgement.

Historical cost accounting

In a time of stable prices, the historical cost system works well. What an asset cost is seldom in dispute, and although the directors have to assess the expected useful life of fixed assets, and their likely disposal value, there is limited scope for subjective judgement. Furthermore, the quality of historical cost accounts has steadily improved over the years, largely thanks to the efforts of the Accounting Standards Committee. SSAPs have considerably reduced the number of options available to company directors and, though some problems do still remain, only accounting theorists would seriously suggest that historical cost be abandoned as the basis of accounting in a period of stable prices.

In a period of substantial price rises (*i.e.*, inflation), people become dissatisfied with historical cost accounting systems for four main reasons:

1. Cost of sales tends to be understated. In historical cost accounts, stock consumed and sold is charged against sales at its original cost, rather than at the cost of replacing it. But the company, to retain the same stock level, has to finance the difference (and would have to do so entirely out of profits after tax were it not for stock relief). This is perhaps most easily understood if we add a few figures. Assume the company has in stock one item which costs £25. It sells it for £40, and replaces the stock for £35. Historical cost accounts say that it has made a profit of £15; but if it is to maintain its original stock level it has to plough back £10 of the "profit" of £15, simply in order to stand still.
2. Historical cost accounts fail to recognise the need for increases in other components of working capital in a time of general inflation. In most companies, debtors are greater than creditors, so, on an unchanged volume of business, "debtors minus creditors" increases with inflation, requiring extra working capital to be provided.
3. Historical cost accounting seeks to write off the cost of fixed assets over their effective lives. It does not set out to provide a fund from which the fixed assets can be replaced at the end of their lives. Nevertheless, in a period of stable prices, sufficient cash could be set aside over the life of an asset to replace it at its original cost. In times of inflation, insufficient is provided in this way to enable the business to replace its assets.
4. Borrowings are shown in monetary terms, and if nothing is repaid, and nothing further is borrowed, borrowings appear stable. Some people feel that this is a distortion of the picture, and that a gain has been made at the expense of the lender (since in real terms the value of the loan has declined) which ought to be reflected in the accounts.

In times of general inflation, profits calculated on historical cost basis tend to be overstated due to inadequate provision for depreciation, and to illusory stock profits. They also present difficulties for the simple reason that the figures are themselves reported in pounds of falling value, so that one year's sales, profits and dividends, are not comparable with those of another; similarly, the balance sheet at the end of one year cannot fairly be compared with that at the end of another without adjustment because they are expressed in pounds of different purchasing power.

Current purchasing power accounting (CPP)

CPP accounting, put forward as a possible system of inflation accounting by ED 8, published in 1973, provides a method of adjusting historical cost accounts to remove the distorting effects of changes in the purchasing power of money. CPP simply adjusts the figures for earlier years by the change in the Retail Price Index, treating previous years' pounds as different currencies to be translated at a rate of (this year's RPI ÷ previous year's RPI). There is one exception: *monetary items remain unchanged.*

ED 8 proposed that CPP accounts should be produced as a *supplementary* statement in company reports and accounts. Although the proposals received quite a lot of support, they were not entirely satisfactory for a number of reasons, in particular because the system greatly enhanced the profits of companies that were heavily borrowed and because nobody knew which set of figures to believe. In the event CPP, as proposed by ED 8, was fairly short-lived, being flatly rejected by the government-appointed committee on inflation accounting, the Sandilands committee.

Current cost accounting (CCA)

Current cost accounting, the system proposed by the Sandilands Committee and over-complicated by ED 18, tries to provide a system of accounting that is better than historical cost accounting whether there is inflation or not. Its two fundamental concepts are:

(*a*) that holding gains (due to the value of assets increasing in monetary terms) should not be confused with the profits from operations, *and*

(*b*) that assets should be shown at their value to the business, not at their "book value" (cost less accumulated depreciation).

While the former is very sensible, some people fear the latter could give the directors too much scope for subjective judgement. It is hoped, however, that the auditing profession will be able to ensure that any estimates of "value to the business" are realistic and properly based.

CCA makes no direct attempt to adjust for the decline in the value of money. In this sense it is not a system of inflation accounting. It reflects the somewhat pedantic view of the Sandilands Committee that "Inflation . . . is not a phenomenon capable of independent and objective measurement" (para. 45 of their report). It is only in the statement of net change in equity shareholders' interests (tacked on by ED 18) that CCA makes any attempt to adjust for changes in the purchasing power of money.

The opposition to ED 18 proved so widespread that members of the Institute of Chartered Accountants in England and Wales voted that current cost accounting should not be made compulsory.

The Hyde Report

As a result of the vote against CCA, the Accounting Standards Committee set up the Hyde Committee to devise interim measures for showing the effects of inflation in the published accounts of listed companies.

The report of the Hyde Committee, published in December 1977, recommended that supplementary information should be provided in the form of three adjustments to the historical cost profit and loss account: a depreciation adjustment, a cost of sales adjustment and a gearing adjustment. These proposals, which have been endorsed by the Stock Exchange and the CBI, provide a useful indication of the effects of inflation on published accounts, but they are only an interim measure, and proposals for a long-term solution are still needed.

INFLATION

Inflation, which to the layman is the decline in the purchasing power of money as the general price level of goods and services rises, is not new, but it has rarely been as rapid in the United Kingdom as it has been in the past few years, when it has affected most aspects of economic life: the standard of living of individuals, investment decisions, wage negotiations, pricing policies, international trade and taxation.

When the rate of inflation appears low (as it

did throughout most of the previous 30 years) there is a tendency for the business community to ignore it completely. Nevertheless, even a modest annual rate, compounded over a number of years, will have a significant effect on the balance sheet and upon the comparability of figures in the accounts generally, and will tend to make a company look as though it is doing better than it really is; for example "Another year of record profits", so often headlined in company announcements in the newspapers, is hardly cause for jubilation if the rate of profits growth is only half the rate of inflation.

It is therefore important that management should understand the effects of inflation on profitability, and that businesses should have clear information on both:

(*a*) the real return being made on capital employed, *and*
(*b*) the adequacy or otherwise of provisions for the replacement of fixed and current assets.

Recent inflation in the United Kingdom

Between 1972 and 1977 the value of the pound halved. During this period the Western world's economic and financial systems were undoubtedly put off balance by the huge rise in oil prices, but it would be quite wrong to put more than a modest part of the blame for the headlong decline of sterling on OPEC (the Organisation of Petroleum Exporting Countries); as Fig. 22.1 shows, the pound since 1972 has declined dramatically against the currencies of most other European countries, showing that the main cause of the United Kingdom's inflation lies within the United Kingdom.

The underlying reason for the United Kingdom's record rate of inflation in the 1970s was that governments allowed the money supply to increase when there was no corresponding increase in the Gross Domestic Product (GDP). As Fig. 22.2 shows, the UK's GDP remained almost static in the mid-1970s, while the money supply almost doubled, so a high rate of inflation was inevitable in that period.

Fig. 22.1 The decline of sterling

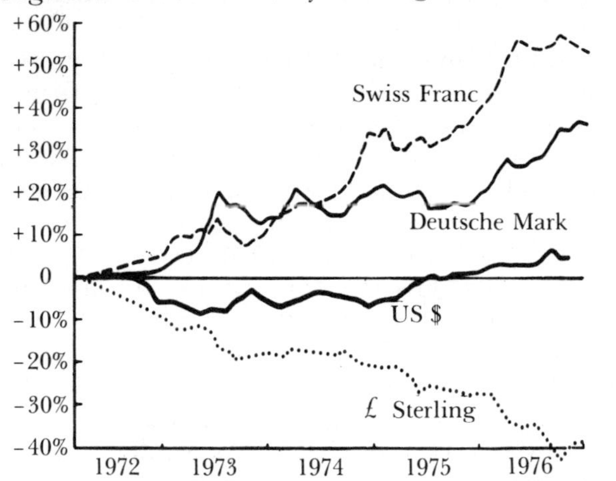

Fig. 22.2 UK money supply and GDP

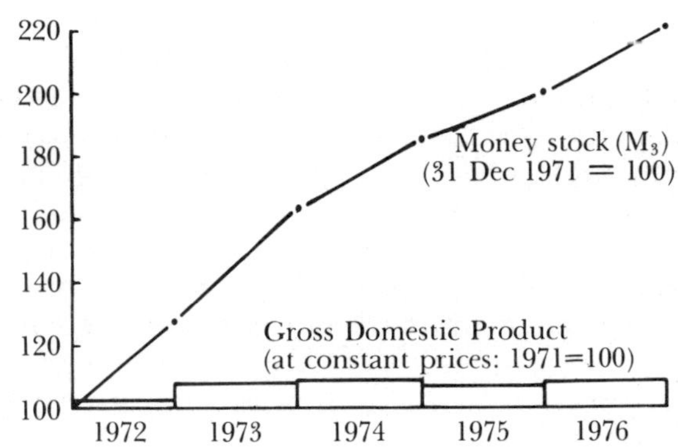

The only really satisfactory solution is to stop inflation; this can only be achieved by suitable government policies; meanwhile, we have to learn to live with inflation, so let us look firstly at the effect inflation has on accounts, and then consider ways of compensating for these effects: *i.e.*, consider various methods of inflation accounting.

HISTORICAL COST ACCOUNTING

Traditionally, companies have prepared their accounts on what is termed the *historical cost convention* – that is to say, items are recorded in terms of purchasing power of the pound at the date when the asset was acquired, the liability was incurred or the capital obtained – though in the United Kingdom there is a growing tendency for companies to revalue some of their assets (normally only freehold land and buildings) to current values. The historical cost convention has the advantage that the recorded historical cost, what was actually paid or received at the time, is rarely in dispute: it can be verified by the auditors or by anyone else examining the books; in contrast, current values, used in alternative methods of accounting, depend on the exercise of subjective judgement, and may therefore be very much a matter of opinion.

The historical cost balance sheet is not, and does not purport to be, a valuation statement. It does not tell us, for instance, what the assets would realise if they were to be sold, either in a forced sale (as in liquidation) or in the normal course of business – and the two figures are likely to be somewhat, and possibly very, different – nor does it tell us what it would cost to replace the assets. In the case of *fixed assets* (which have not been revalued) it shows the cost of the asset, less the depreciation to date, the assumption being that the business will continue long enough for the asset to be written off over its anticipated useful life. Accountants sometimes refer to this as the statement of assets on a going concern basis. (As we described in Chapter 1, one of the fundamental accounting concepts is that the business is a going concern.) *Current assets* similarly appear in historical cost accounts at cost, but in their case it is traditional to write them down to net realisable value should this ever be less than cost. The difference in treatment between fixed and current assets arises for legal reasons. In law a company is not required to write down its fixed assets, and may distribute profits even though its fixed assets are not worth the figure at which they appear in the balance sheet, though this is admittedly not good business practice. The position on current assets is quite different. Any losses on current assets must be written off before a profit can be distributed.

The impact of inflation on historical cost accounts

Inflation makes a three-pronged attack on a company using historical cost accounts:

1. As the cost of fixed assets goes up, the provision for depreciation falls increasingly short of the cost of replacing fixed assets at the end of their useful lives.
2. The amount of working capital required to maintain the same *volume* of business progressively increases.
3. The reported profits are overstated for three reasons:
   (*a*) because of inadequate depreciation of fixed assets;
   (*b*) because, in calculating the cost of goods sold, the closing stock is deducted at inflated prices;
   (*c*) because the profits are stated in terms of money which itself has declined in value.

As Table 22.3 shows, the effect of inflation on the value of money over a number of years is staggering.

Table 22.3 Effect of inflation on the value of money

Annual rate of inflation	*Value of £1 after 5 years*	*Value of £1 after 10 years*
2½%	88.3p	78.1p
5 %	78.3p	61.3p
7½%	69.6p	48.5p
10 %	62.0p	38.5p
12½%	55.4p	30.7p
15 %	49.7p	24.7p
17½%	44.6p	19.9p
20 %	40.1p	16.1p
25 %	32.7p	10.7p

Another way of putting this is to say that with inflation running at 7½% per annum, a modest level by present standards, a company must double its profits every ten years to maintain their real value, and if inflation is up to 15% per annum, profits must be doubled every five years. In fact, we would go further than that: because of the inadequacy of depreciation, the majority of companies should treble rather than double their historical cost profits in those periods in order to hold their own in real terms. Of course, any company that *does* succeed in maintaining real profits in times of high inflation is doing remarkably well.

The effect of inflation – an example

Let us take as our example the "MISCELLANEOUS TRADING COMPANY" (MISCO), whose balance sheet figures for the end of "Year 0" are shown in the company's "Year 1" balance sheet opposite.

Note:

(i)

Fixed assets

At 31 Dec Year 0	*Freehold land*	*Freehold buildings*	*Machinery (note iii)*	*Total*
	£000	£000	£000	£000
Cost	200	500	1,250	1,950
less				
Depreciation	—	100	500	600
Book Value	200	400	750	1,350

(ii) The freehold buildings are all industrial buildings. The straight line method of depreciation is used over the following periods:
Freehold industrial buildings: 25 years
Plant and machinery: 5 years

(iii) The company owns five identical machines, each of which cost £250,000. One is brand new, and the remainder are 1, 2, 3 and 4 years old respectively.

(iv) Taxation and dividends relate to the year being reported upon, and are payable within 12 months.

Consider what the balance sheet would show at the end of Year 1 in two different situations: Situation 1 - no inflation; Situation 2 - 18% inflation. In each case:

[H] the oldest machine is replaced at the end of the year and has no residual value;
[J] the *volume* of stock at the end of the year is unchanged;
[K] the *volume* of goods sold to customers but not yet paid for by them at the end of the year (*i.e.*, Debtors) is the same as it was at the beginning of the year;
[M] the *volume* of goods received from suppliers but not yet paid for by MISCO (*i.e.*, Creditors) is also unchanged.

Situation 1 - no inflation

In the first situation let us assume that there has been *no inflation*, and that the profit and loss account shows:

	£000
Pre-tax profit	300
Taxation (say at 50%)	150
Profit after tax	150
Dividends	100
Retained profit	50

In the balance sheet illustrated:

[B] Reserves would have increased by £50,000 retained profits.
[G] Depreciation on buildings would be £20,000 (4% of £500,000 cost).
[H] Depreciation of £50,000 on each of the 5 machines would have been exactly equal to the cost of one new machine.
[Q] The overdraft would have been reduced by £70,000 (£50,000 retained profits plus £20,000 depreciation on buildings).

Year 1 was not a very spectacular year for MISCO, but it paid a good dividend and managed to reduce its overdraft.

"MISCO" *Balance sheet at 31 December Year 1, Situation 1*

(*Situation 1* - after a year's trading with no inflation.)

		Year 1 £000	Year 0 £000
Liabilities			
Ordinary share capital	[A]	1,000	1,000
Reserves	[B]	550	500
Ordinary shareholders' funds	[C]	1,550	1,500
5% Debenture 1987/90	[D]	600	600
		2,150	2,100
Assets			
Fixed assets			
Freehold land	[F]	200	200
Freehold buildings	[G]	380	400
Plant and machinery	[H]	750	750
		1,330	1,350
Current assets			
Stock	[J]	800	800
Debtors	[K]	1,000	1,000
		1,800	1,800
Current liabilities			
Creditors	[M]	600	600
Taxation	[N]	150	150
Dividends	[P]	100	100
Overdraft	[Q]	130	200
		980	1,050
Net current assets		820	750
		2,150	2,100

Situation 2 – inflation at 18% p.a.

Now let us look at what happens with *general inflation* applying to everything at the rate of 18% p.a. (a normal rate for the United Kingdom in the mid-1970s), and let us assume that:

(*a*) the *volume* of goods sold was unchanged, *and*

(*b*) MISCO was able to increase its selling price whenever it started to sell new stock (*i.e.*, it didn't mark up goods already in stock when suppliers increased their prices).

In order to assess the effect of MISCO's pricing policy, we have to get down to the detail that lies behind the profit and loss account. If stock = 2 months' purchases and is replenished at the end of each month, creditors = 1½ months' purchases and debtors = 2 months' sales, then:

Month end	*Cost price index*	*Purchases*	*Selling price index*	*Sales*
		£000		£000
Jan	101½	406	100	500
Feb	103	412	100	500
Mar	104½	418	101½	507½
Apr	106	424	103	515
May	107½	430	104½	522½
Jun	109	436	106	530
Jul	110½	442	107½	537½
Aug	112	448	109	545
Sept	113½	454	110½	552½
Oct	115	460	112	560
Nov	116½	466	113½	567½
Dec	118	472	115	575
Total for the year		5,268		6,142

Thus:

closing stock = £938,000 (Nov and Dec purchases)

closing debtors = £1,142,500 (Nov and Dec sales)

closing creditors = £705,000 (half Nov and all Dec purchases).

We are, in fact, envisaging prices being steady (at index 100) until 1 January Year 1, and then increasing by 1½ points per month.

The profit and loss account for Situation 2 can now be compared with that for Situation 1, as shown on the facing page.

Redrawing the balance sheet, as in the next column, note that:

"MISCO" *Balance sheet at 31 December Year 1, Situation 2*

(*Situation 2* – after a year's trading with 18% inflation.)

		Year 1	Year 0
		£000	£000
Liabilities			
Ordinary share capital	[A]	1,000	1,000
Reserves	[B]	564	500
Ordinary shareholders' funds	[C]	1,564	1,500
5% Debenture 1987/90	[D]	600	600
Deferred tax	[E]	-	-
		2,164	2,100
Assets			
Fixed Assets			
Freehold land	[F]	200	200
Freehold buildings	[G]	380	400
Plant and machinery	[H]	795	750
		1,375	1,350
Current assets			
Stock	[J]	938	800
Debtors	[K]	1,142	1,000
		2,080	1,800
Current liabilities			
Creditors	[M]	705	600
Taxation	[N]	164	150
Dividends	[P]	100	100
Overdraft	[Q]	322	200
		1,291	1,050
Net current assets		789	750
		2,164	2,100

[B] Reserves would increase by an extra £14,000 retained profit.

[G] Depreciation on buildings would be unchanged at £20,000.

[H] Depreciation on machines would be unchanged, but the new machine purchased at 31 Dec Year 1 would now cost £295,000.

[J] Stock, unchanged in volume, would now be £938,000. The extra £138,000 would reduce the cost of goods sold and thus increase apparent profit by that amount.

[K] Debtors would increase by £142,000.

[M] Creditors would increase by £105,000.

"MISCO" *Profit and loss accounts for Year 1, Situations 1 and 2*

	Situation 1 (without inflation)		*Situation 2 (with inflation)*	
	£000	£000	£000	£000
Sales		6,000		6,412
Opening stock	800		800	
Purchases	4,800		5,268	
	5,600		6,068	
less Closing stock	800		938	
Cost of goods sold		4,800		5,130
Gross profit		1,200		1,282
Depreciation	270		270	
5% Debenture interest	30		30	
Other costs	600		654	
		900		954
Pre-tax profit		300		328
Taxation (say at 50%)		150		164
Profit after tax		150		164
Dividend		100		100
Retained profit		50		64

	£000
[N] The overdraft would increase by:	
[H] the cost of the new machine	295
[J] the increased stock	138
[K] increased debtors	142
	575
but would be reduced by:	
[G] depreciation on buildings	20
[H] depreciation on plant and machinery	250
[M] increase in creditors	105
[N] increase in taxation payable	14
and, assuming an unchanged dividend, by retained profits of £64,000	64
	453

The company's overdraft would therefore increase by £122,000 from £200,000 to £322,000.

It is, we hope, fairly obvious that MISCO could not go on borrowing indefinitely from the bank each year in order to replace assets, to finance increased working capital and to pay dividends. Indeed, with 18% inflation, the company's profits are somewhat illusory.

Tax relief

As discussed in Chapter 13, there are already two tax measures in operation which help offset the effects of inflation. The first measure, capital allowances, which were increased to 100% in the first year in 1972, are designed primarily to encourage capital investment but the second, stock relief, was introduced in the Finance Act 1975, specifically to ease the liquidity problems caused by inflation.

Their effect on MISCO in Situation 2 would be:

1. *Capital allowances* The full £295,000 cost of the new machine would be allowed in the year of purchase, against a provision for depreciation on plant and machinery of £250,000. The difference of £45,000, with Corporation Tax at 50%, would give a deferral of tax of £22,500.
2. *Stock relief* Deferral of tax is allowed on the increase in the value of stock, less 15% of taxable income from trading. In MISCO's case, taxable income from trading = pre-tax profits of £328,000 less £45,000 (the excess of capital allowances over depreciation) = £283,000, so tax deferred = 50% of (£138,000 – 15% of £283,000) = £47,775.

In the balance sheet an item of £70,000 "deferred taxation" would appear at [E] at the end of Year 1 as a source of capital, the figure for taxation would be reduced by the same amount and, when the tax fell due, that much less would be added to the overdraft to pay it. Even so, the overdraft would still increase year by year.

After one year of inflation at 18%, deferred tax would already represent almost 3% of capital employed. After several years of high inflation, such as the United Kingdom experienced in the mid-1970s, it was quite common to find deferred tax representing 20% or 25% of capital employed. Under SSAP 15, companies can now transfer to reserves any deferred taxation which they do not expect to have to pay in the foreseeable future.

Earlier forms of replacement cost accounting

Some companies realised a number of years ago that, even with the modest rates of inflation the United Kingdom experienced in the 1960s, the provision for depreciation was insufficient to cover the cost of replacements, and they therefore made additional provisions for this purpose. Doing so gave a more realistic picture of profitability, but it did not reduce the liability for taxation: the extra depreciation had to be provided for out of profits after tax.

Details of the methods vary, but the basic principle is to revalue fixed assets periodically and recalculate depreciation on the new values. MISCO, for example, might revalue all its five machines at the end of Year 1:

Number of machines	*Replacement cost*	*Age (years)*	*Adjusted depreciation to date (at 20% p.a.)*	*Revised book value*
1	£295,000	0	Nil	£295,000
1	£295,000	1	£59,000	£236,000
1	£295,000	2	£118,000	£177,000
1	£295,000	3	£177,000	£118,000
1	£295,000	4	£236,000	£59,000
5	£1,475,000		£590,000	£885,000

This increases the total book value of the machines by £90,000, and a corresponding credit would be made to reserves, while the depreciation for the year, calculated on the basis of 20% of the total replacement cost (new), would be £295,000, *i.e.*, just sufficient to pay for the new machine.

If MISCO had had a far wider range of plant and equipment than our simple five-machine example, it would be unlikely to go to the trouble and expense of revaluing every year, so an estimated amount of additional depreciation would be provided and placed in a "fixed asset replacement reserve" until the next revaluation.

You will notice that we haven't mentioned the replacement cost of the freehold industrial building: this involves the question of replacement cost *v.* market value, which we prefer to leave until later in this chapter.

CURRENT PURCHASING POWER ACCOUNTING (CPP)

An exposure draft, ED 8 – *Accounting for changes in the purchasing power of money* – was issued in 1973 recommending that companies adopt what has come to be known as current purchasing power accounting (CPP). The main features of ED 8 were that:

(*a*) companies would continue to keep their records and present their basic annual accounts in historical terms, *i.e.*, in terms of the value of the pound at the time of each transaction or revaluation;

(*b*) in addition, all listed companies would present to their shareholders a *supplementary statement* in terms of the value of the pound at the end of the period to which the accounts related;

(*c*) the conversion of the figures in the basic accounts into the figures in the supplementary statement should be by means of a general index of purchasing power of the pound (the Retail Price Index);

(*d*) directors should provide in a note to the supplementary statement an explanation of the basis on which it has been prepared, and should comment on the significance of the figures.

CPP accounting is concerned solely with removing the distorting effects of changes in the general purchasing power of money on accounts prepared in accordance with established practice (*i.e.*, on a historical cost basis). It does not deal with changes in the *relative* values of non-monetary items (which can and do occur in the absence of inflation).

Converting to CPP

The conversion of historical cost accounts to CPP accounts is a three-stage process.

Stage 1
To produce the corresponding figures for the previous year:

1. In the first year in which CPP accounts are produced, the items in the balance sheet at the end of the previous year are first converted into pounds of purchasing power at the end of the previous year. In our example, MISCO, there was no inflation up to 31 December Year 0, so Year 0's balance sheet is already in Year 0 pounds.
2. The previous year's balance sheet is then updated from pounds of purchasing power at the end of the previous year to pounds of purchasing power at the end of this year. This is done simply by multiplying each item by:

$$\frac{\text{Retail Price Index (RPI) at the end of the year}}{\text{RPI at the beginning of the year}}$$

To apply this to MISCO, take the Year 0 column from the Year 1, Situation 2 balance sheet on p. 148, and multiply each item by the factor 118/100 to update them to Year 1 pounds to produce *the Year 0 column* in the CPP balance sheet illustrated opposite.

Stage 2
Items in the balance sheet at the end of the year are converted into pounds of purchasing power at the end of the year:

1. *Monetary items,* which are assets, liabilities or capital which are fixed in terms of pounds regardless of changes in the purchasing power (marked * opposite), require no conversion.
2. *Non-monetary items* (marked † opposite) are adjusted for changes in the purchasing power of the pound since they were acquired or revalued.

In our MISCO example, converting the balance sheet in Situation 2 from the Year 1 historical cost figures shown in p. 148:

[F] and [G]. Freehold land and buildings are both multiplied by 118/100.

[H] Plant and machinery. The machines that are 1, 2, 3 and 4 years old, purchased at stable prices in Year 0 or earlier, and now written down in historical cost figures to £500,000, are multiplied by 118/100 = £590,000, and the brand new machine bought for £295,000 in Year 1 pounds remains unchanged, to give a total of £885,000.

[J] Stock. November's purchases of £466,000 at index 116½ are multiplied by 118/116½ = £472,000. Together with December's purchases of £472,000 already in year-end pounds, this gives a total of £944,000.

[C] Ordinary shareholders' funds (called "total equity interest" in CPP accounting) is the balancing item. It is neither a monetary nor a non-monetary item.

"MISCO" *CPP Balance Sheet at 31 December Year 1, Situation 2*
(*Situation 2* – After a year's trading with 18% inflation.)

		Year 1 £000	Year 0 £000
Liabilities			
Ordinary shareholders' funds	[C]	1,764	1,770
5% Debenture 1987/90	[D]	600*	708
		2,364	2,478
Assets			
Fixed Assets			
Freehold land	[F]	236†	236
Freehold buildings	[G]	448†	472
Plant and machinery	[H]	885†	885
		1,569	1,593
Current assets			
Stock	[J]	944†	944
Debtors	[K]	1,142*	1,180
		2,086	2,124
Current liabilities			
Creditors	[M]	705*	708
Taxation	[N]	164*	177
Dividends	[P]	100*	118
Overdraft	[Q]	322*	236
		1,291	1,239
Net current assets		795	885
		2,364	2,478

Stage 3
The CPP profit is computed by taking the change in shareholders' funds (adjusted for any change in equity capital) as the CPP retained profit (loss) and then working upwards through the profit and loss account to arrive, by calculation, at the pre-tax profit as the balancing figure.

In MISCO's case there was no change in the share capital; the change in shareholders' funds at [C] gives a retained loss of £6,000 and so:

	Year 1 (Historical cost basis) £000	Year 1 (CPP basis) £000
Pre-tax profits	328	258
Taxation	164	164
Profit after tax	164	94
Dividends	100	100
Retained profit	64	(6)

The reconciliation statement

CPP accounts then include a "reconciliation statement" to explain the difference between historical and CPP pre-tax profits. In MISCO's case this would work out as:

	Year 1 £000
Pre-tax profits (historical basis)	328
Adjustments:	
(i) Restatement of stock	(138)
(ii) Additional depreciation on assets	(49)
(iii) Gain in purchasing power on net monetary liabilities	117
Pre-tax profits (CPP basis)	258

Criticisms of CPP

Although, in MISCO's case, the CPP figures give a much better picture than historical cost, CPP accounts can be criticised on a number of grounds. Among these are:

1. Shareholders are faced with a choice between two sets of figures which frequently give very different results. Both cannot be correct. To this accountants respond "Both are correct: they are simply produced in accordance with different conventions".
2. CPP accounting enhances the profits of companies which are heavily borrowed, particularly those showing low profits on an historical cost basis. This is because assets on which little or perhaps no profit is being made are assumed by CPP to be increasing in value in line with inflation (*i.e.*, maintaining their real value), while the money borrowed to acquire them is declining in real value. The more heavily borrowed the company the more the profits will be boosted by CPP, as for example in GRAND METROPOLITAN's 1974 accounts, illustrated here.

GRAND METROPOLITAN *Extracts from 1974 accounts*

	£000
Ordinary shareholders' funds	429,436
less Goodwill	295,361
OSF net of goodwill	134,075
10% CULS 1991/96	121,114
Other loan capital	281,219
Bank overdrafts and short term borrowings	130,396
Total debt	532,729
Earnings per share (historical)	7.3p
Earnings per share (CPP basis)	35.2p

3. The retail price index is not an index of general purchasing power, which does not exist; and it may represent quite badly the effects of inflation upon a particular individual or company.
4. The reconciliation table reconciles figures which are in historical pounds with other figures which are in current purchasing pounds. What kind of pounds are the other pounds in the table? They merely represent numerical differences.

In the event, in spite of being adopted by quite a large number of public companies, CPP accounting was overtaken by the appointment of the Sandilands Committee.

CURRENT COST ACCOUNTING (CCA)

Sandilands and ED 18

In the summer of 1973, shortly before the closing date for comments on the exposure draft on CPP (ED 8), the Government announced that an independent Committee of Enquiry was to be set up to consider the various methods of adjusting company accounts. The Committee was eventually established under the chairmanship of Mr (now Sir) Francis Sandilands and its membership and terms of reference were announced early in 1974.

Provisional SSAP 7
It was expected that it would be some time before the Sandilands Committee could report, so the Accounting Standards Committee (ASC) decided to proceed with its work and prepare a provisional standard for approval by the relevant professional bodies. The standard (PSSAP 7) was described as provisional in view of the existence of the Sandilands Committee and did not involve the binding obligations imposed by other standards.

The recommendations of PSSAP 7 were followed by quite a large number of companies; and proposals for inflation accounting along similar lines were pursued in several other countries, in particular the United States, Canada and Australia.

The Sandilands Report
The Sandilands Committee reported to the Chancellor of the Exchequer and the Secretary for Trade in June 1975 and its report was published three months later: the Committee rejected the proposals contained in PSSAP 7, and recommended instead the development of a system to be known as current cost accounting (CCA).

ED 18
In response to the Sandilands recommendations, the Inflation Accounting Steering Group (IASG, or the "Morpeth Committee") was set up by the accountancy profession under the chairmanship of Mr Douglas Morpeth to coordinate the introduction of CCA, and its proposals for a system of CCA, endorsed by the Accounting Standards Committee, were published by the ASC as an Exposure Draft (ED 18) at the end of November 1976.

Fundamental concepts of CCA

Two concepts may be said to be fundamental to CCA:

(*a*) the separation of *operating profit* from *holding gains*;
(*b*) the statement in the balance sheet of assets and liabilities at their *value to the business*.

Operating profit
Operating profit is the profit which arises from trading operations after deducting:

(*a*) the cost of sales based on the value of the stock consumed at the time it was consumed;
(*b*) the charge for depreciation of fixed assets on the current cost value of those assets.

Holding gains
Holding gains arise through changes in the price of assets over time. They represent the difference between the "value to the business" of an asset at the time and its original cost (less depreciation). Another term for holding gain, used in ED 18, is *revaluation surplus*.

Value to the business
The value to the business of an asset is normally its written-down current replacement cost (current purchase price, less depreciation based on current purchase price). However, when the written-down current replacement cost is higher than both the economic value and the net realisable value, the value of the asset is taken to be the greater of the economic value and the net realisable value. This is probably easier to understand diagrammatically, as shown in Fig. 22.4 below.

Fig. 22.4 Calculation of "value to the business"

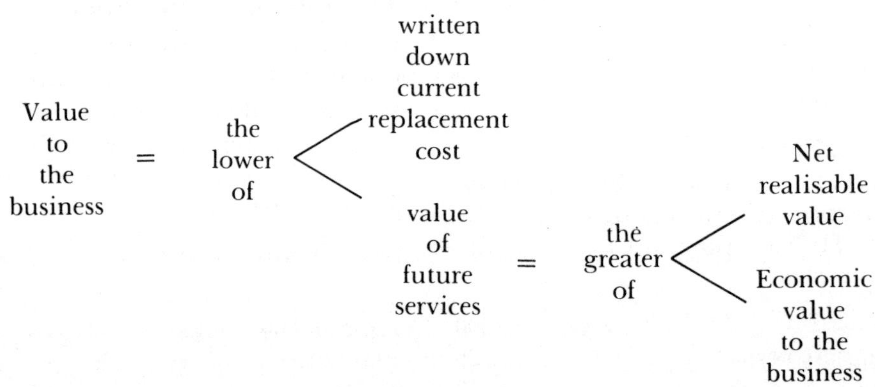

Economic value
Economic value is obtained by:

(*a*) forecasting the future cash flows from employing the asset *and*
(*b*) discounting these flows at a suitable rate of interest to produce the present value of those future cash flows.

Current cost profit
Current cost profit =
Operating profit
plus interest receivable;
minus interest payable;
plus share of associates' profit;
plus investment income.

CCA in practice

CCA is not a system of inflation accounting: it is not concerned with the value of money. The figures in this year's accounts are measured in this year's pounds; those in last year's in last year's pounds, which are not comparable in purchasing power any more than those of HC accounts.

Current cost accounts look very much like historical cost accounts: the difference lies behind the scenes in the accounting concepts upon which they are based. Indeed, it is only the Appropriation Account which looks different. The next few pages use the example of MISCO in Situation 2 (18% inflation) to show what a set of CCA accounts looks like and to explain briefly the workings involved.

MISCO's profit and loss and appropriation accounts for Situation 2 are shown opposite. Note:

Operating profit [X]:

		£000	£000
Historical cost trading profit (£328,000 pre-tax plus £30,000 interest paid)			358
Cost of sales adjustment	(i)	138	
Additional depreciation	(ii)	49	
			187
Operating profit under current cost convention			171

(i) Cost of sales adjustment:
As there was no change in the volume of stock during the year, the current cost of sales = the historical cost (HC) of purchases during the period:

	£000
Purchases during the period	5,268
HC accounts' cost of goods sold	5,130
Cost of sales adjustment	138

(ii) Additional depreciation:
(*a*) Freehold land and buildings:
As ED 18 recommended revaluation of property periodically, let us assume that MISCO had a revaluation carried out on 31 December Year 1:

	HC values	*Revaluation*
	£000	£000
Freehold land	200	236
Freehold buildings	380	448

As the freehold buildings have already been depreciated for 6 years out of an expected useful life of 25 years, the CCA depreciation charge is:

$$\frac{£448,000}{19} = £24,000$$

This gives an additional depreciation charge of £4,000.

(*b*) Plant and machinery:
The price of a new machine rose from £250,000 at 31 December Year 0 to £295,000 at 31 December Year 1. The CCA depreciation charge for Year 1 can be calculated in two ways:

1. On the end-of-year value:
5 machines at 20% of £295,000 = £295,000
2. On the average value during the period:
5 machines at 20% of £272,500 = £272,500

If the second method is used, the difference of £22,500, called "backlog depreciation", is charged to reserves. For MISCO we will use the first method, giving depreciation of £295,000, an excess of £45,000 over HC depreciation.
Total additional depreciation, including £4,000 on freehold buildings, = £49,000.

The appropriation account

In CCA the appropriation account brings together the current cost profit, the year's net surplus or deficit on the revaluation of assets, the appropriation to the revaluation reserve and the dividend. The remainder represents a transfer to or from free reserves.

Net surplus on revaluation of assets [Y]:

		£000
Land and buildings	(i)	108
Plant and machinery	(ii)	135
Stock	(iii)	144
		387

(i) Freehold land
(£236,000 - £200,000) £36,000
Freehold buildings
(£448,000 - (£400,000 - £24,000)) £72,000
(Present value - (31 Dec Year 0 value - CCA depreciation))

(ii) Plant and machinery:
The cost of a new machine has increased from £250,000 to £295,000, so:

	£000	£000
CCA book value at 31 December Year 1: £295,000 x (5/5 + 4/5 + 3/5 + 2/5 + 1/5)		885
CCA book value at 31 December Year 0: £250,000 x (5/5 + 4/5 + 3/5 + 2/5 + 1/5)	750	
less: Depreciation for Year 1 on the CCA year end value	295	
	455	
Add: Cost of new machine	295	
		750
Revaluation gain		135

(iii) Holding gain on *stock*. As the volume of stock is unchanged, holding gain = closing stock - opening stock = £944,000 - £800,000 = £144,000.

"MISCO" *CCA profit and loss and appropriation accounts for Year 1, Situation 2*

(*Situation 2* - After a year's trading with 18% inflation.)

Profit and loss account

		£000
Operating profit for the year	[X]	171
Interest payable		30
Current cost profit before taxation		141
Taxation		(164)
Current cost profit (loss) for the year		(23)

Appropriation account

Current cost profit (loss)		(23)
Net surplus arising from revaluation of assets	[Y]	387
Total surplus		364
Appropriation to revaluation reserve	[Z]	(387)
Net surplus available for distribution		(23)
Dividends		100
Added to (taken from) general reserve		(123)

Appropriation to revaluation reserve [Z]:
We have assumed that, in order to maintain the level of MISCO's business, the directors have appropriated an amount equal to the revaluation surplus (holding gains) for the year.

However, ED 18 left the directors to decide on the amount to be appropriated for the continuing needs of the business, giving them considerable scope for subjective judgement.

The revaluation reserve is shown separately from the general or free reserve - see MISCO's CCA balance sheet, shown here.

"MISCO" *CCA balance sheet at 31 December Year 1, Situation 2*

(*Situation 2* - After a year's trading with 18% inflation.)

		Year 1 £000	Year 0 £000
Liabilities			
Ordinary share capital	[A]	1,000	1,000
Revaluation reserve	[B1]	387	-
General reserve	[B2]	377	500
Ordinary shareholders' funds	[C]	1,764	1,500
5% Debenture 1987/90	[D]	600	600
		2,364	2,100
Assets			
Fixed assets			
Freehold land	[F]	236	200
Freehold buildings	[G]	448	400
Plant and machinery	[H]	885	750
		1,569	1,350
Current assets			
Stock	[J]	944	800
Debtors	[K]	1,142	1,000
		2,086	1,800
Current liabilities			
Creditors	[M]	705	600
Taxation	[N]	164	150
Dividends	[P]	100	100
Overdraft	[Q]	322	200
		1,291	1,050
Net current assets		795	750
		2,364	2,100

Subsidiary statements

Two subsidiary statements were envisaged by ED 18 in an attempt to bridge the gap between CCA and CPP, and to make CCA allow for inflation. They are:

(*a*) a statement of change in net equity interest;
(*b*) an analysis of the gain or loss on holding monetary liabilities and assets.

Statement of change in net equity interest
This statement measures the performance of the company in maintaining the value of its net assets by comparing their change during the year with the increase that would have been needed to maintain the purchasing power of the equity shareholders' funds. In MISCO's case:

	£000
Value of ordinary shareholders' funds at 1 January Year 1	1,500
Increase needed to compensate for the fall in the value of money during Year 1 (18% of £1,500,000)	270
	1,770
Value of ordinary shareholders' funds at 31 December Year 1	1,764
Gain (loss) in value, after ordinary dividends	(6)
Ordinary dividends	100
Total gain (loss) during the year, after allowing for the fall in the value of money	94

Gain (or loss) on monetary liabilities (or assets)
Where funds have moved between monetary and non-monetary items, the arithmetic is somewhat complicated. In MISCO's case, assuming last year's tax and dividends were paid immediately after the balance sheet date, the figures would work out along the following lines:

	£000
Long term liabilities (18% on £600,000 debenture)	108
Bank overdraft (18% on average overdraft of say £386,000)	69
Other (18% on the average of other net current assets of, say, £418,000)	(75)
Total gain	102

Interpreting current cost accounts

Ignoring for the moment the appropriation section, a CCA profit and loss account differs in only two ways from one prepared on a historical cost basis:

(*a*) The cost of sales is adjusted so that inputs of materials, work in progress and finished goods are charged out at their "value to the business" at the moment of sale – so that any holding gains are separated out, and the profit and loss account only shows the "operating profit".
(*b*) The charge for depreciation for the period is based on the "value to the business" of the assets in current terms, and not on their historical cost. This remedies the defect of HC accounts tending to understate depreciation in an inflationary period.

No adjustment is made in the current cost profit and loss account for the changing value of money, so that the corresponding figures are not expressed in pounds of the same purchasing power. Thus, in looking at, say, the figure for sales, one has to make a mental adjustment for changing prices in order to gain some idea of the change in business in volume terms. Unfortunately the Retail Price Index does not always provide a good index of the way in which prices in a particular business have changed. Indeed, most complex businesses would need a series of indices to show how their prices had changed for different products and services, and to show how their costs had changed.

This defect of non-comparable pounds becomes more apparent when one gets to five- or ten-year statements, and it is probably best to use ratio comparisons whenever possible.

In the *appropriation account,* ED 18 suggested that directors should explain the basis and the reasons for the amounts transferred to revaluation reserve. This might have encouraged them to explain what they propose to do with the amounts retained in the business which exceed those necessary to maintain it at its existing size. *i.e.*, to spell out their expansion plans.

Interpreting the statement of net change

Although the CCA balance sheet figure for the equity shareholders' funds does not represent the amount which would be available to them if the company was to be (i) sold as a going concern or (ii) wound up, it does provide us with the best estimate we have of the movement in the interest of equity shareholders when adjusted by the use of an index (the RPI being the most suitable available). But this makes the assumption that the value of the company's net assets should increase in line with the RPI in order to maintain the capital of the business.

Alternatively, it is perfectly reasonable for a company to think in terms of the specific assets it needs: to add up the value of the assets it needed for its business at the beginning of the year, to adjust the value of those assets to the year-end value using specific price indices, and to say that this is the capital it needs at the end of the year in order to maintain its position. Since the prices of individual assets are unlikely to move exactly in line with the RPI, this is likely to give a somewhat different (and some would say a more realistic) answer. It can also be argued that all the money for the increase in the specific price of the assets will not have to come from equity: some can be provided by increasing debt to maintain a constant Debt/Equity ratio.

THE HYDE REPORT

ED 18, although technically impressive and supported by formidable explanatory handbooks, was widely regarded as too complicated, too subjective, and some even felt that it was unauditable. This led to members of the Institute of Chartered Accountants in England and Wales voting at an extraordinary meeting that current cost accounting should not be made compulsory.

As a result of this extraordinary meeting, the Accounting Standards Committee set up the Hyde Committee, with the task of providing guidance, as an interim measure, on how information on the effects of inflation should be provided in the published accounts of listed companies.

The report of the Hyde Committee, entitled *Inflation Accounting – an Interim Recommendation by the Accounting Standards Committee*, was published in December 1977. It recommended that supplementary information should be provided in the form of three separate adjustments to the profits computed on a historical cost basis. Two of these, depreciation and cost of sales, are a simplified form of CCA and the third, gearing, was designed to take account of the effect of net monetary items:

1. *Depreciation* An adjustment should be made for the difference between the depreciation based upon the current cost of fixed assets and the depreciation charged in the HC accounts.
2. *Cost of sales* An adjustment should be made for the difference between the current cost of stock at the date of sale and the amount charged in the HC accounts.
3. *Gearing* The effect of gearing should be shown.

Depreciation adjustment

Where companies have not already developed methods of computing current cost depreciation, the charge may be computed by the use of appropriate industry or asset indices. In MISCO's case, assuming that the indices moved up 18% in the year, the additional depreciation for Year 1 would be £49,000, as calculated for CCA.

Cost of sales adjustment

Some companies may already have appropriate methods of computing the current cost of sales, for example using information from a standard costing system or from base stock or last-in-first-out methods, and if so they should continue to be used.

Otherwise the "averaging method" is recommended, in which the current cost of sales is computed by revising the historical cost of opening and closing stock to the average current cost for the year, using an appropriate index, as illustrated here for MISCO.

"MISCO" *Cost of sales adjustment by averaging method, Year 1, Situation 2*
(*Situation 2* – after a year's trading with 18% inflation.)

Historical cost data (from example on p. 149)	£000
Opening stock	800
Purchases	5,268
	6,068
less Closing stock	938
Cost of Sales	5,130

Index numbers for cost of stock:

1 January Year 1	100
31 December Year 1	118
Average for Year 1	109

To compute cost of sales adjustment:

(i) Revise opening and closing stock to the average current cost for the year:

$$\text{Opening stock} = £800{,}000 \times \frac{109}{100} = £872{,}000$$

$$\text{Closing stock} = £938{,}000 \times \frac{109}{118} = £866{,}000$$

(ii) Compute current cost of sales using the revised stock figures, and deduct HC cost of sales to obtain the cost of sales adjustment:

	£000
Opening stock	872
Purchases	5,268
	6,140
less Closing stock	866
Current cost of sales	5,274
Cost of sales (HC basis)	5,130
Cost of sales adjustment	144

Gearing adjustment

The total liabilities of the company should be compared with its total monetary assets. There are two possibilities: (1) total liabilities exceed total monetary assets *or* (2) monetary assets exceed total liabilities.

1. *If total liabilities exceed monetary assets,* so that part of the operating capability of the company is effectively financed by the net monetary liabilities, an adjustment should be made to reflect the extent to which the depreciation and cost of sales adjustments needn't be provided from current revenue. In this case it is necessary to compute:

$$\frac{\text{Net balance of monetary liabilities}}{\text{Net balance of monetary liabilities plus issued share capital and reserves}} = n$$

For this purpose, the reserves should include the difference between the current value and the HC amount of fixed assets and, if material, stocks, as illustrated for MISCO opposite. The gearing adjustment is then:

n × (depreciation adjustment + stock adjustment)

2. *Where monetary assets exceed total liabilities* an adjustment should be made to reflect the increase in the net monetary assets needed to maintain the scale of operation of the business.
This is done by multiplying the net balance of the monetary assets by the percentage change in the appropriate index during the accounting period.

Thus, the three adjustments recommended by the Hyde Report, as explained in the preceding paragraphs and applied to the case of MISCO in the accompanying examples, would work out for our imaginary company in Year 1 as follows:

	£000
Depreciation	49
Cost of sales	144
Gearing	(57)
Total	136

"MISCO" *Hyde gearing adjustment*

Referring to the HC balance sheet on p. 148 and the CCA balance sheet on p. 155, adjust the HC balance sheet for the difference between the current value and the HC value of:

		£000
Fixed assets (1,569 −1,375)	= 194	200
Stock (944 − 938)	= 6	

Adjusted HC balance sheet

Equity share capital and reserves	1,764
Long-term liabilities	600
Current liabilities	1,291
	3,655
Fixed assets	1,569
Stocks	944
Monetary assets	1,142
	3,655

To calculate the gearing adjustment

(i) Calculate net monetary liabilities:

Long-term liabilities	600
Current liabilities	1,291
Total liabilities	1,891
less Monetary assets	1,142
Net monetary liabilities	749

(ii) Add: issued share capital and reserves 1,764

2,513

(iii) Calculate the gearing proportion:

$$\frac{\text{Net monetary liabilities}}{\text{Net monetary liabilities + share capital and reserves}} = \frac{749}{2,513} = 29.8\%$$

(iv) Calculate the gearing adjustment:

Depreciation adjustment 49
+ Cost of sales adjustment 144 } =

193 × 29.8% = 57

WHERE DO WE GO NOW?

It is generally agreed that any system of inflation accounting should include adequate provision for the cost of replacing fixed assets and should deduct holding gains on stock in the calculation of pre-tax profits, but the assessment and treatment of any benefits derived from holding monetary liabilities in an inflationary period is still open to debate.

Taxation is also a problem: although 100% First Year Allowances give tax relief on the cost of replacing fixed assets, and stock relief is allowed on the increase in the monetary value of stock, both these reliefs are at present only deferrals of tax rather than reductions of tax liability. However, an increasing number of companies are now reducing or omitting to make provision for deferred tax, thus inflating their reported earnings per share and laying themselves open to supernormal tax charges if, in future years, they have to cut back on stocks and capital investment.

The Hyde Committee proposals, which have been endorsed by the Stock Exchange and the CBI, meet the urgent need for listed companies to supply basic information on the effects of changing prices, and provide a possible solution to the question of monetary assets and liabilities, but they are only an interim measure and still leave investors to choose for themselves which of two figures they believe to be "true" profits for the period. This is not a satisfactory long-term solution.

Further proposals are undoubtedly on the way but, after the set-back on ED 18, the introduction and adoption of a comprehensive system of CCA accounting will take well into the 1980s, and CCA is unlikely to become the sole system of accounting unless it is also adopted as the basis for company taxation.

Chapter 23

TRENDS AND RATIOS

This chapter deals with the calculation of trends and ratios, describing each ratio in turn with an indication of the size of ratio one would expect, while the next and final chapter, Chapter 24, contains a suggested pro-forma for analysis, with a line-by-line explanation of each item.

How to tackle the analysis

Now that we have been right through the balance sheet and profit and loss account explaining each component in detail, we come to the heart of the matter: how to set about analysing a report and accounts. We suggest this is best tackled in stages:

1. Take a quick look at the balance sheet and profit and loss account to get a general idea of the size of the company, its capital structure and its profitability. Also look at the historical summary (if provided) to see if the company is growing, cyclical, stagnant or declining, and look at the breakdown of turnover by activity and geographically if one is given. It is also worth while reading any "report to employees" that may be enclosed with the accounts, to help get a general picture of the company before getting down to any detail.
2. Read carefully through the chairman's statement and the directors' report, underlining any interesting points, and then go through the balance sheet and profit and loss account item by item, reading each accompanying "Note" as you go; put a circle round anything unusual. In particular, check the "statement of accounting policies" for anything abnormal and the auditor's report for any qualification or reservation.
3. The trends and ratios should now be calculated. In doing so the analyst should remain on the qui vive for interesting points and not allow himself to get mesmerised by number-crunching, because the figures produced at this stage are not an end in themselves. They are merely a means of helping the analyst assimilate what is happening in the company, providing him with pointers to the reasons behind good or poor performance, and they will often give warning of increasing risk or even of impending disaster.
4. The final stage is the interpretation of the trends and ratios, and the assessment of likely current profits and future prospects. Here the analyst should compare performance with that of similar companies and/or with the industry's averages (using ratios), and should consult other sources of information on the company and on the industry or industries in which the company operates.

The use of percentages and ratios

Any assessment of a company is likely to include a look at:

(*a*) the company's performance in previous years, and
(*b*) a comparison with other companies.

The use of percentages and of various ratios helps in the assessment of trends and in comparisons with other companies, and in particular may highlight aspects of a company that merit closer scrutiny.

Methods of relating items of information

There are four basic ways in which one item of financial information can be related to another:

1. A line-by-line comparison can be made of the current year's accounts with those of the previous year. This is sometimes called *horizontal analysis*.
2. The horizontal analysis can be extended over several years, usually by giving the figure for an item in the first year of the series a value of 100 and relating subsequent years' figures to base 100. This is sometimes termed *trend analysis*.
3. "Common size" balance sheets or income statements can be prepared, each balance sheet item being expressed as a percentage of the balance sheet total and each profit and loss account item as a percentage of sales or earnings. This is sometimes called *vertical analysis*.
4. *Ratios* can be produced by comparing one item in a balance sheet or profit and loss account with another for the same period, or with the current price of the company's shares.

TRENDS

Horizontal analysis – comparison with the previous year

This is possibly the simplest method of comparing one year's figures with another and involves working out the percentage change from the previous year of each main component of the accounts, as in Example 23.1 (ALLIED BREWERIES' 1974 profit and loss account).

Percentage changes in themselves may reveal a certain amount about a company's performance, but they are of most value in prompting further enquiry. The horizontal analysis in Example 23.1 might, for instance, prompt the following questions (letters in brackets refer to lines marked in the example):

[A] Why did *trading profit* fall 5.1% on a turnover which was up more than 20%? Does the directors' report provide an analysis of the various activities of the business and, if so, is one particular area causing the trouble or is it more general?

[B] Was the 13% increase in *finance charges* due to higher borrowings or to higher interest rates or to a combination of both?

[C] Why did *taxation* rise 14% on pre-tax profits down 6.3%? How much of this was due to a change in tax rates? Is part of the increase overseas tax?

[D] *Minority interests* are down 36.7%. Were any subsidiaries sold off during the year, or

Example 23.1 Horizontal analysis of profit and loss account: ALLIED BREWERIES LTD

	1973	1974	*% change*	
	£000	£000		
Turnover	492,800	594,067	+20.5	[A]
Trading profit	66,792	63,390	− 5.1	[A]
Investment income	4,286	4,867	+13.6	
Associated companies	1,055	1,064	+ 0.8	
	72,133	69,321	− 3.9	
Finance charges	9,133	10,319	+13.0	[B]
Profit before taxation	63,000	59,002	− 6.3	[C]
Taxation	25,941	29,562	+14.0	[C]
Profit after taxation	37,059	29,440	−20.6	
Minority interests	703	445	−36.7	[D]
	36,356	28,995	−20.2	
Preference dividends	439	410	− 6.6	
Earned for ordinary and deferred ordinary shares	35,917	28,585	−20.4	
Ordinary dividends	11,498	13,429	+16.8	[E]
Transfer to revenue reserves	24,419	15,156	−37.9	

minority interests bought out? Are any subsidiaries making a loss? (A loss-making foreign subsidiary, or a loss-making UK subsidiary that is less than 75% owned, would also aggravate the tax position).

[E] Does the 16.8% rise in *dividends* reflect board confidence in the future, or was the share capital increased during the year? Or perhaps the interim dividend was increased but the final only maintained, reflecting a downturn in confidence.

These are the sort of questions that should be asked, and answered, by an alert analyst.

Horizontal analysis – half-yearly comparison

The fact that a company's annual figures for sales and profits show an increase on the previous year doesn't always mean that the company's performance is on a rising trend: it may have peaked out *during* the year.

This can be checked quite quickly by looking at the separately published interim results. If the increase over the previous year's first half is larger than the increase for the year as a whole, then there must have been a slowdown in the second half (Example 23.2).

Notice that in Example 23.2 we have compared each half-year in 1977 with the *corresponding* period in the previous year. This is because most businesses are to some extent seasonal, *i.e.*, sales and profits are not evenly distributed between the first and second half. (For example, building materials suffer in the winter, and non-food retailers benefit heavily from Christmas.) Comparison of the second half of a year with the first half can therefore be misleading: in our example the improvement in the first half was clearly not maintained in the second half, although the results for the two half-years of 1977 were very similar.

Example 23.2 Horizontal analysis and comparison of interim figures

	1976	1977	*Change*
	£000	£000	
Year's sales	3,425	3,764	+ 9.9%
Year's pre-tax profits	595	651	+ 9.4%

but the *interim* figures showed:

1st-half sales	1,470	1,880	+ 21.1%
1st-half pre-tax profits	213	316	+ 48.3%

Few companies show their second-half figures, so they have to be obtained by subtracting the interim figures from the full year's figures. In this case:

2nd-half sales	1,955	1,884	– 3.6%
2nd-half pre-tax profits	382	335	– 12.3%

Trend analysis – comparison over several years

Where comparison of a single company's figures is made over more than two years, the normal method is to take the earliest year's figure as 100 and scale subsequent years accordingly, *i.e.*, divide each year's figure by that for the first year, and multiply the result by 100 (Example 23.3).

Example 23.3 Trend analysis: ALLIED BREWERIES LTD

	1970	1971	1972*	1973	1974
Turnover (£m)	384.4	434.5	423.3	492.8	594.1
Index (1970 = 100)	100	113.0	110.1	128.2	154.6

(*Adjusted from a 53-week period.)

Seeing that turnover fell marginally in 1972 might encourage the analyst to examine the trading profit trend:

	1970	1971	1972*	1973	1974
Trading profits (£m)	39.1	46.9	55.4	66.8	63.4
Index (1970 = 100)	100	119.9	141.7	170.8	162.1

(*Adjusted from a 53-week period.)

The fact that trading profits went on rising satisfactorily in 1972 suggests that Allied Breweries may have been concentrating on improving profit margins rather than volume, or had perhaps discontinued some low profitability activities. Reference would need to be made to the 1972 accounts if the analyst wished to pursue this point. (One possible cause was, in fact, extensive rationalisation of the company's public houses in that year).

The use of published historical summaries

Although the five- or ten-year summaries usually included in companies' reports and accounts need to be approached with caution, as we discussed in Chapter 19, most companies go to a good deal of trouble to present as fair a picture *as is possible on a historical cost basis,* and so the published summary can be very useful for a quick analysis of trends, even if slower and more detailed research is subsequently needed.

However, the main drawback to any analysis of trends over several years in times of high inflation is that the figures can be very misleading, with static or even declining performances in *real* terms appearing to have an upward trend in the reported figures.

In using historical cost figures, and pending a generally agreed method of inflation accounting (*see* Chapter 22), a rough idea of the effects of inflation can be gained by comparing the trend of turnover and trading profit with the trend in the Retail Price Index (*see* Appendix 3). Continuing with Allied Breweries in Example 23.4, we have adjusted the Retail Price Index to 100 at the end of September 1970 to coincide with the company's year end.

This admittedly is a very crude adjustment, but it certainly brings the figures much closer to the real state of affairs than no adjustment at all: turnover remained pretty static, while profits rose nicely until 1974, when they dipped sharply.

We will be discussing ratios later in this chapter, but it is perhaps worth pointing out here that where both the items in a ratio are expressed in terms of the currency at the time of reporting, dividing one by the other removes the direct effect of inflation. For example, the ratio of Allied Breweries' trading profit to turnover shows how profit margins slipped in 1974, in Example 23.5.

Trends in rates of growth

One last point before we leave horizontal analysis: the question of growth rates. If the rate of growth is fast, the figures reported year by year can give the impression that the company's growth is accelerating when it is, in fact, slowing down. Consider, for example, the figures of "MIRACLE GROWTH LTD" in Example 23.6.

It is true that the increase in profits each year has been greater than the increase in the previous year in simple or absolute terms, but the compound or percentage growth rate has actually been slowing down each year.

Example 23.4 Trend analysis with adjustment for inflation by RPI: ALLIED BREWERIES LTD

	1970	1971	1972	1973	1974
Turnover	100	113.0	110.1	128.2	154.6
Trading profit	100	119.9	141.7	170.8	162.1
Retail Price Index	100	109.9	117.6	128.5	150.5
Turnover / Retail Price Index	100	102.8	93.6	99.8	102.7
Trading profit / Retail Price Index	100	109.1	120.5	132.9	107.7

Example 23.5 Trading profit/Turnover ratio: ALLIED BREWERIES LTD

	1970	1971	1972	1973	1974
Turnover (£m)	384.4	434.5	423.3	492.8	594.1
Trading profit (£m)	39.1	46.9	55.4	66.8	63.4
Trading profit / Turnover	10.2%	10.8%	13.1%	13.5%	10.6%

Example 23.6 Horizontal analysis of fast growth: "MIRACLE GROWTH LTD"

	1972	1973	1974	1975	1976
Pre-tax profits (£000)	100	130	166	210	260
Year's increase (£000)		30	36	44	50
Percentage increase over previous year		30.0%	27.7%	26.5%	23.8%

Vertical analysis

So far we have discussed only working across the page, comparing each item with the previous year to get the percentage change, or looking at several years to see the trend of an item. If we work vertically, calling the total 100, we can construct "common size" statements giving a percentage breakdown of the account items, as in Example 23.7.

The advantages of this method are, firstly, that the items are reduced to a common scale for inter-company comparisons and, secondly, that changes in the financial structure and profitability of a company can be seen in relation to the capital employed. For example, the change in Allied Breweries' investments and loans between 1973 and 1974 represented a fall of 6.1% of the net assets of the company, while provisions for retirement benefits rose by 3.7% of the company's financing. Had these percentages been expressed in absolute terms – year on year change – they would have been "investments and loans –48.3%" and "provisions for retirement benefits +137.5%", and the perspective of these two movements in relation to the size of the company would have been lost.

Taking a more acute example of the drawback of plain percentage changes (horizontal analysis), a large company with an overdraft of say £100 one year and £1,000 the next would throw up a percentage change of 900%, while a change from zero overdraft would be an infinite percentage change.

The use of vertical analysis over several years helps to show how the financial structure of a company is changing, and it is possible to infer quite a lot from such an analysis even if one has no access to the full accounts of earlier years.

Taking Allied Breweries' capital structure over five years (Example 23.8 opposite), and beginning with the first four lines:

[A] Ordinary shareholders' funds (OSF) as a percentage of capital employed didn't change much between 1970 (54.6%) and 1974 (54.3%), *but*

[B] ordinary capital went up by over 50% in 1972, with no corresponding rise in OSF and a downward movement in reserves, suggesting a scrip issue rather than a rights issue at par (which would have added the same amount to OSF) or a rights issue at a premium (which would have added to reserves as well); in fact a 1-for-2 scrip issue was made in February 1972.

[C] Reserves did, however, jump in 1973. This looks like a revaluation of assets, because we know there was no huge increase in retained profits, and the opportunity was

Example 23.7 Vertical analysis of a balance sheet: ALLIED BREWERIES LTD

			Common size statements	
	1973	1974	1973	1974
	£000	£000	%	%
Assets employed				
Fixed assets	397,091	419,357	80.0	86.8
Investments and loans	64,255	33,218	13.0	6.9
Associated companies	2,547	3,402	0.5	0.7
Net current assets	32,338	27,126	6.5	5.6
	496,231	483,103	100.0	100.0
Financed by				
Share capital	125,948	127,206	25.4	26.4
Share premium	3,519	3,372	0.7	0.7
Reserves	190,694	157,594	38.4	32.6
Shareholders' funds	320,161	288,172	64.5	59.7
Loan capital	125,419	128,155	25.3	26.5
Provisions for retirement benefits	12,741	30,255	2.6	6.3
Deferred taxation	35,033	34,264	7.1	7.1
Minority interests	2,877	2,257	0.5	0.4
	496,231	483,103	100.0	100.0

Example 23.8 Five-year review of capital employed: ALLIED BREWERIES LTD

Year ending September		1970		1971		1972		1973		1974	
		£m	%	£m	%	£m	%	£m	%	£m	%
Ordinary capital	[B]	75.7	23.6	75.9	22.1	116.0	29.4	116.9	23.6	118.2	23.0
Reserves	[C], [D]	126.2	39.3	128.0	37.3	110.4	28.0	194.3	39.1	161.0	31.3
Intangibles		-26.8	-8.3	-27.7	-8.0	-27.3	-6.9	-	-	-	-
Ordinary shareholders' funds	[A]	175.1	54.6	176.2	51.4	199.1	50.5	311.2	62.7	279.2	54.3
Preference capital		9.0	2.8	9.0	2.6	9.0	2.3	9.0	1.8	9.0	1.7
Provisions	[E]	0.3	0.1	12.9	3.8	13.3	3.4	12.7	2.6	30.2	5.9
Minorities		2.0	0.6	2.6	0.8	2.2	0.6	2.9	0.6	2.3	0.5
Tax equalisation account	[F]	9.0	2.8	11.9	3.5	17.1	4.3	20.9	4.2	28.5	5.5
Deferred Corporation Tax		12.2	3.8	11.2	3.2	11.2	2.8	14.1	2.8	5.7	1.1
Loan capital	[G]	113.3	35.3	119.2	34.7	142.2	36.1	125.4	25.3	128.2	24.9
Overdraft	[G]	-	-	-	-	-	-	-	-	31.5	6.1
Capital employed	[H]	320.9	100.0	343.0	100.0	394.1	100.0	496.2	100.0	514.6	100.0

		1970	1971	1972	1973	1974
RPI for September		141.5	155.5	166.4	181.8	212.9
Adjusted capital employed	[J]	320.9	312.1	335.1	386.2	342.0
Debt/Equity ratio	[K]	0.65	0.68	0.71	0.40	0.57

taken to write off all remaining goodwill (Intangibles: arising from paying more than book value for acquisitions).

[D] But in 1974 reserves fell again: something must have been revalued downwards or a loss taken; revaluing downwards the year after revaluing upwards is unusual for a prudently run company, so it was probably an exceptional loss, as we know Allied traded profitably. (In fact the company's 26% stake in TRUST HOUSE FORTE was sold in October 1974 at a loss of just under £31½ million, and was bought back the following day – "bed-and-breakfasted", a device that has since lost its advantages for company taxation purposes).

Moving further down the review:

[E] Provisions jumped in 1974, explained in the 1974 accounts by a transfer of £18 million from revenue reserves for retirement benefits.

[F] Tax equalisation account, deferred tax due mainly to capital allowances exceeding depreciation, has grown steadily, indicating continued capital investment.

[G] The proportion of finance provided by loan capital has fallen, but the company suddenly ran up an overdraft in 1974. A glance at previous years shows that running an overdraft is not normal practice for Allied Breweries, and the reason should be investigated (in fact it was a £42½ million jump in stocks: is this going to escalate and leave the company hard pressed for cash?). In this context Chapter 5 goes into the question of a company's ability to increase borrowings, but a useful indication can be gained by comparing total borrowings with ordinary shareholders' funds, the Debt/Equity ratio [K], one of the key ratios we will now go on to discuss.

One final general point though, before leaving the five-year review: capital employed [H] appears to have grown considerably between 1970 and 1974, helped by the 1973 property revaluation. However, the picture looks rather different if a simple adjustment is made for inflation by *dividing* the capital employed at the end of each year by the Retail Price Index for September each year (taken from Appendix 3) and by *multiplying* it by the Retail Price Index for September 1970. Although this is admittedly very crude, the adjusted figures [J] do show that, in real terms, the company's capital employed is probably fairly static. This is no reflection on Allied Breweries, for many companies are declining in real terms and large companies, whose scope for expansion is limited by their sheer size if not by the Monopolies Commission, do well to hold their own under adverse economic conditions.

It is interesting to see from Appendix 3 how long the Index took to rise a given percentage from its 1962 base, compared with the time taken to reach the same level from the rebasement at 100 in January 1974:

Percentage Rise	*1962 Index*	*1974 Index*
35% (*i.e.*, to 135)	8 years	18 months
70% (*i.e.*, to 170)	11 years	3 years

THE USE OF RATIOS

Choice of ratios

With both a balance sheet and a profit and loss account each containing a minimum of ten to twenty items, the scope for comparing one item with another is enormous, so it is important to be selective, both to limit the calculations required and, more importantly, to make the presentation of the selected ratios simple and readily understandable. No decision-maker wants a jungle of figures, so the ratios chosen should be the key ones, logically grouped.

Logical grouping

Ratios can conveniently be divided into three main groups:

1. *Operating ratios*, which are concerned with how the company is trading, and take no account of how the company is financed.
2. *Financial ratios*, which measure the financial structure of the company and show how it relates to the trading activities.
3. *Investment ratios*, which relate the number of ordinary shares and their market price to the profits, dividends and assets of the company.

In describing these ratios we give what we regard as the most useful and practical definition of each component. Although there is an increasing trend towards standardisation, individual analysts do not always agree on definitions, while companies do not all define ratio components in the same way, and some even "misname" items in their accounts: MARKS & SPENCER, for example, until 1977 labelled pre-tax profit "operating profit", a term which is usually regarded as synonymous with trading profit.

Some companies include a table of key ratios in their report and accounts, *e.g.*, MARLEY in their five-year review, shown in the next column.

These can be useful for looking at trends within the company concerned, but it is preferable to work out one's own ratios by a standard method, so that they form a fair basis for inter-company comparisons. Marley, for example, have never provided for deferred taxation, so the figures they give for earnings per share may not be directly comparable with the e.p.s. of other companies.

MARLEY *Extract from five-year review*

Ratios	1972	1973	1974	1975	1976
Borrowings as % of total capital	24.8%	21.8%	24.0%	23.3%	24.5%
Return on total capital	22.8%	27.4%	20.7%	18.2%	24.9%
Earnings per share	6.8p	9.3p	8.1p	5.9p	11.8p

Typical ratio values

Useful general guidance on the ratio values one might expect to find in various sectors of UK industry is contained in a book called *Industrial Performance Analysis* published annually by Inter Company Comparisons Ltd. Example 23.9 shows an extract from the aggregated balance sheet and profit and loss account data it gives, together with key ratios calculated from this data. Analysts using this book should be careful to note the definitions of each ratio component, and in particular that "total assets" includes goodwill and that "capital employed" does not include overdraft.

Ratios and inflation

As we mentioned earlier, when discussing published historical summaries, where *both* items in a ratio are *monetary* and are expressed in terms of pounds of approximately the same date, dividing one term by the other removes the direct effect of inflation.

For example, Wages/Turnover can fairly be compared from year to year, but Trading profit/Capital employed is distorted to some extent unless fixed assets are revalued or adjusted annually.

Example 23.9 Extracts from Industrial Performance Analysis

The Chemicals and Plastics Industry
Balance Sheet/Profit & Loss

1976/77 Manufacturing

	Toiletries & cosmetics £m	%	Chemicals £m	%	Plastics processors £m	%	Rubber manf. £m	%	Pharma-ceutical manf. £m	%	Paint & printing ink manf. £m	%	Plastics packaging £m	%	Sector totals £m
Fixed assets			**796**	40.0	**153**	39.8	**503**	35.1	**364**	37.4	**148**	27.6	**102**	37.3	**2066**
Stocks			**548**	27.8	**89**	23.2	**456**	31.8	**287**	29.5	**171**	31.8	**71**	25.9	**1622**
Debtors			**532**	26.9	**113**	29.4	**396**	27.6	**253**	26.0	**176**	32.8	**93**	33.9	**1563**
Other current assets			**96**	4.9	**29**	7.6	**78**	5.5	**70**	7.1	**42**	7.8	**8**	2.9	**323**
Total assets			**1972**	100.0	**384**	100.0	**1433**	100.0	**974**	100.0	**537**	100.0	**274**	100.0	**5574**
Current liabilities			**704**	35.7	**153**	39.8	**596**	41.6	**365**	37.5	**208**	38.7	**117**	42.7	**2143**
Capital employed			**1268**	64.3	**231**	60.2	**837**	58.4	**609**	62.5	**329**	61.3	**157**	57.3	**3431**
Total			**1972**	100.0	**384**	100.0	**1433**	100.0	**974**	100.0	**537**	100.0	**274**	100.0	**5574**
Sales			**2588**		**525**		**2017**		**1079**		**807**		**464**		**7480**
Pretax profit			**232**		**41**		**96**		**132**		**55**		**42**		**598**
Exports			**550**		**101**		**352**		**275**		**85**		**72**		**1435**

The Chemicals and Plastics Industry
Chemicals

Rounded totals and weighted averages for 56 companies year ended 7 April

			1976/77	**1975/76**	**1974/75**
Profitability	Profit before tax	£m	232	118	194
	Total assets	£m	1972	1608	1465
	Profit/total assets	%	11.7	7.4	13.2
Profit margin	Profit before tax	£m	232	118	194
	Sales	£m	2588	1956	1859
	Profit/sales	%	8.9	6.1	10.4
Capital usage	Sales	£m	2588	1956	1859
	Total assets	£m	1972	1608	1465
	Sales/total assets	ratio	1.3	1.2	1.3
Return on capital	Profit before tax	£m	232	118	194
	Capital employed	£m	1268	1067	930
	Profit/capital employed	%	18.3	11.1	20.8
Liquidity	Current assets	£m	1176	920	843
	Current liabilities	£m	704	540	535
	Current ratio		1.7	1.7	1.6
Stock turnover	Sales	£m	2588	1956	1859
	Stocks	£m	548	434	404
	Sales/stocks	ratio	4.7	4.5	4.6
Credit period	Debtors	£m	532	399	357
	Sales	£m	2584	1953	1855
(55 companies)	Collection period	days	75	75	70
Export ratio	Exports	£m	550	386	415
	Sales	£m	1981	1499	1421
(50 companies)	Exports/sales	%	27.8	25.8	29.2

OPERATING RATIOS

Most well run companies of any size make extensive use of ratios internally, to monitor and ensure the efficient running of each division or activity.

Companies are not, however, obliged to publish more than overall turnover and profit figures, a limited range of other profit and loss account information, and a geographical analysis of turnover and trading results of operations outside the United Kingdom (*see* Chapter 12).

It is thus usually impossible to make any detailed analysis of operations, although some companies include further information on turnover, net assets and profitability by principal activities or market segments; in addition resort can be made to Companies House for accounts filed by subsidiaries, although these can be misleading if goods and services have been transferred within the group at unrealistic prices or if major adjustments have been made on consolidation. In any case, the accounts of subsidiaries are often not filed at Companies House until some considerable time after the group accounts have been published.

Main operating ratios

1. $\frac{\textbf{Trading profit}}{\textbf{Sales (Turnover)}}$ expressed as a percentage.

where *Trading profit* = profit before interest charges and tax; investment income and the company's share of the profits of associated companies are not included.

and *Sales (Turnover)* = Sales (excluding transactions within the group).

This ratio gives what analysts term the profit margin on sales; a normal figure for a manufacturing industry would be between 8% and 10%, while high volume/low margin activities like food retailing can run very satisfactorily at around 3%. This profit margin is not the same thing as the gross profit margin (the difference between selling price and the cost of the goods sold, expressed as a percentage of selling price) which is unobtainable from most published accounts.

Unusually low margins can be set deliberately by management to increase market share or can be caused by expansion costs, *e.g.*, new product launching, but in general depressed margins suggest poor performance.

Somewhat better-than-average margins are normally a sign of good management, but unusually high margins may mean that the company is "making a packet" and will attract more competition unless there are barriers to entry (*e.g.*, huge initial capital costs, high technology, patents or other special advantages enjoyed by the company). A good example of high margins attracting competition occurred in fitted kitchen furniture in the early 1970s: WRIGHTON, who had been long-established specialists in the business, with a well earned reputation for excellent quality at reasonable prices, reaped the initial benefit as business boomed and reported rising margins:

Year to 31 March	1971	1972	1973
Sales (£000)	3,347	4,096	5,684
Trading profit (£000)	234	364	731
Trading profit ÷ Sales	7.0%	8.9%	12.9%

Fitted kitchen furniture became a conspicuously good growth area, leading to intensified marketing effort by HYGENA and DAINTYMAID, both backed by large parent companies, and by the entry of SCHREIBER, the largest UK furniture manufacturer, and MAGNET JOINERY, door and window manufacturers with about 100 of its own depot outlets in the United Kingdom (before the merger with SOUTHERNS EVANS).

Wrighton's subsequent margins tell the tale of fierce competition and a downturn in housebuilding:

Year to 31 March	1971	1972	1973	1974	1975
Sales (£000)	3,347	4,096	5,684	7,007	6,876
Trading profit (£000)	234	364	731	705	338
Trading profit / Sales	7.0%	8.9%	12.9%	10.1%	4.9%

Trading profit margins are also important in that both management and investment analysts usually base their forecasts of future profitability on projected turnover figures multiplied by estimated future margins.

An alternative definition of trading profit, used by some analysts, is *before* deducting depreciation, the argument being that different depreciation policies distort inter-company comparisons. If this approach is used, then trading profit should also be *before* deducting hire charges, to bring a company that leases rather than owns plant and machinery on to a comparable basis. Our view is that depreciation is a cost and should be deducted in any calculation of profit; we therefore prefer to deal with cases where a company's depreciation charge seems unduly low (or high) by making an adjustment, rather than by adding back every company's depreciation charge.

2. $\dfrac{\textbf{Trading profit}}{\textbf{Capital employed}}$

= **Return on Capital Employed** (ROCE), expressed as a percentage.

This is a most important measure of profitability, for several reasons:

(*a*) A low return on capital employed can easily be wiped out in a downturn.
(*b*) If the figure is lower than the cost of borrowing, increased borrowings will reduce earnings per share (e.p.s.) unless the extra money can be used in areas where the ROCE is higher than the company's average.
(*c*) It serves as a guide to the company in assessing possible acquisitions and in starting up new activities – if their potential ROCE isn't attractive, they should be avoided.
(*d*) Similarly, a persistently low ROCE for any part of the business suggests it could be a candidate for disposal if it isn't an integral part of the business.

ROCE can be calculated either for the company overall or for its trading activities:

Capital employed (in trading) = Share capital + reserves – intangibles + all borrowings including bank overdraft + minority interests + deferred liabilities – associates and investments. Government grants are not included.

Capital employed (overall) Associates and investments are not deducted, while the *overall profit* figure includes income from investments and the company's share of the profits of associated companies, in addition to trading profit.

The figure for capital employed should, strictly speaking, be the average capital employed during the year, but for simplicity's sake it is normally satisfactory to use the capital employed at the end of the year unless there have been major changes. Some companies label the total at the bottom of their balance sheet as "capital employed", but using this figure can be deceptive, in that bank overdrafts and loans repayable within twelve months are netted out against current assets, giving a company that has perhaps an embarrassingly large short-term debt a better ROCE than a company whose debt is more prudently funded long-term.

Another variation used by some analysts is to deduct any cash from the overdraft or, where a company has a net cash position, to deduct net cash in calculating capital employed. Netting out cash against overdraft can be justified where cash and overdraft are both with the same bank and the bank is known to calculate interest on the net figure (overdraft – cash), but in general our view is that if a company feels it prudent to operate with a large cash margin it should be measured accordingly, and that if the company's cash is locked up somewhere (for example, if it has arisen from retaining profits overseas to avoid UK taxation) the situation should be reflected in the ratio.

For example, RUGBY PORTLAND CEMENT showed the following details in its consolidated balance sheet in 1974:

Balance at bankers, money at call and cash in hand	£16,147,220
Bank overdraft	£ 3,343,945

but did not disclose the whereabouts of the amounts involved; we would therefore think it wrong to net out the bank overdraft in this case.

Any upward revaluation of property is likely to reduce ROCE in two ways:

(*a*) it will increase capital employed (the surplus on revaluation being credited to capital reserve), and
(*b*) it will probably increase the depreciation charge, and thus reduce profits.

Similarly, a company that shows government grants as a liability and uses them to offset against the depreciation charges over the life of the assets concerned will show a poorer return on capital employed than a company which shows assets net of any government grants. We recommend that government grants should *not* be included in capital employed, on the grounds that the original investment decision to purchase any asset was (or should have been) made on a net-of-grants basis.

3. $\dfrac{\textbf{Sales (Turnover)}}{\textbf{Capital employed (in trading)}}$

expressed as a multiple.

A rising ratio usually indicates an improvement in performance, *i.e.*, the amount of business being done is increasing in relation to the capital base, but beware of an improvement in the ratio achieved when a company fails to keep its plant and machinery up to date; depreciation will steadily reduce the capital base and improve the ratio without any improvement in sales. Beware, too, of any rapid increase in the ratio, which may well be a warning signal of overtrading, *i.e.*, trying to do too much business with too little capital.

In inter-company comparisons care should be taken to compare like with like: the ratio can be misleading unless the operations of the companies concerned are similar in their activities as well as in their products. For example, a television manufacturing group which is vertically integrated (makes the tubes, electronic circuits and the cabinets and then puts them together) will have much more capital employed than a company which merely assembles bought-out components.

A better measure of performance is that of value added compared with capital employed, but value added cannot normally be found from published information, although the number of companies including a value added statement in their accounts is increasing. Because of the difference in operations that can occur in apparently similar companies we would place more importance on our previous ratio (Trading profit/Capital employed) than on the ratio of Sales/Capital employed.

Our first three ratios are, of course, interrelated:

$$\frac{\text{Trading profit}}{\text{Sales (Turnover)}} \times \frac{\text{Sales (Turnover)}}{\text{Capital employed}}$$

$$= \frac{\text{Trading profit}}{\text{Capital employed}}$$

and the equation helps to illustrate the four ways in which management can increase trading profit in relation to capital employed:

by increasing the first factor by

(*a*) reducing costs
(*b*) raising prices
} by higher profit margins

by increasing the second factor by

(*c*) increasing sales volume
(*d*) reducing capital employed
} by higher output per £1 of capital

The healthy way of reducing capital employed is to dispose of low profitability/high capital parts of the business when this can be done without adversely affecting the remainder, but there is another way of producing the same optical effect other than by running down capital investment, and this is to lease rather than buy premises, plant and machinery (or to sell and lease back fixed assets already owned).

We say optical effect, because if leasing is for long periods, as one would expect for a continuing business, the rental is a fixed charge just as much as interest on the debt that would have been incurred had the property or plant been purchased. Furthermore, although interest rates can fluctuate in either direction, most property rents are subject to periodic reviews that can put the rent up but not down (the technical term is a "ratcheted" rent review, meaning that if the market rate is less than the rent when reviewed the rent stays the same).

Further operating ratios

The choice of further operating ratios depends on what aspect is being examined and the information available. We have chosen four which deal with the size of working capital items (Stocks, Debtors, Creditors and Working capital itself) in relation to Sales, and finally one measuring trading profit as a percentage of wages and salaries.

4. $$\frac{\textbf{Stocks}}{\textbf{Sales (Turnover)}}$$

expressed as a percentage.

Stocks comprise stocks of materials, purchased components, work in progress (net of progress payments) and finished goods.

Except when stocks are built up in anticipation of sharp price rises, well-run companies usually try to carry the minimum stock needed for the satisfactory running of their business: they do so to minimise interest charges on the money tied up in stocks, to save the costs of extensive storage and to reduce the risk of being left with goods that can't be sold due to deterioration, becoming obsolete or going out of fashion. Although some distortion can occur with accelerating growth, because stock is a year-end figure while sales occur throughout the year (on average six months earlier), a rising stock ratio without any special reason is regarded as bad news, reflecting lack of demand for goods and/or poor stock control. A high ratio in comparison to similar companies is undesirable although Stocks/Turnover ratios vary enormously with the nature of a business. At one end of the scale, and apart from advertising agencies and other service industries, ready-mixed concrete companies probably have one of the lowest Stocks/Turnover figures of any industry: aggregates are extracted from the ground when required and the product is delivered the same day, so all that is needed in stock is a supply of fresh cement and fuel, giving a typical Stocks/Turnover figure of 5%. At the other end of the scale a company which maintains depots of finished goods and replacement parts worldwide, like a power transmission and mechanical handling systems manufacturer, can reasonably be expected to have a ratio as high as 50% in order to maintain a first-class service to its customers all over the world.

For an average manufacturing company a Stocks/Turnover ratio of around 25–30% would be reasonable, increasing the larger and more complex the goods made; for instance, a helicopter manufacturer might have stocks and WIP representing 60–70% of turnover and this level could be subject to sharp fluctuations, depending on whether completed helicopters had been delivered to clients just before or just after the end of the year; in contrast, a company making a limited range of nuts and bolts could probably run on a few weeks' stock, though if supplies were subject to interruption and/or shortages it might be prudent to carry more raw materials, and if orders tended to be erratic a higher stock of finished goods would be needed.

If the *Cost of goods sold* is available, it can be used instead of the sales figure and, assuming that stocks are mostly finished goods (*e.g.*, a distribution or retail business), the ratio Stocks/Cost of goods sold can be expressed as so many days or months of stock, or as stock turned over so many times a year, and more accuracy can be obtained by taking the average of the opening and closing stock, as in Example 23.10.

Example 23.10 Calculation of Stocks/Cost of goods sold

	1975	1976	1977
	£000	£000	£000
Year-end stock	1,758	2,272	3,008
Average stock		2,015	2,640
Sales		10,830	12,490
Cost of goods sold		6,270	7,130
Stocks/Sales		18.6%	21.1%
Stocks/Cost of goods sold		32.1%	37.0%
Days of stock		117 days	135 days
Stock turned over p.a.		3.12 x	2.70 x

5 $\frac{\textbf{Debtors}}{\textbf{Sales}}$

expressed either as a percentage or, multiplied by 365, as the collection period in days.

For example, given Debtors of £820,000 and Sales of £5 million:

$$\frac{\text{Debtors}}{\text{Sales}} = \frac{£820,000}{£5,000,000} = 16.4\% \textit{ or}$$

$$\text{Collection period} = \frac{£820,000}{£5,000,000} \times 365 \text{ days}$$

$$= 60 \text{ days}$$

Apart from "strictly cash" businesses like supermarkets, with virtually zero debtors (*e.g.*, TESCO's debtors average about 0.01% of sales), normal terms are payment at the end of the month following delivery, so with 100% prompt payment the average credit given would be between 6 and 7 weeks, making debtors about 12% of turnover. In practice, a figure of 20–25% is quite normal although some companies may, as a matter of policy, give more generous credit in order to give themselves a competitive edge, while others may factor their debts and thus show abnormally low debtors.

A falling collection period is generally a good sign – an indication of effective financial control – but it could show a desperate need for cash, involving extra discounts for cash and undue pressure on customers.

Where extended credit is given by hire purchase facilities provided by the company itself, rather than through a finance company, the HP amount outstanding is usually shown separately, but unless the turnover figure is also broken down it isn't possible to calculate the ratios of HP debtors/HP turnover and Other debtors/Non-HP turnover separately.

6. $\frac{\textbf{Creditors}}{\textbf{Sales}}$

expressed as a percentage.

This gives some indication of the amount of credit a company is allowed by its suppliers, and quite a good indication, providing stock levels and profit margins are reasonably steady and the business is not highly seasonal.

A better measure would be Creditors/Cost of goods purchased, but the cost of goods purchased during the year is seldom disclosed, so the analyst has to content himself with Creditors/Sales. This ratio will still show up any change in credit allowed, so it is the trend which needs to be watched.

A company that is short of cash will be forced to try to get as much credit as it can, despite losing discounts for prompt payment. (*En passant*, any indications of change of suppliers or refusal of credit by suppliers can be an excellent early warning of trouble, because suppliers are usually in very much closer personal day-to-day contact with a company than an analyst or the company's shareholders.)

An alternative ratio to use here is Creditors/Stocks, to see what proportion of the stocks are financed by the company's suppliers. This is of particular interest in retailing businesses, where 80% or 90% is a typical figure for an efficient retailer like MARKS & SPENCER.

In addition, bankers often study movements in the ratio Debtors/Creditors. When things are normal this tends to be stable. Violent change in either direction is a warning signal.

7. $$\frac{\textbf{Working capital}}{\textbf{Sales}}$$

expressed as a percentage
where *Working capital* = Stocks + Debtors − Creditors.

This shows how much capital is required to finance operations in addition to capital invested in fixed assets. It can vary from a tiny 1%, or even negative, for a food retailer to 50% or more for a heavy engineering company, and gives some indication of the likely additional cash needed with increased turnover. A falling ratio indicates the possibility of overtrading.

8. $$\frac{\textbf{Trading profit}}{\textbf{Wages}}$$

expressed as a percentage.

Companies are only obliged to report on the number of employees in the United Kingdom and their wages and salaries, so the comparison can normally only be made with UK trading profits.

Trading profit/Wages gives a direct indication of the effect of wage increases on profits. For example, a company whose trading profit is only 15% of wages is likely to be much more adversely affected by a wage increase of 10% than a company with a ratio of 50%.

Finally, Sales per Employee and Trading profit per Employee are also useful ratios: their trend gives some indication of changing productivity.

FINANCIAL RATIOS

Financial ratios fall into two broad groups, gearing ratios and liquidity ratios. Gearing is concerned with the proportion of capital employed that is borrowed, the proportion provided by shareholders' funds and the relationship between the two, while liquidity ratios are concerned with the company's cash position.

Gearing

Financial gearing can be defined in a multiplicity of ways, the two most common being:

(*a*) the Debt/Equity ratio, shown as Borrowings/Shareholders' funds in the *Investors Chronicle,* and called "leverage" in the United States and elsewhere, and
(*b*) the percentage of capital employed represented by borrowings.

Whatever method is used to compute gearing, a company with "low gearing" is one financed predominantly by equity, whereas a "highly geared" company is one which relies on borrowings for a significant proportion of its capital.

To illustrate (Example 23.11 opposite), let us take the bottom half of three different companies' balance sheets, making two adjustments:

(*a*) deducting any intangible assets in calculating ordinary shareholders' funds;
(*b*) including the bank overdraft and any other borrowings shown under current liabilities (these are normally netted out against current assets in a company's balance sheet, but are just as much a part of capital employed as long-term borrowings are).

As you can see, the Debt/Equity ratio is a more sensitive measurement of gearing than Debt/Capital employed, and it also gives a better indication of the effect of gearing on equity income, known across the Atlantic as the "leverage effect".

Example 23.11 Calculation of gearing and Debt/Equity ratios

		Company A	Company B	Company C
		£000	£000	£000
Ordinary share capital		600	500	250
Reserves		850	800	300
Intangibles		-	-250	-
Ordinary shareholders' funds	[A]	1,450	1,050	550
Redeemable preference capital (3.5%)	[B]	-	100	-
Minorities	[C]	150	150	150
Deferred tax		400	400	400
Loan capital (10%)	[D]	-	150	400
Overdraft (12%)	[E]	-	150	500
Capital employed	[F]	2,000	2,000	2,000
Debt/Equity (Leverage) $\left(\frac{B+D+E}{A+C}\right)$		0%	33%	128%
Debt/Capital employed $\left(\frac{B+D+E}{F}\right)$		0%	20%	45%
Gearing		None	Low	High

Notes:

[B] The treatment of preference shares is a problem: although they are not debt they do carry a *fixed* rate of dividend that is payable ahead of ordinary dividends. On balance we favour treating them as debt if redeemable but otherwise as equity when looking at capital (because it would be misleading to ascribe the same Debt/Equity ratio to a company with say 60 debt/40 equity as one with 60 pref/40 equity).

[C] Minorities have been included as equity in the calculation of Debt/Equity ratios, on the assumption that minority interests in subsidiaries are all pure (non-redeemable) equity.

Leverage effect

The effect of leverage can be expressed as a ratio: percentage change in earnings available to ordinary shareholders brought about by a 1% change in earnings before interest and tax (EBIT).

Suppose each of the three companies in Example 23.11 has a return on capital employed (ROCE) of 10%, and that the rate of Corporation Tax is 50%; then earnings before interest and tax (EBIT) will be as shown in Example 23.12.

Example 23.12 Calculation of leverage effect

	Company A	Company B	Company C
	£000	£000	£000
EBIT	200	200	200
less			
Loan interest	-	-15	-40
Interest on overdraft	-	-18	-60
Pre-tax profits	200	167	100
Tax at 50%	100	83.5	50
Profits after tax	100	83.5	50
Preference dividends	-	3.5	-
Available for minorities and ordinary shareholders [G]	100	80	50
1% change in EBIT	2	2	2
Tax	1	1	1
Available for minorities and ordinary shareholders [H]	+1	+1	+1
Leverage ratio $\frac{H}{G} \times 100$	1.0	1.25	2.0

Leverage, of course, works both ways; if EBIT fell by 50% then earnings available to ordinary shareholders would fall to £50,000 (Company A); £30,000 (Company B); and Company C would be on the verge of making a loss.

Operational gearing

In assessing what level of financial gearing might be reasonable for a company, we must first look at the volatility of profits. This depends to a large extent on the sensitivity of profits to turnover, which we will call operational gearing (although the term operational gearing is sometimes used in the sense of overall gearing to include the effects of financial gearing as well).

The operational gearing of a company can be described as the ratio of the percentage change of trading profit which results from 1% change in turnover, and depends on the relationship between fixed costs, variable costs and net profit, where fixed costs are costs that are incurred regardless of turnover, and variable costs are directly proportional to turnover:

Operational gearing
(Turnover-Variable costs): Trading profit
or (Trading profit + Fixed costs): Trading profit

Example 23.13 (overleaf) demonstrates this.

Example 23.13 Effects of operational gearing

	Turnover	*Fixed costs*	*Variable costs*	*Trading profit*	*Operational gearing*
	£m	£m	£m	£m	
Company D	100	20	70	10	3:1 (100–70:10)
Company E	100	70	20	10	8:1 (100–20:10)

If turnover increases by 10%:

	£m	£m	£m	£m	*Change in profits*
Company D	110	20	77	13	+30%
Company E	110	70	22	18	+80%

This is fine for both D and E, especially for E, which is much more highly geared operationally than D. But, as with high financial gearing, high operational gearing works against a company when turnover falls. Assume a 10% fall in turnover:

Company D	90	20	63	7	-30%
Company E	90	70	18	2	-80%

The effect of gearing can also be illustrated graphically on a "profit/volume chart", as shown in Figure 23.14

Fig. 23.14 Profit/volume chart

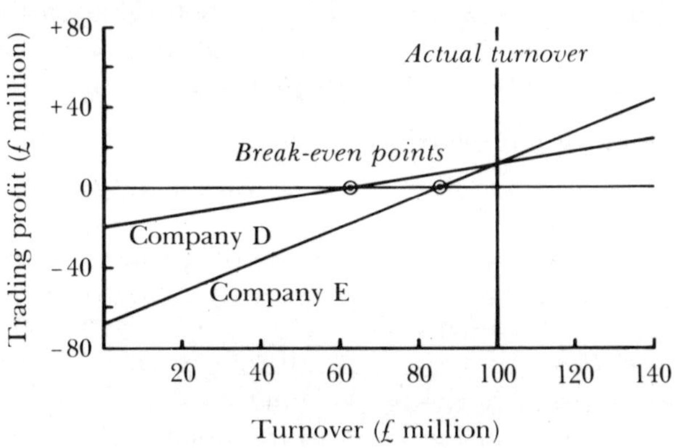

A profit/volume chart is constructed by plotting two points:

(*a*) trading profit against actual turnover;
(*b*) fixed costs against zero turnover

and joining the two points together. The point where this line crosses the horizontal "zero profit" line represents the level of turnover at which the company "breaks even", *i.e.*, neither makes a profit nor a loss. The steeper the gradient of the line the higher the operational gearing of the company. The break-even point can also be calculated:

Break-even turnover

$$= \frac{\text{Fixed costs} \times \text{Actual turnover}}{\text{Actual turnover} - \text{Actual variable costs}}$$

e.g. Company D $= \frac{20 \times 100}{100 - 70} = £66.67\text{m}$

Company E $= \frac{70 \times 100}{100 - 80} = £87.5\text{m}$

It is fairly obvious that a company with high operational gearing aggravates the problem by gearing up financially. Suppose, for instance, that Company E had borrowings that incurred interest charges of £3 million p.a.; Example 23.15 shows the effect on profits.

Example 23.15 Effect of high financial gearing coupled with high operational gearing

Turnover	*Net trading profit*	*Interest charges*	*Pre-tax profits*
£m	£m	£m	£m
100	10	3	7
110	18	3	15
90	2	3	-1

An example of high operational gearing is LONDON BRICK, which until an issue of convertible ULS in an acquisition had no long-term debt, and only ran up an overdraft to finance brick stocks built up during periods of low demand. The profit record shows why the company prudently avoids having extensive debt to service:

LONDON BRICK COMPANY *Six-year profit record*

	1969	1970	1971	1972	1973	1974
Trading profit (£000)	2,285	3,501	6,420	7,315	8,221	3,070
Pre-tax profit (£000)	2,476	3,674	6,634	7,582	8,927	2,670

Imagine what effect the existence of a £20 million issue of 14% ULS would have done to the profits in 1974.

Conversely, the directors of a property company with mainly completed developments let to substantial clients know that they have an assured rental income coming in each quarter, and they would not be considered imprudent to borrow heavily (*i.e.*, gear up) providing the level of interest payments plus running expenses could not exceed the stream of rental income.

We say "could not exceed", because one of the ways property companies get into trouble is by borrowing short-term with a variable interest rate (*e.g.*, on bank overdraft), rather than at a fixed rate; they then get caught out when interest rates go up faster than rental income.

Hidden gearing

Some companies acquire the use of assets by leasing them, an increasingly popular form of off-balance-sheet financing. Where the lease is for several years and the terms do not give the company the option of terminating whenever it chooses, the company has geared itself up just as much as if it had borrowed the money to purchase the assets, except that leasing charges have to be paid rather than interest. Where leasing is thought to provide a significant part of a company's financing, it is worth monitoring the ratio Hire charges/Depreciation as a guide to the extent of leasing and to spot any increase in the proportion of assets leased.

Liquidity

The two ratios most commonly used in assessing a company's liquidity are concerned with current assets (stocks and WIP, debtors and cash) and current liabilities (bank overdraft and any debts due to be settled within the next twelve months):

1. **Current ratio**

$$= \frac{\text{Current assets}}{\text{Current liabilities}}$$

2. **Quick ratio** (*or* "Acid test")

$$= \frac{\text{Current assets - Stock}}{\text{Current liabilities}}$$

Current ratio

The Current or Working Capital ratio is a broad indicator of a company's short-term financial position: a ratio of more than 1 indicates a surplus of current assets over current liabilities. A current ratio of 2 or more used to be regarded as prudent in order to maintain creditworthiness, but in recent years a figure of about 1.5 has become quite normal, and a higher figure isn't necessarily a good sign: it may be due to excessive stocks or debtors, or it may mean that the directors are sitting on an unduly large amount of cash which could be more profitably invested.

When looking at an individual company's current ratio, there is no simple rule of thumb on what the company's ratio "ought" to be, because it so much depends on a number of different factors, including:

1. *The nature of the company's business.* If large stocks and the giving of generous credit terms are normal to the business, the current ratio needs to be higher than the general average, whereas a retail business with only cash sales, no work in progress and with stocks financed mainly by suppliers (*i.e.*, creditors a large item), may be expected to have a lower than average current ratio.
2. *The quality of the current assets.* Stocks, for example, may be readily saleable, *e.g.*, gold, or virtually unsaleable, *e.g.*, half-completed houses in a property slump.
3. *The imminence of current liabilities.* A large loan due for repayment very soon could be embarrassing. It would be acutely embarrassing if gearing was already very high, there was no scope for an equity issue and neither cash nor further overdraft facilities were available. Even that is not perhaps as embarrassing as being unable to pay the wages next week, and next week's wages do not, of course, appear in the balance sheet.

   The key factor is whether a company has scope for further borrowings or is right up against its limits, but facilities available (as opposed to facilities being used) are rarely revealed in annual reports.
4. *The volatility of working capital requirements.* A company with a highly seasonal business pattern, for instance a Christmas card manufacturer or a UK holiday camp operator, may well make use of a much higher average level of borrowings during the year than the balance sheet shows, particularly as companies usually arrange their year end to coincide with low stocks and/or a low level of activity.

Because of these individual factors, the most informative feature of a current ratio is its trend from year to year, *e.g.*, MARKS & SPENCER'S balance sheets over six years (overleaf).

A sharp fall in the current ratio, such as Marks & Spencer experienced in 1974, should always be investigated. In their case it was due mainly to expenditure of more than £40 million on additional properties (compared with £20 million retentions for the year), but this still left a comfortable cash and short-term deposit position of £18 million. The ratio steadied up from 1975 onwards: a further decline could have been cause for concern, especially if the positive cash position had disappeared.

MARKS & SPENCER *Current ratios*

Year end 31 March		1970	1971	1972	1973	1974	1975
Current assets	(£m)	51.5	66.4	61.5	86.4	60.4	70.1
Current liabilities	(£m)	49.9	60.9	60.4	74.6	68.5	77.6
Current ratio		1.03	1.09	1.02	1.16	0.88	0.90

METAL BOX COMPANY *Current ratios*

Year end 31 March		1970	1971	1972	1973	1974	1975	1976
Current assets	(£m)	85.3	100.8	96.4	110.9	150.3	200.7	220.8
Current liabilities	(£m)	44.1	67.3	63.6	96.2	111.5	132.0	130.7
Current ratio		1.93	1.50	1.51	1.15	1.35	1.52	1.69

The consolidated balance sheet of METAL BOX COMPANY shows a much more variable current ratio.

The marked decline in the current ratio between 1970 and 1973 was a clear warning signal, and the trend was reversed by the sale of the company's Baker Street premises for £20.5 million in 1973/4 and an increase in loans of £23 million in 1974/5; a rights issue in the following year, raising £23.3 million, further improved the current ratio.

When calculating liquidity ratios, the balance sheet should be checked to ensure:

(*a*) that current assets do not contain investments other than short-dated Gilts and other near-cash items *and*

(*b*) that all loans and borrowings repayable within twelve months are included in current liabilities, regardless of the original length of the debt: a 20-year debenture redeemable next month is a current liability. Any repayment instalments due within twelve months should also, strictly speaking, be included.

The distortion that can otherwise occur is well illustrated by the consolidated balance sheet of RAGLAN PROPERTY TRUST at 31 March 1975, which showed:

Current assets	£8,072,058
Current liabilities	£4,064,046

suggesting a current ratio of 1.99; but the balance sheet also contained an entry on short-term borrowings of £18,814,843, the composition of which was explained in the note illustrated here:

RAGLAN PROPERTY TRUST *Note to the 1975 balance sheet*

14. Short Term Borrowings

Short term borrowings are represented by secured bank loans and overdrafts which are repayable within 5 years. Of the total £11,785,546 is repayable on demand, £2,773,601 within one year and the balance of £4,255,696 within 5 years.

Thus, the real current liabilities were £18,623,193, the true current ratio was 0.43, and it was hardly surprising to read in the chairman's statement that "the company has been fortunate in being able to retain the support of its bankers throughout the past year".

Quick ratio or acid test

As we have said, not all current assets are readily convertible into cash to meet debts; in particular stocks and work in progress may be able to be run down a certain amount, but not eliminated if the business is to continue. The quick ratio recognises this by excluding stocks from current assets and applies the "acid test" of what would happen if the company had to settle up with all its creditors and debtors straight away: if the quick ratio is less than 1 it would be unable to do so.

Some companies whose normal terms of trade allow them to sell goods for cash before paying for them habitually operate with a quick ratio of well under 1 (0.4 is typical for a supermarket); so it is a poorer-than-average figure compared with other companies in the same industry, coupled with a declining trend, that signals possible trouble ahead. A feature that a low and declining ratio often highlights is a rising overdraft: the question then is, "Are their bankers happy?" Fears in this direction may be allayed by a statement in the annual report about operating well within the facilities available, or by a statement at the time that new money is raised confirming that working capital will be adequate.

A large difference between the current ratio and the quick ratio is an indication of large stocks:

$$\text{Current ratio} - \text{Quick ratio} = \frac{\text{Stocks}}{\text{Current liabilities}}$$

Cash flow

If there is any doubt about the company's liquidity, the cash flow should be examined in as much detail as possible (see Chapter 18). There are two common definitions of cash flow:

Gross cash flow = depreciation plus profit after tax plus increase in deferred tax.

Net cash flow = gross cash flow minus dividends.

The question we need to ask is whether net cash flow in the current year will cover the company's cash requirements.

Cash requirements

There are three main areas to look at in identifying cash requirements:

1. *Repayment of existing loans* due in the next year or two, including convertible loans whose conversion rights are unlikely to be exercised. Loans repayable within twelve months should be (but are not always) shown under current liabilities.
2. *Increase in working capital.* Working capital tends, in an inflationary period and/or when a business expands, to rise roughly in line with turnover. It is useful therefore to use the Working Capital/Sales ratio we described earlier in this chapter to establish the relationship between working capital and sales (Example 23.16).

Example 23.16 Calculation of the Working Capital/Sales ratio

Sales £26m; Stocks £6m; Debtors £4m; Creditors £3½m. Calculate the Working Capital/Sales ratio:

$$\frac{\text{Stocks + Debtors - Creditors}}{\text{Sales}} = \frac{£6½\text{m}}{£26\text{m}} = 25\%$$

Thus if the turnover of this company was expected to increase by 20% in the current year it would be reasonable to assume that unless stocks were unusually high at the last year-end or unless the increase in turnover is not going to follow the company's normal trading pattern, the company is likely to need an increase in working capital of £1.3 million (£26m × 20% × 25%).

---

3. *Capital expenditure requirements.* Companies are required to report the amount of capital expenditure that has been contracted for and the amount that has been approved by the directors but not yet put out to contract.

   The flexibility of the company's capital expenditure programme is important; there is much more risk in building one large process plant than in adding 50 outlets to a retail chain at about the same total cost over, say, 2½ years, because the former, once embarked upon, is a complete liability unless and until it comes on stream while the retail chain's expansion could be curtailed if, say, the economic trends turned downwards and capital expenditure had to be cut a year later, leaving 20 new outlets trading profitably. In general, "great leaps forward" are more risky than step-by-step progress, especially in areas of high technology.

   The size of a single project in relation to the overall size of the company is another inportant factor to watch: a new £25 million process plant that fails to come on stream as planned and loses £5–6 million a year for several years might break a smaller company but would cause no more than mild embarrassment to ICI, and would be regarded as normal in government-financed nuclear power projects.

Cash shortfall

If the net cash flow looks like falling short of the cash requirements we have identified, then the company may have to take one or more of the following steps:

(*a*) increase its overdraft (but is it at the limit of its facilities? – we probably don't know);
(*b* borrow longer term (can it do so within its borrowings limits?);
(*c*) make a rights issue (is its share price at least 20% above par, is it at least a year and preferably two years since its last rights issue, and are market conditions suitable?);
(*d*) acquire a more liquid and/or less highly geared company for paper (*i.e.*, bid for another company using shares);

(*e*) sell some assets (has it any listed investments which could be sold, or has it any activities which could be sold off without seriously affecting the business?);

(*f*) sell and lease back some of the properties used in the business (has it any unmortgaged properties?);

(*g*) cut back on capital expenditure that has not already been put out to contract;

(*h*) tighten credit and stock control;

(*i*) reduce or omit the ordinary dividend, and possibly even the preference dividend too.

If the company takes none of these steps it will run into an overtrading situation, which is likely to precipitate a cash crisis unless, as a last resort, it:

(*j*) reduces its level of trading.

Contingent liabilities: net tangible assets

Contingent liabilities which are large in relation to the net tangible assets of a company or group can, with a run of bad luck (or bad judgement), be a serious threat to the financial stability of a business, and although the great majority of contingent liabilities never materialise, it is prudent to monitor what is going on. In group accounts, contingent liabilities of the parent company in respect of guarantees of borrowings by subsidiaries can, of course, be ignored, because the borrowings concerned are incorporated in the consolidated accounts, but all guarantees for associates and third parties should be included. Leasing commitments, if material, should also be monitored, and the particular points to watch for are guarantees and commitments outside the normal course of business and sharp increases in the amounts involved, as reflected by the ratio Contingent liabilities/n.t.a. BURMAH OIL COMPANY's 1972 accounts, illustrated here, are an example of this.

BURMAH OIL COMPANY *1972 accounts, Note on commitments and contingent liabilities*

(*d*) Three subsidiaries have contractual commitments in respect of tanker in-charters and leased facilities involving hire charges (exclusive of certain operating costs) as follows:

Estimated as payable during:

1973	£ 20 million
1974 to 1977	115 million
1978 to 1982	140 million
1983 and thereafter	215 million

A substantial part of these commitments is already matched by tanker out-charters and other long-term arrangements. Guarantees have been given by the company in respect of the obligations of the subsidiaries and also in relation to certain joint ventures with which they are associated.

The previous year's accounts had shown commitments of £204 million in respect of tanker in-charters, with out-charters of certain vessels covering £127 million, so the absence of any actual figure for out-charters in the 1972 accounts is, in itself, a little suspicious. A reasonable estimate of "substantial" might be say 50%, leaving a £245 million unmatched commitment, equal to about 37% of net tangible assets, compared with 1971's unmatched figure of £77 million, only 12.7% of the net tangible assets that year.

INVESTMENT RATIOS

These are the ratios used by investors when deciding whether a share should be bought, sold or held. Most of them relate to the current price of the share, and therefore vary from day to day. The two most important ones are the Price Earnings Ratio (PER) and the dividend yield.

Price earnings ratio (PER)

$$\text{PER} = \frac{\text{Share price}}{\text{Earnings per share (e.p.s.)}}$$

where *share price* = the middle market price, which is the average of the prices at which shares can be sold or bought on an investor's behalf (the jobber's bid and offer prices respectively),
and *e.p.s.* = Profit attributable to ordinary shareholders ÷ Average number of ordinary shares in issue during year.

The calculation of earnings per share is described in detail in Chapter 14. The analyst will normally calculate two price earnings ratios: the "historical PER", using last year's e.p.s., and the "prospective PER", using his estimate of e.p.s. for the current year; he may also project his earnings estimates ahead to produce a PER based on possible earnings for the following year.

What the PER represents

One way of looking at the PER is to regard it as the number of years' earnings per share represented by the share price, *i.e.*, *x* years' purchase of e.p.s., but this assumes static e.p.s., while in practice the PER reflects the market's view of the company's growth potential, the business risks involved and the dividend policy. For example, a company recovering from a break-even situation, with zero e.p.s. last year, will have a historical PER of infinity but may have a prospective PER of 12 based on expectations of modest profits for the current year, falling to 6 next year if a full recovery is achieved.

The PER of a company also depends not only on the company itself, but the industry in which it operates and, of course, the level of the stock market, which tends to rise faster than reported profits when the business cycle swings up and to fall faster than profits in a downturn. The level of the PER of the *Financial Times* 500 Index shows this very clearly:

	500 Index	*500 PER*
Top of the Bull Market, 19 May 1972	227.30	19.88
Bottom of the Bear Market, 13 December 1974	63.49	3.71

The Actuaries Share Indices table published in the *Financial Times* every day except Mondays also gives the PER for each industry group and sub-section, so any historic PER calculated for a company can be compared with its sector and with the market as a whole, although differences in the treatment of tax by individual companies can cause some distortion here.

In general a high historical PER compared with the industry group suggests either that the company is a leader in its sector or that the share is overvalued, while a low PER suggests a poor company or an undervalued share. In each case check to see if the prospective PER is moving back into line with the sector, as a historical PER that is out of line may be due to expectations of an above average rise in profits for the current year (in which case the historical PER will be higher than average), or to poor results being expected (which would be consistent with a low PER). In addition, if dataSTREAM is available (*see* Chapter 21), it is worth checking the company's relative PER history to see where the current PER Relative (the PER in relation to the PER of the *Financial Times* 500 Share Index) lies in relation to its historical range.

Another useful rule of thumb is to be wary when a PER goes much above 20. The company may well be a glamour stock due for a tumble or, if it is the PER of a very sound high-quality company, the market itself may be in for a fall. One exception here is the property sector, where PERs are normally very high because property companies are, in the main, highly geared and use most of their rental income to service their debt, leaving tiny e.p.s.; investors buy property company shares for their prospects of capital appreciation, not for their current earnings.

Dividend policy and the PER

As the price of a share is influenced both by the e.p.s. and the dividend, a company's dividend policy affects the PER.

In the past it has been fashionable in some companies to pay tiny dividends so that they could plough back most of their profits to finance further growth. Shares in these companies were very popular with private investors, for whom capital appreciation was much more of an attraction than highly taxed dividends.

Today the market has swung away from the private investor, who is currently a net seller of investments, towards yield-conscious institutional investors, for whom good solid income can be equally or more attractive than hopes of high capital appreciation in the future. Thus the shares of a company that distributes a sizeable proportion of its profits to shareholders may stand higher in the market than the shares of a company paying very modest dividends. However, in times of high inflation, a company distributing a large proportion of its reported profits (calculated on a historical cost basis) will tend to lose credibility if dividends are believed to exceed real earnings.

Dividend yield

As described in Chapter 13, dividends under the Imputation System are actually paid net of tax at the basic personal rate, and carry an associated tax credit. Dividend yields are based on *gross* dividends per share, that is, on the dividends actually paid plus the associated tax credit; if the gross equivalent of a net dividend paid is not given in the report and accounts, it can be obtained by grossing up, *i.e.*, by dividing the net dividend by (1 – basic tax rate expressed as a decimal):

$$\text{Gross dividend yield (\%)} = \frac{\text{Net dividend in pence per share} \times 100}{(1 - \text{basic tax rate}) \times \text{Ordinary share price in pence}}$$

The associated tax credit depends on the basic rate of tax at the time the dividend was paid (not the rate in the year it was earned), and the rates on the interim and final dividend may be different, *e.g.*,

Basic rate of tax increased from 33% in 1974/5 to 35% in 1975/6.

December 1974 Interim dividend = 2p net,

$$\text{grossed up} = \frac{2}{0.67} = 2.985\text{p gross}$$

July 1975 Final dividend = 3p net,

$$\text{grossed up} = \frac{3}{0.65} = 4.615\text{p gross}$$

Total dividend = 5p net = 7.600p gross

Dividend yield (with a share price of 50p) =

$$\frac{7.6}{50} \times 100 = 15.2\%$$

Dividend cover

Providing the company is in a normal tax position with reasonably steady and mainly UK earnings, so that all the profits after tax can be distributed net with full tax credit, then, as Example 23.17 shows:

$$\text{Dividend cover} = \frac{\text{Earnings per share}}{\text{Net dividend per share}}$$

Example 23.17 Calculation of dividend cover

With a basic rate of personal tax of 35% and a Corporation Tax rate of 50%:

	Modest dividend	*Maximum dividend*
	£000	£000
Pre-tax profits	2,000	2,000
Corporation Tax	1,000	1,000
Profits after tax	1,000	1,000
Ordinary dividends	400	1,000
Retained earnings	600	Nil
Tax payable		
ACT: 35/65ths of net dividends	215	538
Mainstream tax	785	462
Total tax	1,000	1,000
Issued equity = 10m shares		
Earnings per share = $\frac{£1\text{m}}{10\text{m}}$	10p	10p
Net dividend	4p	10p
Dividend cover	2.5 x	1.0 x

Example 23.17 is very straightforward, but when foreign tax on overseas earnings becomes significant, the maximum net dividend a company can distribute out of a year's profits is no longer the e.p.s. but something less, due to ACT absorbing UK tax liability that would otherwise be available for UK relief on overseas tax, and the cover has to be worked out at a gross level.

Full distribution

Example 23.18 opposite illustrates the dividend cover calculated on a "full distribution" basis.

As explained more fully in Chapter 13, the maximum distributable gross dividends ("full distribution earnings") are the lesser of:

(*a*) "Nil distribution" after-tax profits, grossed up; *or*

(*b*) Total pre-tax profits, *less*
   (i) Minimum mainstream tax on UK pre-tax profits, charged at (CT rate – basic tax rate) and
   (ii) Foreign tax payable if all overseas profits are remitted to the United Kingdom.

$$\text{and dividend cover} = \frac{\text{Full distribution e.p.s.}}{\text{Actual gross dividend}}$$

Payout ratio

Before the introduction of the imputation system this ratio could be defined as the dividends distributed (gross) expressed as a percentage of the profits after tax, or as the reciprocal of the dividend cover, which gave the same answer.

Under the imputation system the payout ratio is less straightforward. Providing the company would not incur any extra tax liability on full distribution, the payout ratio is still the reciprocal of the dividend cover, but if full distribution increases the tax charge a difference arises. Taking the "modest dividend" situation in Example 23.18:

(*a*) $\text{Payout ratio} = \frac{\text{Net dividends}}{\text{Profits after tax}} = \frac{400}{1{,}000} = 40\%$

(*b*) $\text{Reciprocal of dividend cover} = \frac{1}{2.36} = 42.4\%$

As the payout ratio reflects, by implication, the amount retained by the company, (*a*) seems the better definition as the company does, in fact, retain 60% of attributable profits if it pays out 40% in dividends.

Example 23.18 Calculation of dividend cover: full distribution

Taking our previous Example 23.17, but assuming that half the profits are earned overseas and bear foreign tax (including any withholding tax on remission) at 40%, then the maximum distributable gross is:

Pre-tax profits	£2,000,000
less UK minimum mainstream tax	£150,000
Foreign tax	£400,000
Full distribution	£1,450,000

65/100ths of this full distribution figure will be distributed as net dividends (£942,500), together with 35/100ths as the associated tax credit (£507,500).

With 10 million shares the full distribution earnings per share = 14.5p, while the modest 4p net dividend's gross equivalent, with a 35% basic rate of personal tax = 4 × 100/65 = 6.15p and

$$\text{dividend cover} = \frac{14.5}{6.15} = 2.36 \text{ times}$$

The overall tax position would be:

	Modest dividend £000	*Maximum dividend (i.e. full distribution)* £000
Net dividend	400	942.5
Tax credit (ACT for company to pay)	215	507.5
UK pre-tax profits	1,000	1,000
CT liability	500	500
less ACT (max. 35% of UK pre-tax)	215 [a]	350 [A]
Mainstream tax (minimum 15%)	285 [b]	150 [B]
Overseas pre-tax profits	1,000	1,000
UK CT liability	500	500
less Remaining ACT	–	157.5 [C]
Max. credit for overseas tax	500	342.5
Overseas tax	400 [d]	400 [D]
Unrelieved overseas tax	–	57.5
Mainstream tax	100 [e]	
Total tax	(a+b+d+e) 1,000	(A+B+C+D) 1,057.5
Profits after tax	1,000	942.5
Issued equity = 10m shares		
Gross dividends	615	1,450
Gross dividends per share	6.15p	14.5p
Dividend cover	2.36	1.0

Net asset value (n.a.v.)

This shows the book value of assets attributable to each ordinary share:

$$\text{n.a.v.} = \frac{\text{Ordinary shareholders' funds (OSF)}}{\text{Number of ordinary shares issued}}$$

Although the n.a.v. figure is *very* dependent on the balance sheet values of assets being realistic, it does give some indication of how much the price of a share depends on the ability of the company to generate profits and how much is backed by assets.

The net asset value is one reference point used in deciding on terms for an acquisition, assuming the potential biddee's assets are fairly valued or are adjusted for the purpose of the calculation. Where property has been revalued but the new value is only shown in a note to the accounts, *i.e.*, the surpluses have not been credited to reserves, analysts will often show two figures, *e.g.*, "n.a.v. = 73p (94p including property revaluation)."

Chapter 24

PRO-FORMA GUIDE TO ANALYSIS

Although historical information summaries and analyses of company accounts are readily available from Extel Cards and dataSTREAM, for those fortunate enough to enjoy these excellent services, there really is no substitute for poking around the accounts to spot, for example, when a company decides to stop making provisions for deferred tax (because its dividend would look terribly thinly covered if profits suffered a normal tax charge?), or when a loan repayable within twelve months, by *not* being included in current liabilities, makes the liquidity ratios look very much better than they really are.

This chapter provides a pro-forma to help you poke round systematically and to work out key ratios. The first three sheets are designed for the analysis of a single year's accounts, and the remaining five sheets present a summary of a company's record over five years, to show the long-term trends of key ratios and percentages.

Analysts' views on the treatment of some items do vary, and this pro-forma is only one way of tackling the figures: it should be modified, adapted and extended to suit individual tastes, providing users are consistent in their treatment of items so that figures produced are on a fair basis for inter-company comparisons.

The following line-by-line notes, which provide cross-references to the relevant sections in earlier chapters, should be read in conjunction with the pro-forma. (It should be noted that some of the pro-formas have lines which are numbered but left blank: these are to accommodate any special items which may occur in individual cases.)

ANALYSIS SHEET 1 – PROFIT AND LOSS ACCOUNT

The main purpose of this sheet is twofold: to see if reported profits are distorted in any way and to examine the effect of an abnormal tax charge. This is done by "normalising" pre-tax profits and applying a standard tax charge to produce "normalised" e.p.s. Any difference between normalised e.p.s. and reported e.p.s. then serves as a crude indication that something is unusual about (but not necessarily wrong with) the tax charge and/or something is abnormal about the way in which the company reports its profits.

Line 1. Turnover or Sales
This figure should include excise duty, but should not include transactions within the group or VAT (*see* p. 66).

Calculation of trading profit

Companies are not obliged to report their trading profit; some do not do so, and those who do may define it in different ways (*see* p. 68). This part of the pro-forma enables a standard trading profit to be calculated by working back from pre-tax profits.

Line 3. Adjustment to pre-tax profits
Although SSAPs have done much towards standardising the treatment and presentation of accounts, a number of companies include

variations from normal practice which can make a significant difference to reported profits. These may arise in a number of ways:

(*a*) The provision of *extra depreciation* to allow for the inflated cost of replacing assets; this is an eminently sensible practice, but the extra depreciation should be added back into profits for inter-company comparisons.

(*b*) *Capitalising expenses* and amortising them over the years in which benefits are expected to accrue, rather than charging the expenses at the time they were incurred. It may look fair for example, to capitalise the cost of relocating a factory and to spread the charge over several subsequent years when the relocation will be saving rent, transport costs, etc., but the move may not turn out to be a success financially. The risk of capitalising expenditure was demonstrated only too clearly when ROLLS ROYCE, in capitalising research and development expenditure, relied on future profits from a new aero-engine and these profits did not materialise.

The standard accounting practice on research and development, SSAP 13, requires expenditure on research and development to be written off in the year of expenditure, except for specific projects where commercial success is reasonably assured (*see* p. 65). We would also favour writing off all expenditure on intangible assets (*e.g.*, relocation, staff training, advertising campaigns, etc.) and any expenditure a company has capitalised in this way during the year should be deducted from pre-tax profits.

(*c*) *Capitalising interest.* When a company builds a new factory it is reasonable to capitalise interest on money borrowed for the project during construction as this would be included in the capital cost if the project was put out to contract or a newly completed factory was purchased, but if completion is delayed or the start of production is postponed because of lack of demand, then interest on the investment should be written off as an expense (*see* p. 65).

Another variation of capitalising interest is on land banks and on sites awaiting development or redevelopment; the risk here is that the original cost plus subsequent interest may easily exceed the market value of the asset in its present condition, although some might argue that if the company has succeeded in "rolling up" the interest on the associated debt (has been allowed to add the interest to the capital sum borrowed, rather than paying it when due), then it is reasonable to capitalise the interest on the other side of the balance sheet (*i.e.*, add it to the book value of the asset concerned).

We feel that the capitalising of interest before construction has started or after planned completion should be treated with suspicion, and we recommend that any interest that has been capitalised in these circumstances should be deducted from pre-tax profits.

(*d*) *Extraordinary losses.* As we have already discussed (on p. 87), the definition of extraordinary items as opposed to exceptional items (*see* p. 88) leaves a certain amount of scope for differences of opinion. For example, the treatment of losses on foreign currency borrowings (*see* p. 115), and the details of items the company has treated as extraordinary need careful examination: any "non-extraordinary" items should be deducted from reported profits.

(*e*) *Extraordinary profits.* The converse to (*d*) may apply when a company makes profits other than in the normal course of business and does *not* treat them as extraordinary. The profits on any extraordinary items, for example on the sale and leaseback of properties or on the redemption of debt, should be excluded from pre-tax profits.

All these variations, except extra depreciation, tend to boost the reported profits of the company and should be viewed with healthy scepticism. In many cases they are genuine differences in practice, consistently and openly applied, in which case the analyst should adjust the profits to avoid getting an unduly optimistic view of the company, but there is also an unfortunate tendency for companies to adopt "expediency accounting" to paper over the cracks when profits are crumbling. If there is any suspicion of this, a fine toothcomb is needed to check:

(*a*) the auditors' report for qualifications;
(*b*) the statement of or note on accounting policies (usually contained in Note 1 to the accounts) for any changes;
(*c*) extraordinary items;
(*d*) movements to and from reserves.

Line 4. "Normalised" pre-tax profits
These are the reported pre-tax profits, Line 2, adjusted by Line 3 to correct for any variations from normal reporting practices.

Line 5. Interest paid
This is on all borrowings (p. 65) including overdraft, as shown in the accounts, plus any rolled-up interest that has been deducted in Line 3.

Line 6. Earnings before interest and tax (EBIT)
This figure is used in the calculation of return on capital employed (ROCE) in Line 103 at the bottom of this sheet.

Line 7. Associates
This is the group's share of the pre-tax profits of associated companies (p. 110).

Line 8. Income from Investments
This includes dividends received and interest from deposits. Dividends are shown gross, *i.e.*, plus associated tax credits (p. 69).

Line 9
Some analysts add back depreciation to arrive at trading profit. If this is done, hire charges should also be added back.

Calculation of normalised earnings per share

As discussed in Chapter 13, there are many factors that can make a company's tax charge plus deferred tax differ from the standard rate of Corporation Tax applied to pre-tax profits, and the influence of these factors tends to vary from year to year.

Some companies may have a permanently low tax charge after providing for deferred tax, but unless sufficient information is available for this to be reasonably estimated (for instance, where there is a significant element of franked income), a rough and ready practical rule is to apply a full tax charge to "normalise" profits to obtain "normalised" e.p.s. for inter-company comparisons.

The difference between "normalised" e.p.s. and the e.p.s. reported by the company gives a measure of the effect of an abnormal tax charge, and of any variations from normal practice in reporting pre-tax profits. (It is then often useful to try to identify the major factors causing this difference: if, for example, a low tax charge is due to overseas earnings not being remitted to the United Kingdom, is this because the company is keen to reinvest overseas or because the foreign country has restricted or forbidden remission?)

Lines 11 and 12. Taxation payable and Transfer to deferred tax
The figure for taxation given in the profit and loss account should be broken down into the tax the company has to pay and the amount transferred to deferred tax: details are usually given in a note. If a company's policy is not to make a full provision for deferred tax, the accounts should give a figure for what the full deferred tax provision would have been, and that figure should be used in Line 12. If no figure is given for deferred tax, leave Line 12 blank.

Line 13. Tax normalisation
This is the amount required to make

$$\frac{\text{Line } (11 + 12 + 13)}{\text{Line } 4}\ \%$$

= standard rate of Corporation Tax.

Line 15. Minorities
This is the share of profits of the minority shareholders in subsidiaries not wholly owned by the company. In theory the profits attributable to minorities should be adjusted here to reflect a standard tax charge in the subsidiaries concerned, but this usually involves extensive research at Companies House. A crude adjustment can be made by grossing up Minorities at the reported rate of tax and then applying a standard tax charge.

Line 17. Preference dividends
These are paid and shown net of the basic rate of Income Tax (p. 86).

Line 18. Normalised profits attributable to ordinary shareholders
This is the attributable profit, having adjusted pre-tax profits to conform to normal reporting practices and having applied a standard tax charge.

Line 19. Ordinary shares in issue
This is the average number of ordinary shares in issue during the year, *i.e.*, the number of ordinary shares which a company should use in its e.p.s. calculations; it normally appears in the accounts in a note on e.p.s.

Line 20. Extraordinary items, as reported
Extraordinary items are items not arising in the normal course of business, and in a company's accounts are added or subtracted below the line, *i.e.*, after the profit on which earnings per share are calculated.

Line 22. Normalised earnings per share
Line 18 divided by Line 19. The difference between this figure and the reported e.p.s. is, as we have said, a measure of the effect of any abnormal tax charge and of any variations from normal practice in reporting pre-tax profits.

Line 24. Reported fully diluted earnings per share
Companies are not obliged to report fully

diluted e.p.s. unless dilution is material, but they can easily be calculated if required, as we describe on p. 96. A similar calculation can be made using normalised profits attributable to ordinary shareholders to obtain normalised fully diluted e.p.s., but in practice the effect will be very similar to the effect on reported e.p.s., unless normalised profits differ widely from reported profits.

Line 25. Extraordinary items per share
This is just a convenient way of expressing extraordinary items to see if they are significant in relation to earnings per share.

Line 26. Dividend per share
As reported (*i.e.*, net of tax), expressed in pence.

Lines 27 and 28. Dividend cover and Normalised cover
In straightforward cases where Corporation Tax liability is not affected by the proportion of profits distributed (*i.e.*, where ACT on full distribution can be entirely offset against Corporation Tax, without penalty, *see* p. 81) the covers can be obtained by dividing the reported e.p.s. or normalised e.p.s. by the dividend. If full distribution increases the tax liability, usually owing to overseas earnings, the dividend cover becomes complicated and, if not shown in the accounts, can only be calculated approximately (p. 82).

Profitability ratios

The ratios in Lines 101 and 102 are measures of trading performance, and so they are based on capital employed in trading (*see* p. 169), while ROCE (return on capital employed) in Line 103 is for the overall performance of the company, and is therefore based on the overall capital employed.

ANALYSIS SHEET 2 – ASSETS EMPLOYED

This page contains two key ratios, the current ratio and the acid test, both of which can be seriously distorted if current assets are overstated and/or current liabilities are understated. Care should therefore be taken to adjust for any incorrect classification: for example, the inclusion of a housebuilder's land bank as a current asset if it comprises more than a few months' supply of building land, or the exclusion from current liabilities of a long-term debt that falls due for repayment within twelve months.

Line 29. Land and buildings
The accounts will give the net book value (cost or valuation less accumulated depreciation). Unfortunately the figure for capital employed and thus the return on capital employed can be very much distorted by the assets being shown at unrealistically low values, and this distortion is most likely to occur when a high proportion of land and buildings have not been revalued in the last few years, so the details of revaluations, contained in the notes to the accounts, should be checked to see if valuations are reasonably up to date.

Line 30. Surplus on revaluation
Companies sometimes report that they have had revaluations of land and buildings carried out, but have not written up the assets accordingly in their books. In these cases the surplus arising on revaluation can be added separately in Line 30 to produce a more accurate figure for capital employed, with a balancing entry on Analysis Sheet 3. Alternatively, Line 30 may be renamed to show a more detailed breakdown of fixed assets, *e.g.* where a company shows an unusual category of assets peculiar to the nature of its business, for example "Orchards" in the case of H.P. BULMER, the cider company. If this is done, a balancing entry is not, of course, required on Analysis Sheet 3.

Line 31. Plant and equipment
This is normally shown at cost less accumulated depreciation, but a few companies revalue these assets periodically as part of replacement cost accounting systems (p. 150). Where this is found, a "normal" figure based on historical cost less accumulated depreciation may not be readily available, in which case note should be

made that capital employed will be overstated in comparison with other companies.

Line 32. Investment grants
If investment grants are shown separately (as opposed to being deducted from the cost of an asset when it is acquired, *see* p. 35), they should be deducted from the book value of fixed assets. If they have been included in the figure for reserves, they should also be deducted on Analysis Sheet 3 in calculating NTA attributable.

Line 34. Associates
This figure is the cost of any investment in associated companies, less any amounts written off, plus the investing group's share of the post-acquisition retained profits and reserves of the associated companies (see Chapter 16).

Line 35. Other investments
These are usually long-term investments, sometimes described as "trade investments". In our view this figure should include all investments that cannot readily be converted into cash at a price guaranteed within narrow limits; *see* comments on Line 39, and Chapter 7.

Line 36. Stocks and WIP
See Chapter 8.

Line 37. Debtors
Where debts to the company have been settled by bills of exchange which the company is holding to maturity, and the amount involved is shown as "bills receivable" (p. 57), this may be included in the figure for Debtors.

Line 38. Cash
See comments on Line 46.

Line 39. Other liquid assets
These are near-cash items such as government securities and local authority bonds due for redemption or repayment within twelve months. Longer dated gilt-edged securities may be included on the grounds that they are easily saleable although prices may fluctuate, but holdings of ordinary shares should not be included in current assets as their value can easily fall and, even if quoted, the shares may not be marketable in any quantity.

Line 41. Creditors
Where creditors have been paid by bills of exchange which have not yet fallen due, the amount outstanding may be shown separately in the accounts as "bills payable" (p. 57); in the pro-forma we include it with Creditors.

Line 42. Taxation
This is the taxation payable within the next twelve months, and includes the ACT payable on proposed dividends.

Line 45. Sub-total
This sub-total is struck before the inclusion of overdraft and acceptance credits so as to avoid these two items being deducted from assets in the calculation of capital employed (*see* p. 169). Both items are types of debt and are included in Analysis Sheet 3 as methods of financing.

Line 46. Overdraft
Some analysts net out any cash against the overdraft (that is, deduct cash from the overdraft), thus showing a lower figure for overdraft and reducing the figure for capital employed. Where it is known that a company's bank nets out cash balances in calculating interest charges on overdraft, netting out can be justified. On the other hand, if cash balances are retained in overseas subsidiaries, or if the management chooses to maintain cash balances that are independent of overdrafts elsewhere in the group, it is not realistic to net them out (p. 169).

Line 47. Acceptance credits
Although derived from bills of exchange, acceptance credits are only another method of borrowing (p. 57) and can be treated in the same way as an overdraft; that is, by adding them in the Financing table on Analysis Sheet 3, rather than netting them out against assets in calculating capital employed on Analysis Sheet 2.

Line 49. Trading capital employed
This is the sum of all assets except Associates and Other investments (and Intangible assets, which are dealt with on Analysis Sheet 3), less all current liabilities except overdrafts and acceptance credits.

Line 50. Overall capital employed
Associates on Line 34 and Other investments on Line 35 are added to Line 49.

Lines 105 to 110. Ratios
Each of these ratios is described in Chapter 23.

ANALYSIS SHEET 3 – FINANCING

Line 51. Ordinary capital
The total nominal value of both ordinary and deferred shares which are fully paid. Where shares are partly paid, the total paid up should be shown separately.

Line 52. Share premium account
The details of premiums paid on the issue of shares for more than their nominal value (*see* p. 16) is usually the first item in the note on Reserves.

Line 54. Intangibles
The most common intangible item is Goodwill (the cost of obtaining control in an acquisition over and above the value of assets acquired, *see* p. 101), but any other intangible item included in a company's accounts (*e.g.*, patents) should also be deducted here.

Line 55. Net tangible assets attributable
These are the net tangible assets attributable to the ordinary shareholders.

Line 30. Surplus on revaluation
This is the balancing entry for any surplus on revaluation shown in Line 30 on Analysis Sheet 2.

Lines 56 and 57. Redeemable and other preference shares
Redeemable preference shares need listing separately, as we count them as debt in the capital structure of the company because they eventually have to be repaid.

Line 58. Minorities
This represents the interest of minority shareholders in partially owned subsidiary companies.

Line 59. Deferred taxation
This is mainly due to capital allowances being given to the company for tax purposes faster than the company applies depreciation in its accounts, and to stock relief (p. 76).

Line 60. Other provisions
Other provisions may include provisions made for pensions and product guarantees.

Lines 62 to 67. Loans
The best way of presenting information on loan capital and other loans depends very much on the debt structure of the company; it may be useful to show:

(*a*) The division between loans repayable in less than five years and over five years, which Schedule 2, para. 8(d) of the Companies Act 1967 requires to be reported.
(*b*) Debenture, unsecured loan stock, convertible loan stock, bank loans and other loans.
(*c*) The breakdown between sterling denominated and foreign currency loans.

Lines 46 and 47. Bank overdraft and acceptance credits
As already discussed, these two current liabilities are *not* netted out against assets in Sheet 2, but are included here in Sheet 3 as part of a company's financing.

Line 68. Total debt
This includes redeemable preference shares (Line 56), all loans (Lines 62 to 67), bank overdraft (Line 46) and acceptance credits (Line 47).

Line 69. Capital employed
This figure should be the same as Line 50, Overall capital employed, on Analysis Sheet 2. The cause of any discrepancy should be found and corrected.

Line 70. Net asset value
This is the book value of the assets attributable to each ordinary share:

$$\frac{\text{Line 55}}{\text{Line 51}} \times \text{Nominal value of ordinary share}$$

Further calculations can be made to obtain a fully diluted net asset value (*i.e.*, allowing for paying up partly paid shares, for converting convertibles and for exercising warrants), but in practice the difference this makes is seldom significant.

Line 71. Net asset value plus revaluation
Line 30 from Analysis Sheet 2, any surplus on revaluation that has not been written into the books, is added to Line 55 in calculating the net asset value.

Line 72. Contingent liabilities
This is an item all on its own, usually to be found tucked away near the end of the notes to the accounts; it is easily overlooked but can be very important (*see* p. 60). The figure that is required is the total of commitments and contingencies *outside* the group; that is, not including guarantees of borrowings by subsidiaries but including, for example, guarantees on behalf of associated companies.

Line 114. Contingent liabilities as percentage of net tangible assets
This ratio shows the extent of contingent liabilities outside the company or group in relation to its equity base. (A figure of more than 2–3% is unusual, and worth further investigation.)

Analysis Sheet 1 Profit and loss account

Company:		Year to			
Line		19...	19...	% Change	Remarks
		£....	£....		
1	**Turnover or sales**				
Calculation of trading profit					
2	Reported pre-tax profits				
3	± Adjustments to pre-tax profits				
4	"Normalised" pre-tax profits				2 ± 3
5	+ Interest paid				
6	= Earnings before interest and tax				4 + 5
7	- Associates				
8	- Income from investments				
9					
10	= **Trading profit**				6 - 7 - 8
Calculation of "normalised" earnings per share					
4	"Normalised" pre-tax profits				From 4 above
11	- Taxation payable				Total to equal
12	- Transfer to deferred tax				standard rate
13	± Tax normalisation				tax charge
14	= **Normalised profits after tax**				4 - 11 - 12 ± 13
15	- Minorities				
16	= Profits attrib. to company				14 - 15
17	- Preference dividends				16 - 17
18	= **Norm. profits attrib. to ord.**				
19	Ordinary shares in issue				Average for year
20	Extraordinary items				
21					
22	Normalised e.p.s.				18 ÷ 19
23	Reported e.p.s.				
24	Reported f.d. e.p.s.				
25	Extraordinary items per share				20 ÷ 19
26	Dividend per share				
27	Dividend cover				
28	Normalised cover				
Profitability ratios					
100	Trading profit/Sales				10 ÷ 1 as %
101	Trading profit/Capital employed				10 ÷ 49 as %
102	Sales/Capital employed				1 ÷ 49 as %
103	ROCE				6 ÷ 50 as %
104					

Analysis Sheet 2 Assets employed

Company:		Year to			
Line		19...	19...	% Change	Remarks
		£....	£....		
Fixed assets					
29	Land and buildings				
30	+ Surplus on revaluation				
31	+ Plant and equipment				
32	- Investment grants				
33	= Total fixed assets				29 + 30 + 31 - 32
34	Associates				
35	Other investments				
Current assets					
36	Stocks and WIP				
37	+ Debtors				
38	+ Cash				
39	+ Other liquid assets				
40	= Total current assets				Sum of 36 to 39
Current liabilities					
41	Creditors				
42	+ Taxation				
43	+ Dividends				
44	+ Other current liabilities				
45	± Sub-total				Sum of 41 to 44
46	+ Overdraft				
47	+ Acceptance credits				
48	= Total current liabilities				45 + 46 + 47
49	Trading capital employed				33 + 40 - 45
50	**Overall capital employed**				34 + 35 + 49
Ratios					
105	Current ratio				40 ÷ 48
106	Acid test				(40 - 36) ÷ 48
107	Stocks/Sales				36 ÷ 1 as %
108	Debtors/Sales				37 ÷ 1 as %
109	Creditors/Sales				41 ÷ 1 as %
110	Working capital/Sales				(36+37-41) ÷ 1 as %

Analysis Sheet 3 Financing

Company:		Year to			
Line		19...	19...	% Change	Remarks
		£....	£....		
51	Ordinary capital (Nominal value each:)				
52	+ Share premium a/c				
53	+ Other reserves				
32	− Investment grants				Only if in reserves
54	− Intangible assets				
55	= n.t.a. attributable				51+52+53−32−54
30	Surplus on revaluations				From Analysis Sheet 2 (if any)
56	Redeemable preference shares				
57	Other preference shares				
58	+ Minorities				
59	+ Deferred tax				
60	+ Other provisions				
61	**= Sub-total**				Sum of 57 to 60
Loans					
62	+				
63	+				
64	+				
65	+				
66	+				
67	+				
46	+ Bank overdraft				From Analysis
47	+ Acceptance credits				Sheet 2
68	**= Total debt**				56+(62 to 67) + 46 + 47
69	**Capital employed**				55 + 30 + 61 + 68
70	Net asset value (n.a.v.)				(55 ÷ 51) × Nominal value
71	n.a.v. plus revaluation				(55 + 30) ÷ 51 × Nominal value
72	Contingent liabilities				
Ratios					
112	Debt/Equity				68 ÷ (55 + 58) as %
113	Debt/Capital employed				68 ÷ 69 as %
114	Contingent liabilities/n.t.a.				72 ÷ 55 as %

SUMMARY SHEET 1 – SUMMARY OF PROFIT AND LOSS ACCOUNTS

In practice it can be confusing to show normalised figures mixed in with figures actually reported, so the only special figures shown in the profit and loss summary sheet are:

(*a*) adjustments – to indicate reporting variations;

(*b*) normalised e.p.s. – to show the effect of (*a*) and the application of a standard tax charge.

Where a company's reported profits do not require adjustment it may be found satisfactory to dispense with Analysis Sheet 1 and the calculation of normalised e.p.s.: the summary can then be compiled direct from the accounts, as the figure for percentage of pre-tax profits taken by taxation will show up any abnormal tax charge.

Summary Sheet 1 does not, however, allow each item's percentage change from the previous year to be shown unless the % column provided is used for that purpose instead of showing each item as a percentage of reported pre-tax profits.

SUMMARY SHEET 2 – SUMMARY OF ASSETS EMPLOYED

This summary sheet gives a slightly compressed version of the information in Analysis Sheet 2, and shows each item as a percentage of capital employed instead of the percentage change from the previous year. Here again the summary sheet can, with practice, be compiled straight from a company's accounts.

SUMMARY SHEET 3 – SUMMARY OF FINANCING

This is the counterpart to Summary Sheet 2 and similarly, with practice, can be completed straight from a company's balance sheet without using Analysis Sheet 3.

SUMMARY SHEETS 4 AND 5 – SUMMARY OF SOURCES AND APPLICATIONS

As discussed in Chapter 18, the contents and the presentation of source and application statements vary considerably from company to company, so it can be useful to put the information provided into a standard format. It may also be useful to look at the pattern over the years, in particular at the use of external financing (funds from other sources), the growth in working capital and the trends in liquidity. As with earlier sheets, these formats should be adjusted to taste and to cater for any special features of the company being examined.

In general our formats follow those in the Examples in SSAP 10, except that Applications of funds are shown as positive amounts on Summary Sheet 5, rather than negative amounts on the same sheet as Sources.

Note, in particular, that Line S1 on the Sources page is Profit before tax *less* minorities. If minorities have not been deducted by the company than dividends paid to minorities should be inserted as an application (Line A3) and there will be no minority retentions on Line S6. As the treatment of minorities illustrates, the Sources and Applications pro-formas will often need modification to cater for the very varied information given by individual companies.

Summary Sheet 1 Summary of profit and loss accounts

Company:		Year ending											
Line		19...		19...		19...		19...		19...		19...	
		£....	%	£....	%	£....	%	£....	%	£....	%	£....	%
1	**Turnover or sales**												
10	Trading profit												
8	+ Investment income												
7	+ Associates												
5	– Interest paid												
3	± Adjustments												
2	**= Reported pre-tax profits**		100		100		100		100		100		100
11	– Actual tax												
12	– Deferred tax												
	= Reported profit after tax												
	– Reported minorities												
	± Profits attrib. to company												
17	– Preference dividends												
	± Profits attrib. to ord												
	– Ordinary dividends												
	= Retentions												
20	Extraordinary items												
22	Normalised e.p.s.												
23	Reported e.p.s.												
24	Reported f.d. e.p.s.												
Profitability ratios													
100	Trading profit/Sales												
101	Trading profit/Capital employed												
102	Sales/Capital employed												
103	ROCE												
101													

Summary Sheet 2 Summary of assets employed

Company:		Year ending											
Line		19...		19...		19...		19...		19...		19...	
		£	%	£....	%	£....	%	£....	%	£....	%	£....	%
29	Land and buildings												
30	+ Surplus on revaluation												
31	+ Plant and equipment												
32	− Investment grants												
33	**= Total fixed assets**												
34	Associates												
35	Other investments												
36	Stocks and WIP												
37	+ Debtors												
38	+ Cash												
39	+ Other liquid assets												
40	**= Total current assets**												
41	Creditors												
42	+ Taxation												
43	+ Dividends												
44	+ Other current liabilities												
45	**= Sub-total**												
46	+ Overdraft												
47	+ Acceptance credits												
48	**Total current liabilities**												
49	Trading capital employed												
50	**Overall capital employed**		100		100		100		100		100		100

Ratios

105	Current ratio						
106	Acid test						
107	Stocks/Sales						
108	Debtors/Sales						
109	Creditors/Sales						
110	Working capital/Sales						

Summary Sheet 3 Summary of financing

Company:		Year ending											
Line		19...		19...		19...		19...		19...		19...	
		£....	%	£....	%	£....	%	£....	%	£....	%	£....	%
51	Ordinary capital												
52	+ Share premium a/c												
53	+ Other reserves												
32	– Investment grants												
54	– Intangibles												
55	= n.t.a. attributable												
30	Surplus on revaluation												
56	Redeemable preference												
57	Other preference shares												
58	+ Minorities												
59	+ Deferred tax												
60	+ Other provisions												
61	**= Sub-total**												
62	+												
63	+												
64	+												
65	+												
66	+												
67	+												
46	+ Bank overdraft												
47	+ Acceptance credits												
68	**= Total debt**												
69	**Capital employed**		100		100		100		100		100		100
70	Net asset value (n.a.v.)												
71	n.a.v. + revaluation												
72	Contingent liabilities												
Ratios													
113	Debt/Capital employed												
114	Contingent liabilities/n.t.a.												

Summary Sheet 4 Summary of sources of funds

Company:		Year ending					
Line		19...	19...	19...	19...	19...	19...
		£....	£....	£....	£....	£....	£....
S1	Profits before tax (less Min.)						
S2	± Extraordinary items						
S3							
Non-monetary Adjustments							
S4	+ Depreciation						
S5	+ Other provisions						
S6	+ Minority retentions						
S7	– Retained in associates						
S8	± Exchange adjustments						
S9							
S10							
S11	+ Disposal of fixed assets						
S12	+ Sale of subsidiaries						
S13							
S14	**= Generated from operations**						
Funds from other sources							
S15	+ Rights issue of shares						
S16	+ Other issues of shares						
S17	+ Increase in loans						
S18	– Decrease in loans						
S19							
S20	+ Sale of investments						
S21							
S22							
S23	**= Sources total**						

Summary Sheet 5 Summary of application of funds

Company:		Year ending					
Line		19...	19...	19...	19...	19...	19...
		£....	£....	£....	£....	£....	£....
A1	Tax paid						
A2	+ Dividends						
A3							
A4	+ Purchase of fixed assets						
A5	+ Purchase of subsidiaries						
A6	+ Investment in associates						
A7	+ Purchase of investments						
A8							
A9	Goodwill written off						
A10							
A11	+ Increase } in working						
	– Decrease } capital						
A12	+ Increase } in net						
	– Decrease } liquid funds						
A13	= **Application total**						
Working capital							
A14	Increase (decrease) in stocks						
A15	Increase (decrease) in debtors						
A16	(Increase) decrease in creditors						
A11	Net increase (decrease)						
Liquidity							
A17	Increase (decrease) in cash						
A18	(Increase) decrease in overdraft						
A12	Increase (decrease) in liquidity						

APPENDICES

APPENDIX 1 – CURRENT SSAPs AND EDs

The following Statements of Standard Accounting Practice and Exposure Drafts were current in March 1979.

		Date of issue
SSAP	Explanatory foreword (Revised May 1975)	Jan 1971
SSAP 1	Accounting for the results of associated companies (Amended Aug 1974)	Jan 1971
SSAP 2	Disclosure of accounting policies	Nov 1971
SSAP 3	Earnings per share (Revised Aug 1974)	Feb 1972
SSAP 4	The accounting treatment of government grants	Apr 1974
SSAP 5	Accounting for value added tax	Apr 1974
SSAP 6	Extraordinary items and prior year adjustments (Revised Apr 1975)	Apr 1974
SSAP 8	The treatment of taxation under the imputation system in the accounts of companies (revised Dec 1977)	Aug 1974
SSAP 9	Stocks and work in progress	May 1975
SSAP 10	Statements of source and application of funds	Jul 1975
SSAP 12	Accounting for depreciation	Dec 1977
SSAP 13	Accounting for research and development	Dec 1977
SSAP 14	Group accounts	Sept 1978
SSAP 15	Accounting for deferred taxation	Oct 1978
ED 16	Supplement to "Extra-ordinary items and prior year adjustments"	Sept 1975
ED 18	Current cost accounting	Nov 1976
ED 21	Accounting for foreign currency transactions	Sept 1977
ED 22	Accounting for post balance sheet events	Feb 1978
ED 23	Accounting for contingencies	Nov 1978

APPENDIX 2 – PRESENT VALUE

£1 received in a year's time is worth less than £1 received today, because £1 available today could be invested to earn interest for the next twelve months. If £1 now could be invested at a rate of interest i (expressed as a decimal), it would be worth £$(1 + i)$ in a year's time. If the £$(1 + i)$ at the end of the year was left invested, it would be worth £$(1 + i) \times (1 + i)$ = £$(1 + i)^2$ at the end of the second year, and £$(1 + i)^3$ at the end of the third year, and so on; in other words, it would earn compound interest at the rate of i per annum.

Present value is like compound interest in reverse: the value of £1 received in a year's time is worth £1 ÷ $(1+i)$ now, and £1 in two years' time is worth £1 ÷ $(1+i)^2$ now, and so on. For example, if i (known as the discount rate), is 10% p.a., then the present value of £1 received in a year's time is £1 ÷ (1+0.10) = £0.9091. Similarly the present value of receiving £1 in two years' time is £1 ÷ $(1.10)^2$ = £0.8264, and £1 in 3 years' time is £1 ÷ $(1.10)^3$ = £0.7513, and £1 in n years' time is £1 ÷ $(1.10)^n$.

Tables of *present values* are available for various rates of interest and periods of years. The table below is a very simplified and abbreviated version of one:

Present value of 1 in n *years' time*

n	*Rate of interest (the discount rate)* 1%	2%	3%	4%	5%	10%	15%
1	.990	.980	.971	.962	.952	.909	.870
2	.980	.961	.943	.925	.907	.826	.756
3	.971	.942	.915	.889	.864	.751	.658
4	.961	.924	.889	.855	.822	.683	.572
5	.951	.906	.863	.822	.784	.621	.497
10	.905	.820	.744	.676	.614	.386	.247
20	.820	.673	.554	.456	.377	.149	.061

Present value tables refer to the value of 1, rather than the value of £1, because they can be used for any currency: the 1 may be $1, DM1, 1 peseta or 1 of any other currency you care to name.

The present value concept (also known as discounted cash flow, DCF) can be applied to any streams of future income and to repayments of capital. For example, £20 nominal of 5% loan stock redeemable in three years would be worth the interest payments of £1.00 at the end of each year plus the £20 in three years' time, all discounted at 10% per annum, to give a present value of:

$$\frac{£1}{(1.10)} + \frac{£1}{(1.10)^2} + \frac{£1}{(1.10)^3} + \frac{£20}{(1.10)^3}$$

$$= £0.909 + 0.826 + 0.751 + 15.026 = £17.512$$

The calculation of the present value of a steady stream of income can be assisted by the use of annuity tables, an annuity of 1 for n years simply being an annual payment of 1 for n years; such a table is set out below.

In our previous example, the present value of £1 per annum for 3 years, discounted at 10%, could have been obtained from the annuity table: 3 years at 10% = 2.487.

In practice, interest on fixed-interest securities is usually paid half-yearly in arrears (*i.e.*, at the end of each half-year), and so the half-yearly discount rate, which is the square root of the annual rate, is used to discount each half-yearly interest payment. In addition, stock is usually traded in units of £100 nominal, so £100 of 5% Loan Stock with three years to redemption, discounted at 10% per annum, would have a present value of:

$$\frac{£2.50}{(\sqrt{1.10})} + \frac{£2.50}{(\sqrt{1.10})^2} + \cdots + \frac{£2.50}{(\sqrt{1.10})^6} + \frac{£100}{(1.10)^3} =$$

$$2.3837 + 2.2728 + \cdots + 1.8784 + 75.1315 = £87.8734$$

Annuity table: present value of an annuity of 1 for n *years*

n	*Rate of interest (the discount rate)* 1%	2%	3%	4%	5%	10%	15%
1	.990	.980	.971	.962	.952	.909	.870
2	1.970	1.942	1.913	1.886	1.860	1.736	1.626
3	2.941	2.884	2.829	2.775	2.723	2.487	2.283
4	3.902	3.808	3.717	3.630	3.546	3.170	2.855
5	4.853	4.713	4.580	4.452	4.329	3.791	3.352
10	9.471	8.983	8.530	8.111	7.722	6.145	5.019
15	13.865	12.849	11.938	11.118	10.380	7.606	5.847

APPENDIX 3 – RETAIL PRICE INDICES SINCE 1970

Retail price indices, as published in the Government Statistical Service's *Monthly Digest of Statistics,* were until 1974 based on 100 at 15 January 1962. On 15 January 1974 the Government Statistical Service rebased the index at 100 and published figures accordingly thereafter; these figures are shown here in parentheses, below their January 1962-based equivalents. To prolong the usefulness of this table for quick reference, space has been left for the reader to fill in later figures as they become known. The necessary adjustment to the old (January 1962) base can be made by multiplying the current figure by 1.918.

Mid-month	1970	1971	1972	1973	1974	1975	1976	1977	1978	1979
Jan	135.5	147.0	159.0	171.3	191.8 (100.0)	230.0 (119.9)	283.6 (147.9)	330.6 (172.4)	363.5 (189.5)	397.4 (207.2)
Feb	136.2	147.8	159.8	172.4	195.1 (101.7)	233.8 (121.9)	287.3 (149.8)	333.9 (174.1)	365.6 (190.6)	400.6 (208.9)
Mar	137.0	149.0	160.3	173.4	196.8 (102.6)	238.4 (124.3)	288.8 (150.6)	337.1 (175.8)	367.9 (191.8)	
Apr	139.1	152.2	161.8	176.7	203.5 (106.1)	247.6 (129.1)	294.4 (153.5)	345.8 (180.3)	373.2 (194.6)	
May	139.5	153.2	162.6	178.0	206.4 (107.6)	258.0 (134.5)	297.6 (155.2)	348.5 (181.7)	375.3 (195.7)	
Jun	139.9	154.3	163.7	178.9	208.5 (108.7)	263.0 (137.1)	299.2 (156.0)	352.1 (183.6)	378.2 (197.2)	
Jul	140.9	155.2	164.2	179.7	210.4 (109.7)	265.6 (138.5)	299.7 (156.3)	352.5 (183.8)	380.0 (198.1)	
Aug	140.8	155.3	165.5	180.2	210.6 (109.8)	267.1 (139.3)	304.0 (158.5)	354.2 (184.7)	382.4 (199.4)	
Sept	141.5	155.5	166.4	181.8	212.9 (111.0)	269.4 (140.5)	308.0 (160.6)	356.2 (185.7)	384.0 (200.2)	
Oct	143.0	156.4	168.7	185.4	217.1 (113.2)	273.3 (142.5)	313.5 (163.5)	357.7 (186.5)	385.7 (201.1)	
Nov	144.0	157.3	169.3	186.8	221.0 (115.2)	276.5 (144.2)	318.0 (165.8)	359.4 (187.4)	388.4 (202.5)	
Dec	145.0	158.1	170.2	188.2	224.2 (116.9)	280.0 (146.0)	322.2 (168.0)	361.3 (188.4)	391.6 (204.2)	
Annual average	140.2	153.4	164.3	179.4	208.1 (108.5)	258.5 (134.8)	301.3 (157.1)	349.1 (182.0)	378.0 (197.1)	

INDEX